ON IMMIGRATION

Surveying Biblical Teaching on Issues of Immigration

Immigrants, Foreigners, and Strangers

CHRISTOPHER B. HARBIN

© 2015

Published in the United States by Nurturing Faith Inc., Macon GA, www.nurturingfaith.net.

Library of Congress Cataloging-in-Publication Data is available.

978-1-938514-62-3

All rights reserved. Printed in the United States of America

TABLE OF CONTENTS

Initial Words on Immigration v

SECTION ONE
Special Themes and Passages Regarding Immigrants 1

SECTION TWO
Passages Containing Specific Terminology for Immigrants 23

SECTION THREE
Other Pertinent Themes and Texts 89

    Summary Conclusions 147

    Further Reading 149

    About the Author 151

—En Español—

    Palabras Iniciales Referentes a la Inmigración 153

PARTE UNO
Temas y Pasajes Especiales Referentes a Inmigrantes 155

PARTE DOS
Pasajes que Utilizan Términos Específicos para Inmigrantes . 179

PARTE TRES
Otros Textos y Temas Pertinentes 249

    Conclusiones Sumarias 311

    Para Más Lectura 313

    Sobre el Autor 315

INITIAL WORDS ON IMMIGRATION

The issue of immigration is an old one. It is also a current issue in politics in the United States of America, as it is around the entire world, from Europe to Latin America, Africa, Australia, and Asia. As from time immemorial, it is an issue that pertains to how we treat and interact with people of some other group, identity, ethnicity, or origin who enter our sphere of life. The Hebrews, later Jews, had a history with the concept of immigration, specifically tied to their own beginnings in the person and experience of Abraham, their preeminent forefather, the patriarch of both faith and nation. His classification as an immigrant, sojourner, or foreigner was enshrined in the oldest statement of faith and identity in the Hebrew scriptures: "A wandering Aramean was my father." This was the core statement at the heart of understanding themselves as a nation and their position among the other nations of their world.

This text will not attempt to deal with the politics of immigration in the national or international arena. It may be pertinent to highlight how some of the biblical issues and discussion play out on the political scene, but we will focus essentially on the relevance of the biblical text to the issue of immigration from a more personal perspective. While there may be biblical implications for national policy, the focus of this text will be on what the Bible has to say to the church and those who comprise the church. What does the Bible have to say in reference to our interactions, attitudes, and reactions to immigration and immigrants?

One may notice that many of the biblical discussions related to immigration are equally applicable to concerns of racism and race relations. This is because, at heart, the issue is one and the same. Immigration from a political standpoint is about dealing with the often undesired presence of the "other," however we might define such a category. It is about how we treat those who are from a different race, religion, background, region, language, culture, or ethnicity.

In the United States of America, this discussion has played out historically in relation to the native peoples of the continent, the French, the Spanish, the Tory, the slave, the Irish, the Catholic, the Italian, the Jew, the Chinese, the communist, the Japanese, the Hispanic, the carpetbagger, the African, the Yankee, the rebel, the redneck, the hillbilly, the Muslim, the Arab, and so forth. At issue was never the precise nature of the group under observation, but the concerns regarding the group as different and somehow perceived to be a threat. In almost every case, we have devised terms for immigrant population groups that denigrate them, casting them in the category of unwanted, unfit, and undesired.

This has generally been the condition of the immigrant, both here and around the world. To qualify as an immigrant in this sense, one does not even need to cross a border, enter a new nation, or speak a different language. One simply needs to be an outsider among a people who view and consider one as different. One might be a foreigner, or simply a stranger.

Often as not, the church has remained mostly silent on the issue of dealing with these groups the larger society has often attempted to exclude or place in some controlled category.

Before dealing with the specific biblical texts using terminology related to immigrants, foreigners, or refugees, we will look at some larger themes in the Bible pertaining to immigrants and foreigners. Some of these texts may not use the specific terminology, but equally apply to issues pertaining to immigrant populations.

SECTION ONE

Special Themes and Passages Regarding Immigrants

This text is written in three main sections. First, we will deal with some overarching biblical themes on immigrants, foreigners, and strangers. Next, we will look at the biblical passages that use terminology specific to immigrants, foreigners, refugees, and strangers. We will categorize these by the larger themes into which they fall. Finally, we will look at a series of other stories, texts, and characters whose lives and treatment have implications for our own relationship to and understanding of outsiders and how God wants us to treat them.

The theme of immigrants, foreigners, and strangers is an expansive one. This text will simply be an introduction to the theme as dealt with throughout the Bible.

"Remember That You Were Slaves in Egypt"

This refrain, "Remember that you were slaves in Egypt," was to be a constant reminder to the Hebrews dealing with foreigners in the midst of Israel. The people were to remember how their own forefathers were mistreated and how they would have wished to have been treated differently. This refrain called the nation to a higher ethic of empathy toward outsiders, who were naturally powerless in the midst of a society to which they did not belong. The frequent call to memory was a call to place themselves in the shoes of those they considered other.

The Hebrews were to remember that they once belonged to the same category of immigrant, or outsider. In fact, the very term Hebrew appears to have originally meant "slave." To be a slave is to have one's humanity reduced to that of being property, chattel, or merchandise without the full autonomy of being for consideration as a person. It is to be considered less than others. Along with the degrading of personhood, slavery categorizes one as having less worth and value than other people, which is the essence of our definitions of otherness.

Escaping from Egypt, the people who would become the Hebrew nation were nothing more than a rag-tag band of former slaves. In the eyes of the world, their personal worth and corporate identity were categorized by their having been slaves, and therefore of lesser importance than other peoples. It was in their freedom, garnered by Yahweh's intervention through Moses, that they became something akin to a nation, a sovereign people. While being slaves made them less than human and of lesser importance, Yahweh's intervention turned the tables. God took this group deemed worthless and transformed them into a nation with a new identity as the people belonging to Yahweh.

As a nation of former slaves, they were to remember that a life of slavery was not something to look down on so much as an occasion to recognize that one person was truly no better than another. Before Yahweh, all should bow equally as slaves and servants. They were only special because of Yahweh's grace of intervention on their behalf. Otherwise, they would still have been slaves in Egypt for generations to come. It was in part because of their no-account status that Yahweh had heard and rescued them in the first place. They had no special standing, other than a claim to being in part the descendants of one to whom God had promised blessing.

Abraham had been a landless wanderer, a migrant, a nomadic herdsman, a sojourner in a land to which he could never claim title. The nation as a whole came from the same background upon leaving Egypt. Escaping Egypt as slaves, they entered a land that was not theirs by any right of law or inheritance. Even their founding scriptures designated the land as not belonging to them. They were simply entering the land of Yahweh to serve as stewards of this land of Yahweh's promise and blessing. It was from this backdrop that they were to look upon others. At the end of the day, if any class of people should be despised, it would be that slave class, of which they wholly participated from the beginning of their exodus.

"There Shall Be One Law"

Mosaic Law was not designed to favor those with power, wealth, land, or status. Its intent was to deal with all equitably. This phrase, "There shall be one law," was used in specific relation to how the law dealt with and should treat people without status. They were to be granted the same degree of respect and value as any other individual. The rights and value given to any individual should be given equally to all before the Law.

Law in most any land may begin from such a lofty ideal of treating all with standards of equality. At best, however, this tends toward being an ideal reading of law, which rarely, if ever, reaches the high standards its crafters sought. The Declaration of Independence of the United States of America claims some of these lofty ideals of equality. The man who drafted said declaration, however, held both men and women as slaves. With one hand he wrote of equality, yet with the practice of his life he kept a separate classification of some as being somehow less than others.

For Jefferson, the clash between ideals in his writing and his practical life extended to his treatment of women as well. He was no different from the other founding fathers in regarding only men as citizens of the newly forming sovereign state. They crafted laws that sought to hold out for concerns of equality, yet they themselves never quite reached their own ideals due to a failure to truly understand equality.

Hebrew legal code was no different. Sure, there are plenty of texts that point to the higher ideals of equal treatment under the law, yet these are tempered with others that fail to reach the same lofty ideals. There should be one law equally treating all, but human nature interferes, along with the lapses in cultural and social comprehension of how to apply those same ideals in daily practice. Even so, it is the higher ideal set forth in Scripture that should hold our attention. We must be aware of failure to reach God's full will and purpose, yet we strive on toward the higher goal set before us.

"What Does Yahweh Require of You?"

Micah's call to justice was a reminder for Israel that worship was about so much more than sacrifice, offering, and praise. It was about the way we treat one another, giving special attention to the oppressed or voiceless within the larger society: the widows, orphans, poor, and immigrants.

This was a refrain not limited to Micah. It was a standard and purpose to which Israel as a whole was to rise. Justice was the category sorely lacking for an enslaved populace in Egyptian bondage. The lack of justice among the nations was already decried in the Abraham narratives regarding Sodom and its treatment of foreigners. Justice was defined as doing what is right, not necessarily what is legal.

Under legal definitions of the day, a foreigner, such as the visitors who came to Abraham and Sodom, had no rights. They were completely at the mercy of the people they encountered, both by law and by custom. The Genesis traditions posit that Abraham was righteous or just in his dealing with foreigners, as he responded to them on the basis of their needs for food and shelter, giving no regard to considerations of their personal worth, position, importance, or status. Abraham simply met their needs. Sodom, by contrast, dealt with strangers on the basis of what they might gain from them in the face of lack of legal restraint.

Widespread among the nations of the day was the concept of justice being reflected in how one treats foreigners, widows, orphans, and the poor. This was Micah's concern, as it was the concern of the Genesis narrator and the ethicists of Babylonian and Ugaritic cultures as well. Unfortunately, just like in Israel, very few lived up to the ideal standards of justice they promoted in their words. It was this failure that prompted prophets like Micah to recall Israel to the standards of Yahweh.

"Render unto God What Is of God"

The specific terms here in the Greek give the notion that Jesus was speaking of questions of origin. What comes from or belongs to God is what we are to return to God. We may think of concerns of life and spirituality, but to the Jewish mind Jesus' words carry a much broader and deeper meaning. They apply to a much larger reality, including both what we might consider spiritual and material. To the Jews of the first century, much of what we term physical—for example, our breath—they considered spiritual. To them, breath was a God-given lease on life, a direct connection with God in something as common as each act of breathing.

Jesus calls us to respectfully return our all to God, even while we fulfill our legal obligations to governments. At the same time, he places emphasis on looking beyond questions of personal rights and personal welfare to our responsibilities toward others. Our obligations before God toward others are not to be trumped by any competing authority, regardless of what authority that might be.

At the heart of Jesus' words is the understanding that our all belongs to God. He calls us to place everything that has origin in God in subjection to God's will and purposes. As far as Jewish law was concerned, even the land belonged to Yahweh. The food gathered from the fields came from God, who sent rain, owned the field, and caused the seed to germinate, grow, and bear fruit. The cattle and flocks gave birth due to God's initiative and creation. The breath of each one hinged upon God lending life and breath for each inhalation.

Given this backdrop, there is nothing one might claim as personal property, for all of life depended and depends upon the divine gift of life and all that sustains life. If we are no more than stewards of God's gifts, we have nothing of our own to protect and hold back from another of God's creatures. Instead, all at our disposal begins and remains in God's care and at God's direction.

"Render unto Caesar"

The coin presented for "tribute" in Jesus' discussion regarding paying tribute to Rome bore the image of Caesar. It bore Caesar's image because it was coined by Caesar, or under Caesar's authority. It was minted to allow for easier commerce with a standardization of prices, weights, and measures. Jesus' words here echo the concept that what Caesar has provided or originated belongs to Caesar at the end of the day. If Caesar demands tribute in the coin of Rome's making, its giving is no more than returning what had come from Caesar in the first place. Those questioning Jesus about the practice were caught up with the issue of the term being tribute. As such, it was viewed from Roman perspective as recognizing the legitimacy of Rome and its domination as a matter of the strength of Roman deities.

From religious perspectives, the very coin of tribute should not have been in circulation in Israel in light of the commandment against graven images, if one wanted to be legalistic about it. It should, therefore, have been returned to Rome without question. At issue, however, was not the dignity or righteousness of Rome, but the fact that the Jew had a greater allegiance to Yahweh than to material wealth or its originators.

To the first-century Jew, returning Roman coin in tribute meant a blatant disregard for their sense of oppression at the hands of Rome. It pained them to follow these requirements of Roman occupation, for it reminded them of Rome's power over them, just as Rome intended. Jesus, however, seems to recognize that while Rome oppressed the Jews, they also provided certain benefits. He was willing to look beyond the Jewish sense of oppression under Rome as simply a minor issue. They had no power to change the political structures under which they lived, but Jesus was not as concerned with political structures as they and we tend to be.

In a democratic system of government, one must recognize that the citizen has both a responsibility to and for government. There was no such pattern for Jesus' hearers. There was one in Rome, but the Jews were kept out of that process. Jesus referenced a government that was often seen as oppressive. In such a situation, Jesus' words call one to obey, even at personal cost to oneself, yet one is to give an even higher allegiance toward God. Rome or any other governing structure would fall in second place behind God, even though tribute might be exacted.

If a law is just or unjust, the individual is required to follow it or at least be prepared to accept its consequences. In the context of Jesus' teaching, however, there is interplay between God's authority and that of human authorities. We must look beyond simply this text on tax or tribute to recognize that there are plenty of instances when the demands of God run counter to the demands of state. In any such case, believers are called to live in submission to God first, just as we see in the example of Jesus, the apostles, and the early church.

Ending Oppression

It is the Christian believer's responsibility before God to work to end the oppression of others, though we are to accept the oppression we face personally. While this oppression might be called out and recognized for what it is, the believer's responsibility is to accept it. We see this principle working out in Paul's life, where he goes so far as to deny himself certain rights for the higher calling of serving God and working for the welfare of others. We see this in the actions of Peter and John, who are arrested in the temple after healing a lame man under Jesus' authority. We see it in Jesus' example as well.

Paul writes on behalf of an escaped slave, calling on a brother in Christ to treat the slave not as chattel, but as an equal. He then goes on to claim responsibility for any financial damage the slave owner has incurred in the case of the escapee. Paul willingly accepts injustice to himself in order to champion release from oppression for another. He does work directly to topple a social structure as a whole, but he works on the individual level to seek a higher plane of interaction among believers.

For his own life example, he accepts punishments that are oppressive. Peter and John joyfully do the same, counting the experience as an opportunity to share in the sufferings of Christ Jesus. At the same time, the apostles work to create within the community of new believers a higher ethic, which would lay a foundation for a new standard of behavior.

Paul wrote that in Christ there are no distinctions according to the social order of the world. As such, there are no grounds to justify the oppression of others. The new community of believers in Acts gathered under radically new parameters. These left no room for oppression of any second category of persons in their midst or of those outside their community. Initially, oppression stopped within the scope of the church's influence. They could easily control it within their own community, so that is where they began "acting" to end oppression. By extension and influence, their actions would change the society around them as well.

Championing Justice

Biblically, justice is about equity and providing for those who are most likely to be oppressed by any system of power. Those without recourse and voice are the ones we are challenged to protect the most. Doing what is right is another expression of justice, as it pertains to establishing equity and care for the needs of others. Godly justice understands that God is sufficient to provide ample resources to meet the needs of all.

For the Hebrews becoming a nation in Yahweh's land, justice was about turning the tables on the status quo of the societies they encountered. They were to act differently, abiding by a wholly distinct set of norms from the established societies. They were not to pretend to own the land, so to exclude others. Instead, they were to live as stewards of God's bounty. The produce of the land was to meet the needs of all: the landless, the voiceless, the powerless, and the disenfranchised. This was the central trait of justice they were to seek.

Hebrew society was to look after its weakest segments, with special attention to those who otherwise would not even find consideration as belonging to the society. In the midst of voices crying out for vengeance upon the landholders and the unjust, uncaring legal framework of the settled peoples, the Hebrews were not to simply become the new wave of oppressive power brokers. They were to establish a wholly new community based on completely new standards.

They did not achieve these ideals, but the ideals were nonetheless stated in law and by the mouths of the prophets. The king was to champion the cause of the weak and oppressed, just as Nathan called David to account for his misdeeds. The nation was to depend upon Yahweh to meet its needs, not to build structures to empower greed and build power. Its security was to be based on caring for the weak and depending on Yahweh's sufficiency to care for the nation as it championed the cause of justice for all.

Loving Mercy

Loving mercy was to be the faithful's measuring rod alongside the justice of equity. Mercy is the standard whereby law is judged and the higher standard established for a Christian's behavior. Micah deals with justice and mercy as working hand in hand, beyond the bounds of any legal prescription. This is also the way Jesus implemented his care for the needy in his midst. Our actions and attitudes should be governed by mercy as well as justice.

Shakespeare highlighted mercy as a higher calling for a king in his quality of mercy speech in The Merchant of Venice. The words did not come from the Bible, but their concepts might be associated with several of its passages, most notably in 2 Kings 6, where Elisha leads an enemy army blind into Samaria and places them helpless into the hands of the king. He restores their sight, then has them fed and released to go home. The result is thirty years of peace.

Again, this is the higher ethic found in the biblical record. It was a stretch not only for the biblical characters, but for us as well. It is the attitude we find in Paul's acceptance of the persecution he faced while offering no recrimination or curse in defiance. Instead, he offers salvation and forgiveness to his jailer in Philippi. Justice, peace, and forgiveness are wrapped in mercy as integral to the gospel message of love for one and all.

We see Jesus applying principles of mercy to release many from oppression, in spite of Jewish prejudices against differing peoples. He offers grace to a Syro-phoenician woman, a Jewess with a flow of blood, sight to the blind, and healing to a Samaritan leper. His display of mercy knows no bounds of nationality or religious definitions of dignity, worth, or value.

"Love Your Neighbor"

The term neighbor did not normally refer to a foreigner, but that is precisely how Jesus reinterprets it in the parable of the good Samaritan. He addressed responsibility to care for the needs of the immigrant, enemy, or stranger on the same lines one would care for a child, spouse, or parent in need. Love seeks to meet the needs of others, without concern for definitions of the other's worth.

While this was in one sense the intent of the original command Jesus quoted in context of the parable, the traditional interpretation limited its application to others of the same Israelite community. They discounted immigrants, strangers, second-class community members, the poor, and the "unimportant." It has ever been the same in communities the world over.

Our standard use of the concept of neighbor not only limits definition of the term, but also how we interact with others. We seek out those who are most like us, who are family or friends, and treat them with deference, while looking askance at anyone outside our comfortable definitions of community. It is to this natural human practice that Jesus directs his interpretation in the good neighbor parable. Our love is supposed to include all our neighbors, not simply those whose identity and lifestyle confirm our personal self-worth and sense of well-being.

To further complicate matters, Jesus places in the role of good neighbor the hated enemy of the Jew, the Samaritan who had mixed Judaism with other religious traditions and intermarried with people outside the promise to Abraham. They were deemed not simply a filthy people who were unfaithful to God; they were seen as traitors to the traditions of Abraham and Moses. Even so, it is this class of undeserving, unworthy people that Jesus places in a position to teach those within the scope of God's love and acceptance, a love we are called to emulate.

Equality in Christ

In Christ Jesus, there is no distinction of rank, position, or prominence, except in terms of service. Paul is very clear on this in Galatians, as is Luke in Acts. Even Matthew begins his Gospel building on this theme about Messiah coming through a questionable genealogy, including foreigners such as Dinah, Rahab, Ruth, and Bathsheba. To top it off, God's announcement of Jesus' birth is given to astrologers from Eastern lands, seemingly from the region of Babylon.

This concept of equality builds on a theme begun in the Old Testament with God's benevolence toward immigrants, strangers, outsiders, and those cast off by society. All are of equal worth in Christ Jesus. We see him ministering to the outcasts of Israelite society as well as to people beyond Israelite society. There are Roman soldiers, Samaritans, and Syrophoenicians who receive the same quality of mercy and care as those from within the bounds of Judaism.

Jesus then spoke of sheep from other folds, ostensibly of those who were not Jews but needed access to the good news of God's acceptance.

Jesus took women into his inner circle, as evidenced in the conversation with Mary and Martha at Lazarus's house. He placed fishermen, tax collectors, and women in the same band of his followers, entrusting them with the intimate details of the good news to be shared. He included in the list of disciples both Palestinian and Hellenistic Jews. He did not simply ignore the social distinctions separating classes, genders, and ethnicities; he obliterated them. He showered one and all not simply with tolerance or acceptance, but with the full grace and mercy of God.

What Jesus preached and lived, Peter and Paul built on throughout the descriptions in Acts. Peter learned to accept all Gentiles as acceptable to God beyond the demands of circumcision and laws of ritual purity. Paul struggled with many who pressed for distinction on the grounds of circumcision. He went on, however, to defend distinctions of language, culture, and even gender as meaning nothing in light of the news of God's lavish character of grace.

Genesis 18–19

The visitation of Abraham contains themes of justice in accord with the standard definitions of the day. Judging one's righteousness was generally held to be visibly reflected in how one dealt with specific categories of people: immigrants, strangers, widows, children, and the poor. This was a concept held in common among the Hebrews as well the majority of their neighbors, just as cultures the world over still pride themselves today on being a very hospitable people.

The visitors who came to Abraham were outsiders, immigrants of some class, though most likely traveling as part of an unmentioned entourage. He received them with honor, spreading a generous table before them and placing himself in the category of servant to address their needs. The people of Sodom, by contrast, interfered with Lot's attempts at hospitality, seeking to abuse the strangers who had come into their midst. As far as the story goes, this was positive proof of the unrighteousness of Sodom and Gomorrah's inhabitants. The major point of the story seems to contrast hospitality to strangers with the abuse of the powerless as a visible measure of one's righteousness.

There are plenty of other biblical passages that deal with this same theme. The New Testament picks up on the concept of hospitality to strangers (likely to be read as foreigners or immigrants) in reference to this passage where Abraham hosts messengers of Yahweh without even recognizing it. It also portrays Jesus dealing positively with outsiders, foreigners, and immigrants without condemnation, but meeting their needs.

The Babylonians and other nations viewed the level of one's hospitality to go hand in hand with one's character of righteousness and justice. Ugarit, a city of the northern coast of Palestine, left texts that use the refrain of treating widows, orphans, strangers, and the poor as a measure of one's righteousness. This concept would have been widely understood throughout the Middle East, not simply among the Hebrews. In every case, the peoples did not necessarily live up to the standards they claimed, but they did understand that the way one treated outsiders demonstrated one's true character.

They knew that how one treated those who were powerless spoke much more of one's character and integrity than did following a series of laws. As has been said in other circles, the measure of a man is not how he treats his equals and superiors, but how he treats those he considers inferior. Along these lines, Abraham and Lot passed the test with flying colors, while Sodom and Gomorrah failed miserably.

Philoxenia

There is a word that shows up in only a couple of New Testament passages, specifically Romans 12:13 and Hebrews 13:2. This term is normally translated as "hospitality," but its sense is a little more than mere hospitality as we tend to think of it. It is a conjunction of two Greek words, one for love and the other for stranger. Though the concept here indeed entails a certain kind of hospitality, it is a special category of hospitality extended toward a stranger.

Paul, writing to the Romans, speaks of our responsibility to serve strangers with those actions and attitudes that flow from a sense of abundant hospitality. For Paul, this is an integral part of the Christian's service as an outflow of having offered up our lives as sacrifices in service to Christ Jesus.

The author of Hebrews speaks in a similar manner, mentioning that other characters had offered hospitality to strangers and in so doing had received angels as their guests. Obviously, the passage refers most specifically to Abraham and Lot, but it also makes reference to others, like the widows who received Elijah and Elisha, who were messengers of God (the terms translated as angel in both Hebrew and Greek simply mean "messenger").

It is not the case that every time a text translates a word with the term hospitality that the underlying Greek is this same term. In Acts 28:7, the term is philophronos, to think in a kind, friendly, or loving manner. In the majority of cases, hospitality is treated by example, not with the use of specific terms. In 1 Peter, the text reflects the concept of extending hospitality toward those who compose the church. It is in Romans and Hebrews that hospitality toward strangers is specifically dealt with.

For Paul and for the author of Hebrews, it is not enough that the believer accept immigrants, that they be extended friendship, and that they be treated justly. The believer should likewise assume the responsibility to extend hospitality to immigrants or strangers who are in need. They would apply this principle to bringing them inside one's home to care for them. There is no room here for screening on issues of dignity, immigrant status, or levels of behavior. The responsibility here lies completely with the believer as part of one's service to Christ, with no concern for the character of the immigrant in need. This is a far cry from our more standard practices of hospitality.

Zipporah

Moses not only took a wife from Midian; he also tied himself to the family of a prophet outside the known categories of Abraham's descendants. Jethro, his father-in-law, apparently served the same God of Abraham, though he was not of the same lineage. He accepted Moses as a Hebrew refugee from Egypt. Moses then created familial ties with this priest of Midian, married his daughter, and lived with him as an immigrant. Later in Exodus, he received Jethro as a visitor and took advice from him on organizing the nation administratively. We see in Jethro a model for treating an immigrant as well as Moses reciprocating the lesson of caring for another without making an issue of the distinctions of lineage and culture.

It is notable that Moses married Zipporah by the fact that the text mentions her by name. We know nothing of Joshua's wife, nor that of Aaron, Samuel, and Eli, but we have a name for Moses' wife, seemingly because of her foreign status. We will find a different name in the Exodus text for a wife for Moses, likely indicating that he had more than one wife, but greater mention is made of this one, a stranger to the nation forming among the descendants of Jacob.

Amid a host of texts that speak of the need for the nation of Israel to keep itself pure in marriage, there are several women of foreign origin who figure prominently enough in the greater characters of Israelite history. Zipporah is one of them, but she is definitely not the only one. What may mark her as different from the others is that she is of a family who likewise serves Yahweh as the one true God. She is the daughter of Jethro, priest of the Most High God. It is this relationship to Yahweh that is of much greater significance in her life and her full participation in the life of the new nation forming in the wilderness.

Rahab

In Joshua 2 we find the story of Rahab, who, while not technically an immigrant, is found outside the bounds of God's people. She chose to identify with the band of Hebrews who were entering the country. In dealing mercifully with Joshua's two spies, she begged participation within the nation of Yahweh. Her inclusion overlooked her position as a temple prostitute in a pagan religion as well as her national origin. She was allowed to choose to become part of Yahweh's people. Not only was she accepted by the spies, but we find out that she ended up being one of King David's ancestors (Matthew 1:2–6).

Rahab's name will be found again in Matthew's list of Jesus' family members. He will take pains to point out that this woman who was an outsider and should have been condemned to death for her lifestyle finds grace and participation within Israel.

Though of a foreign people, she finds inclusion within the new nation simply because she recognizes the validity of Yahweh's claim to sovereignty and victory against her own people and gods. She asks to participate in the newly forming nation and then takes steps to assist Joshua's spies in their flight from Jericho's king. She is not judged by her ethnicity, but by her actions to seek inclusion within the nation of Israel, giving her life in service to Yahweh.

If any Old Testament character's inclusion within the life of Israel should shock us, this would be that character. She was a foreigner, pagan, idolatrous, a prostitute working in the service of the fertility gods of her people. Despite all of this, she finds God's grace to be sufficient to take her at her moment of need and bring her a new opportunity for a new identity and a new lease on life.

Ruth

The book of Ruth is an implicit critique of Israelite society's contempt for the foreigner. Ruth is shown as a foreigner who accepts allegiance to the God of Israel. In the course of her story, she shows herself to be more worthy than many, if not most of the Israelites around her. She is then portrayed as a vessel through whom comes one of God's most revered servants, King David, her great-grandson (Ruth 4:13–20).

Ruth was a foreigner. Not only a foreigner, she was from the land of Moab, considered the worst of Israel's enemies. Her people had denied the haggard band of Hebrew slaves' passage through their land in their journey through the wilderness in flight from Egypt. Moab was officially not supposed to be forgiven for their opposition to the Hebrews. Even so, it is in the character of this young woman that Israel finds a lesson for its own lack of faithfulness to Yahweh.

Ruth joined her mother-in-law in returning to Israel with a degree of loyalty few could match. She cast her lot with Naomi, even when Yahweh had not demonstrated much care for this poor widow whose sons had also died. Ruth pledged to remain with and care for Naomi in returning to Israel, placing her own needs aside to care for her immigrant mother-in-law, then to become an immigrant within Israel in her own stead.

It takes courage to become an immigrant, leaving all one knows behind. To do so as a widow and attached to another widow takes a whole new level of courage and faith in a God who has not shown the kind of faithfulness we would like to see. As such, Ruth demonstrates a level of faith and trust virtually unknown in Israel and sets the bar for Israelite faith in Yahweh.

Bathsheba

The widow of Uriah the Hittite, Bathsheba was taken as wife by King David after his repentance and the death of their illegitimate son. She then becomes mother to David's heir, King Solomon. Technically, she should not have found such acceptance, due to certain laws in Israel, yet she enters the lineage of Jesus' ancestors, per Matthew's description (Matthew 1:2–6).

Bathsheba was either an immigrant herself, or she had stooped to marry an immigrant, contrary to the expectation and legal proscriptions for Israel. As with the Ruth and Rahab stories, immigrants find a place in God's grace. There would appear to be an element of progress here in God's revelation, as God works beyond the limitations apparent in sections of Israelite society and law.

It was one thing for King David to take Bathsheba as a wife; he had many wives and concubines. What is most noteworthy here is that she rose to being the future king's mother. This position was not granted her as mother of David's eldest son. David placed her in this position in apparent compensation for having abused her while she was still the wife of Uriah.

The prophet Nathan was in agreement with such a blessing for her. Though her immigrant status should have overruled her receiving such a boon, Yahweh does not seem to care for the same issues that concerned the legal structures of Israel. The laws were supposed to have come from Yahweh, yet it seems that Yahweh is not as concerned with legal code as with being free with granting participation and blessing in the covenant and promise to Abraham. After all, the promise was that all families of the earth would be blessed in Abraham. That extended to include all Gentiles, foreigners, strangers, and immigrants.

Naaman

In 2 Kings 5, Elisha healed an enemy who had come to Israel to seek healing. The man was a foreigner and servant to a foreign king who was a declared enemy of Israel. God chose to heal Naaman through Elisha's intervention, demonstrating the grace and power of Yahweh. While the

Israelite king did not demonstrate confidence in Yahweh, this foreigner learned faith in his interaction with Yahweh's prophet.

Jesus pointed to this story as an example of God's grace lavished upon some who did not technically belong to the chosen people. He referenced this in response to his own healing of those outside the boundaries of Jewish society. He used the story to demonstrate that he was within not only the will of Yahweh to minister to those beyond Judaism. He was following the very patterns Yahweh had already established of bringing others into the fold of the people named by God as chosen.

The king of Israel viewed Naaman's coming to Israel for healing as a veiled threat, a stratagem to gain a justifiable reason to declare war against Israel. Elisha looked upon Naaman not as a threat, but one with a need, a need Yahweh could meet. While the king viewed the situation out of a perspective of fear and uncertainty, Elisha looked upon the situation as an opportunity to demonstrate Yahweh as worthy of the title of God in and for Israel as well as before the nations all around.

From the story in 2 Kings, we find that Naaman never was a threat, though many considered him such. He was a man with a need, seeking for a long-shot solution to his problems. As in the case of so many modern immigrants, he was simply looking for a way out of the dilemma life had handed him. Elisha was confident that Yahweh could provide that solution and treated him from a position of confidence God was faithful to back up.

Jonah

Jonah is, among all the prophets, the one who is specifically called to become an immigrant in lands belonging to Israel's enemies. Worse than that for him, Jonah does not want to fulfill God's purposes, yet God forces him to obey.

The book of Jonah is all about attitudes regarding immigrants, foreigners, and other nations. Its message counters certain Jewish attitudes against enemy nations in describing their contrast to Yahweh's love for all of creation, including nations, plants, and animals. God's desire is for love, mercy, and forgiveness to reign unhindered by determinations of who may be considered worthy or unworthy. It is a message of the equal worth before God held by all nationalities and ethnicities, regardless of any extenuating circumstances.

Jonah did not hold with such concepts of equal worth of all people. Though he was a prophet of Yahweh, his attitudes did not fall in accord with the attitude of his own God. From the beginning of God's call to send him to Nineveh, he found himself in opposition to Yahweh's purposes. He runs not because he does not believe God loves the Ninevites, but because he fears that Yahweh does indeed love them.

He is sent to preach repentance to Nineveh, though when he actually arrives, he couches the message in terms of condemnation and impending doom. By the next chapter, however, we see that all along, he understands that mercy is an integral part of the message. There is opportunity for repentance and forgiveness. There is an inherent message of grace behind the message of condemnation.

While Jonah desired Nineveh's condemnation, Yahweh was interested in their restoration. Jonah feels himself justified in his attitudes toward Nineveh as they were known to act in extreme cruelty against his own people and their other enemies of war. God, however, is unwilling to allow for such attitudes to be arrayed against others. Jonah knows that; he just does not want to accept the implications of such knowledge. It is one thing for God to love them, but another for him to allow that love to flow through him. Regardless of our justifications in placing people in categories of being unworthy of grace and mercy, God neither deals in such categories nor accepts that we continue to maintain such attitudes ourselves.

Flight to Egypt

Jesus' infancy flight to Egypt with his parents places him in the category of what today would be an "undocumented immigrant." While legislation regarding immigration was much more fluid in the time period and context, Jesus would have arrived in Egypt with his family as one who was dependent on the mercy of the resident majority population.

They did not deal in visas and border crossing checks as we do today. They did, however, define citizenship in accord with the Greek concept of being born in the right families within a city or region. Along with those categories of citizenship was the fact that those who might come in from beyond such categories had little to no rights or protections in the legal systems of the day. The outsider was at the mercy of those who belonged.

Along the lines of Abraham's visitors who made their way to Sodom, those who were not members of the local society could not count on any system of rights or protections that the local populace did not decide to grant.

The Roman Empire did not get involved in disputes of the kind, except as concerned its own citizens. A Jew might be born in territory controlled by the empire, but that was not enough to grant citizenship rights. Instead, there were many degrees of importance granted individuals in accord with their origin or ethnicity as well as the place in which they happened to be. Jesus in Egypt lived devoid of many protections he might have had in Judea, even if Herod at the time desired to have him killed. As an immigrant in a foreign territory, his existence, rights, and freedoms were limited to that of a second- or third-class individual, even if he were not on the level of a slave.

The Canaanite Woman

The whole chapter of Matthew 8 is devoted to the issue of Jesus' dealings with immigrants, foreigners, and the otherwise unworthy in and around Israel. The category of "unclean" in accord with purity laws is one of the major issues that Jesus is addressing here. Purity here has to do with one's ritual standing for participation in temple and synagogue worship. Matthew 9 continues the theme, dealing with a woman with an issue of blood, "sinners," and a leper.

It is in chapter 15, however, that Jesus travels beyond Israel to seek out a Canaanite woman with whom he can show the disciples by example how the grace of God is sufficient to extend beyond the bounds of Jewish society. He reaches out to those a Jew would naturally neglect as unworthy of attention and alien to God's grace.

Jesus had told the disciples that true cleanliness or ritual purity had nothing to do with eating the right foods or following certain Mosaic codes of conduct. Ritual purity in actuality had much more to do with issues of the heart, one's center of decision. When they could not truly understand his words about clean and unclean foods, clean and unclean people, he left the region and entered a different land, where all the people should have been categorized by Jews as ritually impure or unclean.

It was here (as an immigrant or foreigner) that he encountered the Canaanite woman who, from Jewish perspective, had no legitimate claim for God's mercy and healing. She begged his intervention, and he first of all offered her the traditional Jewish response: there is only grace and mercy for those on the inside of the boundaries established by Judaism. If she became clean and part of the fold, then maybe she might be worthy to beg something of God.

Her response is noted for the sake of the disciples and us readers. God's grace is sufficient for there to be scraps or crumbs left over for the unworthy.

Jesus took this answer and recast it in terms of his own teaching to the disciples. Her internal faith had nothing to do with concerns of the externals of purity laws and rituals. It had to do with matters that lay beyond what Judaism could categorize. Though she was part of an unholy nation, God's grace reached her willingly and saw her as worthy of the attention of God's mercy and love.

Philemon

Paul did not campaign against the institution of slavery. He does, however, cast the institution of slavery in his letter to Philemon in a very different manner than that of the modern norm. He encouraged Philemon to treat his slave as an equal in Christ Jesus, no longer according to the sociopolitical standards of the day. He enjoined him to ignore his legal rights in order that the grace of Christ Jesus might take over his attitudes and actions concerning the escaped slave returning to him. Such attitudes proposed by Paul ran counter to the manner in which the society and legal code addressed individuals, their rights, and their inherent value.

Slavery in that day and age was a different institution than that of the transatlantic slave trade of not long ago. It was still not a humane treatment of people and placed many in the category of chattel or property. At the same time, however, it did allow individuals to take on slavery as a means to care for their physical and economic needs when they faced extreme circumstances along the lines of current bankruptcy laws. Slaves were still property, yet they had certain rights and were not deemed to be less than human.

Paul, however, establishes in this short letter a completely new take on the person of the slave. The slave here is to be held as a brother in Christ, a person of equal worth and value. The way Philemon treats his slave is viewed as a reflection of Philemon's treatment of Christ Jesus, who dwells within the person of his slave. There is no concept here of simple property, even though Paul recognizes that the escaped slave has likely caused his owner some kind of economic damage. His personhood in Christ, however, should trump any economic concern Philemon might have. Paul goes so far as to ask that any damage be placed on his own account, one that Philemon would not be likely to charge.

Paul reminded Philemon that he himself owed Paul a debt he was unable to pay, even as he owed a debt to Christ Jesus. It is under this framework that Philemon is enjoined to look upon his slave now: he is a person for whom Christ died and in whom Christ Jesus lives. That is cause enough to consider any and all persons as having equal or higher worth than ourselves, regardless of the category in which our society might desire to place them.

"Multiply and Fill the Earth"

There is another set of texts, specifically beginning in Genesis, which deal with a wholly other category, in which immigration becomes central to God's plan. Repeatedly, God tells humanity to scatter, multiply, and fill the earth. By so doing, we are to fulfill God's plan for creation to be teeming with life and human life the world around.

Abraham is called to immigrate to a new land he does not know. In a related manner, Philip, Barnabas, Silas, and Paul are called to new lands on mission for Christ. In texts like Matthew 23, the disciples are warned of the impending destruction of Jerusalem, upon which they were to scatter throughout the world with this gospel. Becoming immigrants was often linked with fulfilling God's purposes for us as individuals and as the people of God. Becoming missionaries requires that we step into the category of immigrant in some other society.

In our looking upon immigrants in our own midst, we must also look to those occasions in which we are called to live as immigrants in other lands or support those sent by God into other lands as immigrants. Unfortunately, we are often loathe to look upon others with the same attitudes we want others to look upon us when the shoe is on the other foot.

Philip, Paul, Silas, Peter, Barnabas, Luke, John Mark, and many others were sent out as emissaries of the gospel to other lands. Jesus himself took the disciples to regions outside of Israel, healing the Gerasene demoniac in Mark 5 and sending him to another region to spread the word of God's work in his life. In Matthew 28 and Acts 1, the disciples are charged with taking God's message to all nations, making disciples of them. For this to occur they would have to become immigrants or wanderers like Abraham.

We are the product of people like these disciples of old who left one land for another. Europeans left for shores in the New World, Africans have left their shores for Europe, and Asians have left their own land for others. While these migrations over the centuries have not necessarily been urged specifically by God's decree, they are consistent with God's message throughout the Pentateuch that humanity is to fill the world, multiplying and spreading out in new ways. Whether we like it or not, the immigrants in our midst are fulfilling this commandment of God.

SECTION TWO

Passages Containing Specific Terminology for Immigrants

In this next section, we will look at the breadth of biblical passages that use specific terminology for immigrants, foreigners, or refugees. As noted above, there are other passages that are pertinent to the topic, even if they do not use the specific terminology. For instance, Matthew 15 speaks of the Canaanite woman, but in that context it is Jesus and the disciples who find themselves in the category of immigrants or foreigners, though neither term is used.

I have taken a master list of passages using the specific terminology and organized them according to ten larger identified themes. I have listed these themes in descending order of how often each theme occurs. For each defined passage, I have listed the range of verses and then offered a summary statement of the importance of the passage regarding the issue of immigration and the treatment of immigrants, specifically in accord with the themes being developed.

Some of the passages listed below fall under more than one thematic heading. Therefore, those passages will be listed again under each pertinent category. All told, there are 182 passages in the Bible using specific terminology translated as immigrant, foreigner, refugee, stranger, or wanderer. I am not counting the number of times these specific words occur, but the number of passages that contain the terms. I list, for example, Genesis 17:3–13 as one passage, though the terms in question appear more than once in that one range of verses. This same passage also deals with more than one theme and will therefore be referenced more than once.

God's Blessings Are for All Peoples
(91 Passages)

God's blessings are available for all people, without distinction.

This group of texts looks beyond issues of nationalism, recognizing that God wills to include all peoples within the bounds of love, grace, acceptance, and blessing. This message will become clearer in the New Testament than it is in the Old, but it has definite origins within the Old Testament. Those voices simply tended to be drowned out by others crying for concerns of superiority in nationalism.

God extends grace beyond Israel's borders or definitions of nationality. Some of these texts, such as Acts 2, will refer to Jews living around the known world of the Roman Empire. Others will show how God's people have always been defined by broader categories than the standard definitions used by Israelite society. This is made clear both in the promise to Abraham of God's will to bless all nations as well as in the inclusion of various foreigners within the core identity of the people of Israel, most notably in expressions of David's lineage.

Genesis 17:3–13. God's promise includes that Abram will be the father of many nations. The land in which he lived as an immigrant would one day belong to his descendants. Beyond that, however, all the families of the earth would find blessing in what God planned to do through him.

Exodus 12:43–49. The foreigner was not to participate in eating the sacrificial lamb if they had not participated in the redemption of the Hebrews from Egypt. If they had become part of the people through circumcision, they were considered fully a part of the people and were required to participate fully. The only distinction allowed here is based on one's participation in the redemption process. Otherwise, all are equal before God, and nationality itself becomes negligible. Immigrants who have not participated in the covenant are allowed to do so, as God's blessings are available to them as well.

Exodus 20:10. The Sabbath was given as a blessing and respite to the Hebrews on the basis of being able to trust Yahweh with sufficient provision for them to take a day to rest. This blessing was to extend to the immigrants, who would normally have been expected not to enjoy the same freedoms and blessing as the rest of the population. Rather than being a lower class of people who God did not care to bless, they are given protection here in the law on the basis of God's care for them.

Exodus 23:12. Immigrant workers were not to be placed in a category inferior to work animals. They are given the same category of protection and blessing as that of the national residents. While there is recognition that immigrants are natural targets for oppression, neither they nor animals are to suffer forced labor any more than those protected as belonging to the land. God's design is to bless and protect them all equally.

Leviticus 17:8–16. A distinction is made between living in the land and belonging to God's people. There is no sense that an immigrant is not allowed to become part of God's people, but conversion must occur prior to enjoying the position of full participation in the covenant agreement. Covenant protections are still extended as well as certain ethical demands and restrictions that would apply to all.

Leviticus 19:10. Gleanings are to be left for the poor, including immigrant refugees. This is part of God's abundant provision for the needs of all. This provision should be considered as enough to care for every person, regardless of their status.

Leviticus 23:22. Again, gleanings are to be left for the poor, including immigrant refugees. The stress through repetition here reinforces the fact that God plans to provide for everyone without distinction.

Leviticus 24:22. There is but one law that should apply equally to all, native or immigrant alike. This law is for the benefit of the entire society. Immigrants are to find rescue, redemption, and provision alongside all others.

Leviticus 25:4–7. The seventh year's unplanted harvest would be sufficient to care for the slaves, servants, and immigrant refugees. God's provision was planned to care for the needs of all, beyond those deemed of greater import by society.

Leviticus 25:35. An Israelite coming to poverty should be treated with the mercy due to any immigrant refugee. There is no distinction made here, although strangely the concept assumes the good treatment of the immigrant above the treatment of the poor.

Numbers 9:14. Immigrants should celebrate Passover along with Israelites. The message and associated blessings of Passover were available to all, without distinction due to one's ethnic, cultural, or national origin. The whole point of the exodus was that God took a band of slaves to form a new nation from them.

Deuteronomy 5:14. Even the immigrants should participate in the day of Sabbath rest, along with all native born and work animals. This was deemed a blessing stemming from God's provision and here extended to all in Israel.

Deuteronomy 10:18–19. God is merciful toward orphans, widows, and immigrant refugees, setting an example for the people in remembrance of their having lived as refugees and slaves in Egypt. God's blessings and protections extend to all.

Deuteronomy 14:27–29. Gifts for the care of the Levites should extend to cover the needs of orphans, widows, and refugees. This is a use of offerings directed by God to care for people beyond the limits of national identity.

Deuteronomy 16:9–11. The harvest feast should be shared with widows, orphans, Levites, and immigrant refugees. All are to share in the blessings of God's bounty, with no regard to national origin.

Deuteronomy 16:13–15. The feast of tabernacles was to be celebrated in the company of families, slaves, orphans, widows, Levites, and immigrant refugees. This feast was a reminder of living as wanderers in the wilderness. Immigrants are here encouraged to participate in this celebration of God's provision.

Deuteronomy 24:14–15. There is here a repetition of the rule of equality between the native born and immigrants. The poor must be paid daily with the warning that injustice in this regard will be handled by God's intervention. God wants to provide for all.

Deuteronomy 24:17. One must not mistreat a refugee or an orphan nor ask a widow's cloak as collateral. God's protections against discrimination and oppression were to cover all members of the society equally, including the foreigners.

Deuteronomy 24:19–22. Leave the gleanings in the field for the poor, refugees, orphans, and widows. All the vulnerable were to be recipients of God's bounty and blessings, even when they had not entered the covenant agreement with Yahweh.

Deuteronomy 26:11–14. To the feast of thanksgiving, they were to invite the priests and refugees living in the land. The triennial tithe would be given to priests, immigrant refugees, orphans, and widows. Notice that the injunction here is for the landholders to share with the vulnerable landless.

Deuteronomy 27:14–26. Amid a list of curses toward those mistreating others in need of protection, a curse is called upon those who mistreat immigrant refugees, widows, and orphans. This is God's curse, as God wants the bounty and justice of the land to be shared with all people.

Deuteronomy 29:11. All were gathered for ratification of the covenant, including the immigrant laborers who were set to forced labor on behalf of the nation. While there is some inconsistency here to these actions, an underlying principle is that the covenant blessings were for the benefit of all.

Deuteronomy 31:12. All are to celebrate the feast, including immigrant refugees, in order that they might learn to respect and obey God. It was God's desire that all become participants in the covenant agreement and recipients of its blessings.

Joshua 8:33–35. Immigrants were included in the gathering of Israel for the priestly blessing before the ark of the covenant. The participation of the immigrants was in part to teach them the norms of Yahweh, but also that they might seek full inclusion.

Joshua 20:9. The creation of cities of refuge were to apply equally for the protection of immigrants as for the native born. There is but one law for all, applying equal protections as well as responsibilities with no sense of discrimination.

1 Kings 8:41–43. Solomon pleads with God to use the temple to reach all nations from the temple's impact among immigrants living within Israel. This is in accordance with God's declared will to bless all peoples.

2 Chronicles 6:32–33. God is asked to heed the prayers of immigrants when they should pray at the temple, answering them in order to lead other to faith in Yahweh from among all nations of the world.

2 Chronicles 30:25. The Passover celebration was extended for an extra week because the celebration was taken up with joy by all, including the immigrant population. God was happy with their participation in this covenant celebration of God's blessings.

Job 29:16. Protection and defense of the poor and immigrant are cast here as signs of righteousness and justice. True righteousness does not discriminate between categories of people and their supposed levels of dignity and value.

Psalm 18:43–45. This is a reiteration of David recognizing that God had placed him in a position of respect before immigrant peoples. It was God's will to be known by all nations, regardless of the distinctions we might consider important.

Psalm 94:6. Injustice is framed here as killing widows, murdering orphans, and massacring immigrant refugees. There is no sense that it might be less unjust to discriminate toward some people on the basis of some category or another. Injustice is still injustice.

Psalm 107:4, 40. The Hebrew wilderness wandering is cast here as oppressive and difficult, yet God is pictured as ready to rescue the needy wanderer. God used the condition of wandering to chastise the people, preparing them for their future. The sole criterion for access to God's help is crying out in need..

Isaiah 14:1. Upon God's restoration of Israel, many immigrants will come as refugees to join the nation being refashioned. God would offer them inclusion, just as many other immigrants had found inclusion under the blessings of covenant with Yahweh.

Isaiah 56:3–7. There is here a promise of security for the immigrants who come to worship Yahweh. God desires that the temple be a place of prayer for all nations, not simply for those who are of Abraham's biological lineage.

Jeremiah 7:3–7. A major part of repentance includes enacting justice for the oppressed, including immigrant refugees, widows, and orphans. Doing what is right by the vulnerable of society is in accord with God's definitions of justice and righteousness.

Jeremiah 22:3. Yahweh's demands of righteousness are summed up in the care for the oppressed, immigrants, orphans, widows, and the innocent. Immigrants are specifically included as they fall under the scope of God's protection.

Ezekiel 14:7. Yahweh's judgment announcement includes the immigrants in the land as responsible alongside Israel for disobeying Yahweh and idolatry. They are cared for by God, who also holds them equally accountable with Israel.

Ezekiel 44:7–9. The people were leaving the temple worship of Yahweh in the hands of immigrants who had not assumed the covenant responsibilities with Yahweh. The stress here is on the identification with Yahweh, not immigrant status. God's blessings were available to all, but there were responsibilities attached to those same blessings.

Ezekiel 47:21–22. Land apportionment was to include the natural-born children of immigrants. They were to enjoy the same rights as any other Israelites, specifically including an allotment of land on an equal basis as any other native-born individual.

Matthew 4:15. Those in the foreign lands were also to hear God's announcement along with Israel. God's desire was that the message and blessings of the good news would reach all peoples equally, without regard to national distinctions.

Matthew 8:10–12. Jesus finds an immigrant whose belief (trust) is greater than that of any in Israel. He mentions that other nations would be accepted in the final day ahead of many in Israel, as being native born was not as important as entering into a life of faith in God.

Matthew 10:18. Jesus warned the disciples that they would face persecution and danger from both Jews and foreigners. They would be required to bear witness to Jesus before all. The very rationale behind their going before the authorities from God's perspective was to bear the gospel.

Matthew 12:18–21. God's servant here is called to proclaim God's justice to all nations. This will be a message of hope for all peoples, not simply a message of hope for the Jews. All nations are covered in God's blessings and gospel.

Matthew 15:21–28. Jesus deals with a foreigner, exclaiming over her faith and using her as an example that it is his will to deal in grace without respect to nationality, standing, or issues of ritual purity. Ritual purity concerns were about religious distinctions to set some apart as of greater worth or dignity than others. Jesus is unconcerned with such issues.

Matthew 25:31–46. The final judgment of nations will reflect how they treated the hungry, thirsty, poor, stranger, unclothed, sick, and imprisoned. This judgment is upon all nations, including people the world over and their treatment of all. This is a judgment of both condemnation and blessing.

Mark 5:18–20. Jesus' ministry reaches outside the bounds of Israel, sending a man on mission to an entire non-Jewish region. There is here no respecting of borders, but the gospel is presented as a benefit for any and all.

Mark 7:24–28. Jesus' ministry again takes him outside the borders of Israel. He makes a point of ministering to one who was considered inferior due to her status as a non-Jew. Grace reaches out to all without distinction.

Luke 2:32. Messiah is figured here to become an expression of light and hope for all the nations, not simply for the Jews. This is a message of inclusion, as Gentiles are determined to fall under God's banner of blessing, promise, and provision.

Luke 4:16–20. The oppressed (including immigrants) were the essential target of Jesus' preaching of redemption, freedom, and release. Jesus was unconcerned with issues of nationality or immigrant status, for God's love is for all.

Luke 4:25–27. Elijah had been sent to care for a foreign widow, not an Israelite. Naaman, another foreigner, was the only leper cured in Israelite history. God did not withhold blessings from them on the basis of their nationality or lack of belonging.

Luke 10:33–35. It is the Samaritan foreigner who stopped to help the injured man in the parable. He is the answer to the question, "Who is my neighbor that I should love as myself?" From Jesus' standpoint, nationality is of no consequence in God's blessings.

Luke 17:18. The foreigner here sets the bar for giving thanks, as the native born are too wrapped up in the demands of protocol. The Samaritans were considered beyond redemption in the eyes of Jews, but Jesus has no qualms in reaching out to them.

Acts 9:15. God's purpose for Paul was to send him as an emissary of the gospel to the nations beyond that of the Jews. He would become both an immigrant and a burden-bearer to carry a message of hope to all peoples of the world.

Acts 10:45. It was a shock to the Jews to discover validation for the gospel not only to be presented to the Gentiles, but for them to receive it along with the confirming presence of the Holy Spirit. This character of God's breath infusing their lives was to them incontrovertible proof of God blessing efforts to preach grace to all nations without distinction.

Acts 11:1. News of the gospel being preached through Peter to people who were still Gentiles made its way back to Jerusalem. It was a big issue for these Jewish believers, as they had not expected that the gospel would cover people who had not first become Jews.

Acts 11:18. On receiving reports that the Gentile converts had experienced the coming of God's spirit upon them, these Jewish believers were silenced. They were uncomfortable with sharing God and faith in Jesus with Gentiles, but recognized that God called them beyond the bounds of their comfort.

Acts 13:43. Both Jewish and non-Jewish converts followed Paul. He did begin his preaching among Jews in the cities where he taught, but he rapidly shifted to the Gentiles when the Jews turned on him. He accepted them under the gospel with no qualms.

Acts 13:46–48. The Jews in Paul's and Barnabas's hearing did not like the fact that these missionaries would take their message beyond the limits of Judaism. They wanted this message kept in house, rather than making it available to any without requirements that they first become Jews. The non-Jews, however, were thrilled to hear and receive Paul's preaching.

Acts 14:27. Paul reported back regarding the extension of the gospel to the nations beyond Judaism. This news was well received by many, even though it was still an astonishing step for the early church to accept. Receiving Gentiles would mean accepting them without distinction in their own midst, which was a stretch.

Acts 15:3–23. Here, Paul and Barnabas return to Jerusalem to report on their ministry among the Gentiles as well as to seek advice regarding a conflict that had arisen in light of their ministry. The assembly in Jerusalem was not completely happy with details regarding ministry among the Gentiles, but they found themselves forced to recognize God's presence and action among these converts who had not adopted Judaism. The end result of the council was that these Gentiles did not need to be forced to become Jews, but simply to live according to faith and the grace offered by Christ Jesus, which had already covered them.

Acts 17:19–21. The Athenians and immigrant residents there liked to hear new ideas presented. Paul preaches to both the resident and immigrant populace. Such distinctions made no difference in his presentation of the gospel.

Acts 18:6. Paul felt himself forced to take a stand against some of the Jews who were struggling with his teaching. In his reply, he shares openly that his ministry will proceed among Gentiles, since the Jews of the synagogue were unwilling to accept his teaching. They did not like his branching out into the Gentile community.

Acts 21:19. We find Paul once again reporting on his ministry among other peoples. The full blessings and participation in the gospel were made available to all different national groups in the course of Paul's ministry, all from a starting point in God.

Acts 21:25. There is affirmation here of the Jerusalem council decision regarding the Gentile converts. They were not to have been pressed to fully become Jews, but were asked to honor certain Jewish prescriptions against idolatry, eating blood, and sexual immorality.

Acts 22:21. Luke here describes an occasion when Paul recounts the story of his call to serve Jesus. He tells how God had called him with the specific mission to send him to Gentile populations around the world.

Acts 26:17. Paul would encounter persecution in the course of his ministry. This would come from both Gentiles and Jews. God would, however, protect him along the way, offering guidance and protection in the course of his faithful ministry among all peoples.

Acts 26:20–23. Paul recounts elements of his ministry reaching around to peoples from various places and backgrounds. He preached at Damascus, then around the Roman Empire, being called by God to preach to both Jews and Gentiles alike.

Acts 28:28. Finally in Rome, Paul has the opportunity to present the gospel once again to Jews. As they refuse his message, he once again returns to preach the gospel of Christ Jesus among those who are not Jews.

Romans 1:13. It had long been Paul's desire to preach the gospel in Rome, just as he had preached it in many other nations. He was assured that God intended the gospel to be a message open to all, regardless of any national identification.

Romans 3:29. Paul reminds his Roman readers that God is not simply the God of Israel, as though that were an exclusionary title. God is likewise the God for all nations around the world. Rather than being owned by a nation, God is sovereign over all.

Romans 9:22–30. The purpose of the gospel is in part to make us righteous, specifically to justify us before God on the basis of grace and faith. This comes not at any human initiative, as though the Gentiles had pursued God. Rather, this was all at God's instigation—God desiring freely to offer salvation and redemption to all peoples.

Romans 11:11–13. Paul argues here with regard to distinctions between Jews and Gentiles. He is not ready to consider that the Jews are trash any more than that the Gentiles are. The gospel has come to both from God's initiative. Both Jews and Gentiles find acceptance from God on an equal basis.

Romans 11:25. Paul does not want Gentiles believing they are more important than Jews, any more than Jews that they are more important than Gentiles. God's salvation has been offered freely without regard to nationality. As salvation is a gift based on grace, it has nothing to do with any human category of being more worthy or valuable than another.

Romans 12:13. The believers are to share resources with other Christians as well as to invite strangers into their homes. The term here for hospitality actually means the love of strangers or foreigners. The love of the gospel is to reach beyond concerns of nationality and even beyond concerns of knowing the people to whom we minister.

Romans 15:9–18. God's salvation was extended to Gentiles on the same basis as it had been extended to Jews. Paul points to various Old Testament passages that speak to the issue of God's care to redeem people from all the nations.

Romans 15:27. Paul considered it only proper that Gentile believers recognize their responsibility to care for Jews who were suffering economic distress from a famine. He further links this responsibility to a sense of duty to those through whom God's message of salvation had come.

Romans 16:4. There were other believers who were now present in Rome who had sacrificed on behalf of taking the gospel to the Gentiles. They had placed their lives at risk, just as Paul had done, recognizing along with Paul that the gospel extended God's blessings and provision toward all categories of people.

1 Corinthians 14:21. God would speak through immigrants and foreigners in unknown languages, all the while being ignored. God is willing to utilize people regardless of their nationality, but the greater issue is whether one will accept God's message and blessing.

2 Corinthians 11:26. Paul has been in danger from countrymen and foreigners alike. He preached to all, but also was the brunt of persecution from both Jews and Gentiles. Nationality played little to no factor in determining a response to Paul and the gospel.

Galatians 1:16. God revealed Jesus to Paul with the very specific purpose of using Paul to take the gospel to Gentiles around the world. This was not a secondary purpose for God, but something important enough for which to commission Paul.

Galatians 2:2. Paul's preaching ministry among the Gentiles was not something he hid from other believers. He had the support of the Jerusalem church elders, before whom he had explained in detail the message he shared. They had given him their backing.

Galatians 2:8–9. Paul's Gentile ministry was supported by various leaders in the Jerusalem church. They recognized Peter's ministry essentially among Jews and cast Paul's ministry along a similar vein among the Gentiles.

Galatians 3:8. Paul reminds his Galatian readers that God had spoken the same message of salvation by grace through faith from the earliest days of Abraham. The manner in which Abraham found favor with God and salvation was the same manner by which the Gentiles were to find salvation.

Galatians 3:14. As God had granted a promise to Abraham that all families of the earth would be blessed through him, so the Gentiles of Paul's ministry were receiving the blessing of God's spirit poured out in their lives.

Ephesians 2:11–19. Before God, the Ephesians are no longer foreigners, but belong to God's people, the family of God. God is in the business of changing the categories of our belonging, as we are called to belong first and foremost to God and only secondarily to any nation or political entity.

Ephesians 3:1–8. God has called all nations to participate equally in Christ Jesus of the very same inheritance. National distinctions are nonexistent from God's perspective. They are categories of human invention, which God does not validate.

Colossians 1:27. It was God's will to offer the gospel to Gentile nations. The hope of this good news was a message of redemption whereby Christ would live in the believer. This was a new announcement as far as the Jews were concerned, but it covered all Gentiles who would accept God's offer of redemption.

1 Thessalonians 2:16. Paul's ministry to the Gentiles was not without serious opposition. He credited the actions of his opponents as sin. They would have to answer not to Paul, but to God for standing against God's purposes of redeeming all peoples.

1 Timothy 2:7. It was God who had appointed Paul as a preacher and apostle to the Gentiles. This was not a position he had taken on at his own initiative. Indeed, he and many other Jews had fought against such a message. Rather, this was a new initiative of God that made many uncomfortable.

2 Timothy 4:17. Paul recalls some of the persecution he had suffered in order to proclaim the gospel among Gentiles. He had been rescued from violence against him on more than one occasion through God's intervention. God still wanted him to complete that original purpose.

Hebrews 13:2. Hospitality should be extended to strangers, even as some heroes of faith did in the past and thereby received God's messengers as guests. We are enjoined to share God's blessings with all, along with the concept that in so doing we receive the fullness of God's blessings.

Immigrants Should Be Treated with Equality
(73 Passages)

One should treat immigrants with equity.

We could break this group of texts into two themes, one regarding the general treatment due to immigrants and the second pertaining to legal prescriptions that one same law applies to both the immigrant and the natural-born Israelite. Many of these texts do indeed specifically state these biblical ideals and mandate that all people be treated with equity, regardless of national, political, and social conventions. As a whole, however, a command to treat immigrants and foreigners as one would treat the natural born is still a command along the same principles of equal treatment.

God's love and grace are available to all, so we are enjoined to work toward the equal treatment of any and all people, regardless of social definitions, "for in Christ there is neither slave nor free, male nor female, Jew nor non-Jew, but all are one in Christ." This is the principle at the heart of these various passages.

These texts do not refer simply to the fact that the law should treat immigrants and nationals equally. They concern themselves with the specifics of practical application of those principles. Israel rarely lived up to these principles, as can be seen in the conflict between Jews and Samaritans in the gospels. Even so, these texts are rather clear about what should have been the attitudes of God's chosen people.

This second largest grouping of biblical passages using terminology for immigrants, foreigners, or refugees requires equality of treatment for immigrant or foreigner and the resident population of Israel. There is little to no room here for any sense of special privilege to accrue to the national population in contrast to the immigrant. They should be deemed as equals in respect to both the benefits and the requirements of the law.

This principle flies in the face of Roman law, as it did for the laws of the nations around ancient Israel. In Abraham's day, each city made its own laws, yet the norm was that only its citizens found protection by those same laws. This same concept extended to the larger political entities that were created throughout Palestine over the next few centuries.

While Israel shared with other nations a concept of defining righteousness in light of how the voiceless were treated, it is to my knowledge the only nation whose legal code addressed the issue of equality.

Genesis 17:3–13. God's pact includes that Abram will be father of many nations (nationalities/peoples). The land in which he is an immigrant will one day belong to his descendants. The rule regarding circumcision should apply to offspring, slaves, and foreigners (slaves or servants of his retinue), for one law applied equally to all without distinction.

Exodus 12:14–20. The central Hebrew festival of identity (Passover) was to be celebrated by all as requirement for presence in Israel. No distinction was to be made regarding the resident status of an individual. The same law that should to apply everyone equally.

Exodus 12:43–49. The foreigner was not to participate in eating the sacrificial lamb if they had not participated in the redemption of the Hebrews from Egypt by accepting the pact with Yahweh. In a sense, they were still enslaved with a lesser status, awaiting redemption. If they had become part of the people through circumcision, they were considered part of the people and must participate fully. The only distinction allowed here regards one's participation in the redemption process. Otherwise, all are equal before God; nationality itself is negligible. Immigrant residents and Israelites must obey the law alike.

Exodus 20:10. Sabbath was given as a blessing and respite to the Hebrews on the basis of being able to trust Yahweh with sufficient provision for them to take a day to rest. This blessing was to extend to the immigrant, who would normally not have been expected to enjoy the same freedoms and blessing as the rest of the population. Here is a prohibition against taking advantage of the immigrant, treating such workers as belonging to an inferior class of person with lesser rights.

Exodus 22:21. Here we find a command to respect and not mistreat (oppress) refugees due to their status as immigrants. The basis for protection again is related to empathy from the Hebrew experience of having been oppressed as immigrants in Egypt.

Exodus 23:9–12. Refugees may not be enslaved or oppressed because of their immigrant status. Immigrant workers may not be placed in a category inferior to that of work animals. They are to receive the same category of protection and blessing as the national residents. While there is recognition that immigrants are natural targets for oppression, neither they nor animals are to suffer forced labor any more than those protected for belonging to the land.

Leviticus 16:29–31. The same commandment will serve for both the refugee as well as the native born. There are requirements here for equality of treatment, specifically mentioning immigrant populations.

Leviticus 17:8–16. A distinction is made between living in the land and belonging to God's people. There is no sense that an immigrant is not allowed to become part of God's people, but conversion must occur prior to enjoying the position of full participation in the covenant agreement. Covenant protections are still extended, as well as certain ethical demands and restrictions that would apply to all. There must be equal respect offered to God. Concerns with ritual purity apply equally to all.

Leviticus 18:24–26. A mandate here concerns both immigrants and the people to follow one same code of conduct. There is no distinction made in terms of responsibility before the law or God's demands.

Leviticus 19:10. Gleanings in the fields are to be left for the poor, including immigrant refugees. Mercy is not to be limited by one's immigrant status. There is recognition here that God's provision is sufficient to provide for all without distinction.

Leviticus 19:33–34. Refugees and immigrants are to be treated just as well as any other members of the nation, loved just like any other on the basis of empathic experience. As one would desire to be treated as an immigrant or refugee elsewhere, so should one treat others.

Leviticus 20:2–3. Judgment on an immigrant must obey the same rules as on the native born. There is to be no distinction made. The inference is that the tendency would be leniency toward the native and prejudiced injustice toward the immigrant. This is deemed completely unacceptable.

Leviticus 22:18–25. Commands here are given regarding acceptable sacrifices that should apply to all, regardless of their immigrant status. God specifically allows for the participation of immigrants in the worship life of Israel, even if they have not come to participate in the covenant with Yahweh.

Leviticus 23:22. Gleanings are to be left for the poor, including refugees (immigrants). There is to be no distinction with regard to who might benefit from the gleanings left behind in the field. God's concern is to meet the needs of all, without distinction.

Leviticus 24:22. There is but one law that should apply equally to all, native or immigrant alike. The law should not be used to oppress or to benefit one group over another, regardless of concerns over citizenship or immigration status.

Leviticus 25:4–7. The seventh year's unplanted harvest should be sufficient even to care for the slaves, servants, and refugees. These lower classes of society are to receive the benefits of God's provision, just like the rest of the population.

Leviticus 25:35. An Israelite coming to poverty should be treated with the mercy due to any refugee. There is no distinction. It seems somewhat odd that an immigrant might be treated better than a native-born poor person, yet the issue here is simply that of equality, regardless of one's status.

Numbers 9:14. Immigrants should celebrate Passover along with Israelites. There is one law that should apply equally to all. Even though the Passover was a special festival of Hebrew identity with God's redemption from Egypt, all are to be included on an equal basis.

Numbers 15:11–16. There is to be but one law that applies equally to the native born and the immigrant. All should be treated according to the same measure of their worth before God.

Numbers 15:24–29. There is one same law that is to apply to native born and immigrant alike. They must find equal treatment before the law on the basis of their equal value before God, and their lesser status in society required greater protection for them.

Numbers 19:10. Laws of ritual purity should apply alike to both the native-born and the immigrant segments of the population. They share equally in responsibility toward approaching God in honor, obedience, and respect.

Deuteronomy 1:16–18. The law should operate with equality, showing no preference for rich or poor, native born or immigrant. All classes and categories of people should be treated according to the very same norms as equals.

Deuteronomy 5:14. Even immigrants should participate in the day of Sabbath rest, along with all native born and work animals. These blessings of respite guaranteed and decreed by Yahweh were to be shared with all equally.

Deuteronomy 14:27–29. Gifts given for the care of the Levites in the temple should extend to care for the orphans, widows, and refugees (or immigrants) of the entire society. There is no allowance for determining any preferential treatment for any class of persons.

Deuteronomy 16:9–11. The harvest feast should be shared with widows, orphans, Levites, and refugees (immigrants). There is to be a sense of equality in relation to God's provision to cover the needs of all.

Deuteronomy 16:13–15. The feast of tabernacles should be celebrated in the company of families, slaves, orphans, widows, Levites, and refugees (immigrants). All are to be included as participating in the community of Israel.

Deuteronomy 24:14–15. There is here a repetition of the rule of equality between the native born and immigrants. The poor, regardless of their immigrant status, should be paid daily with the warning that injustice in this regard will be handled by God's intervention.

Deuteronomy 24:17. Do not mistreat a refugee or an orphan nor ask a widow's cloak as collateral. The sense is both that these voiceless in society are most likely to suffer abuse as well as the fact that they are to be granted equality of worth in accord with all of the society.

Deuteronomy 24:19–22. The people were to leave the gleanings in the field for the poor, refugees, orphans, and widows. They were to remember that they were once slaves in Egypt. The lower classes were just as much a part of Israelite society as any other and of equal worth as recipients of God's provision.

Deuteronomy 26:11–14. To this feast of thanksgiving, the people were to invite the priests and refugees (immigrants) living in the land. The triennial tithe was to be given to priests, refugees, orphans, and widows. This was a distribution of God's provision in equality for all.

Deuteronomy 27:14–26. Amid a list of curses toward those mistreating others in need of protection, a curse is called upon those who mistreat refugees, widows, and orphans. These are the most likely oppressed in any society, but designated as being under God's special protection.

Deuteronomy 29:11. All were gathered for the ratification of the covenant, including the immigrant laborers who were set to forced labor on behalf of the nation. They were to share the same blessings of Yahweh's inclusion and the acceptance granted to any other member of the community.

Deuteronomy 31:12. All were to celebrate the feast, including refugees (immigrants), in order to learn to respect and obey God. God's blessings reflected in the feast were to be shared with equity among all.

Joshua 8:33–35. Immigrants were included in the gathering of Israel for the priestly blessing before the ark of the covenant. They were being charged with the same terms of observance as well as sharing the same terms of blessing with all others.

Joshua 20:9. Designating cities of refuge as protection from persecution and revenge were to benefit immigrants as well as the native born. There is but one law for all, applying equal protections as well as equal responsibilities.

2 Samuel 22:44–46. David recognized that God was empowering him and giving him respect beyond the bounds of nationalism. God's blessings and reach included foreigners within and beyond the bounds of Israel.

1 Kings 8:41–43. Solomon pleaded with God to use the temple to reach all nations due to the temple's impact among immigrants living within Israel. All were to be recipients of knowledge of Yahweh as well as to participate in the blessings of the covenant.

2 Chronicles 6:32–33. God was asked to heed the prayers of immigrants when they should pray at the temple, answering them in order to lead to faith in Yahweh among all nations. There is a greater interest here in sharing the blessings and covenant between Yahweh and other nations in terms of equal value before God.

2 Chronicles 30:25. The Passover celebration was here extended a full week, as the celebration had been taken up with rejoicing by all, including the immigrant population. They were obviously invited to join in the celebration, seeing themselves as having been redeemed from oppression along with the Hebrews.

Esther 4:11–14. Speaking and acting on behalf of an oppressed people is required by justice and of greater importance than self-protection. The term for foreigners is used here in reference to the fact that all peoples of the empire knew of the prohibition to enter the king's inner court on penalty of death.

Job 29:16. Protection and defense of the poor and immigrant are cast as signs of righteousness and justice. Immigrant status is oppressive by nature, but true justice requires equality of treatment before the law.

Psalm 94:6. Injustice is framed here in relation to killing widows, murdering orphans, and massacring refugees (immigrants). Justice would call for equality of treatment and value to be given to all without distinction.

Isaiah 11:12. God would gather the nations and the refugees of Israel and Judah. There is a sense here of God's desire to treat all from the same definition of value. There is no privilege or special consideration for the chosen people.

Isaiah 14:1. Upon God's restoration of Israel, many immigrants would come as refugees to join the nation. This recalls the initial formation of Israel from slaves who left Egypt along with the Hebrews, as well as God's larger will to offer redemption to all peoples without distinction.

Isaiah 14:32. God would be announced as providing refuge for the poorest of the people in Jerusalem. Among the poorest is almost always the immigrant community, as they are generally the easiest targets for economic oppression and injustice.

Isaiah 56:3, 6–7. There is promise of security for the immigrant who comes to worship Yahweh. God desires to grant security to all with no deference paid to the resident born above the immigrant in the land.

Isaiah 58:7. Justice means to provide food and refuge, clothing, and other such aid to any in need. The intent here is to include any and all with no regard to social categories of worth. The main issue is simply identifying the needy.

Jeremiah 7:3–7. A major part of repentance includes enacting justice for the oppressed, including refugees (immigrants), widows, and orphans. Repentance in regard to oppression implicitly means accepting the fact that all are of equal worth and our oppression is contrary to those principles of equality.

Jeremiah 22:3. God's demands of righteousness are summed up in caring for the oppressed, immigrants, orphans, and widows and protecting the innocent. Immigrant status is oppressive by nature, just as the other conditions listed here. Righteousness or justice requires treatment based on equality.

Jeremiah 25:20. God's judgment on the nations would include the immigrants living in those nations. They participated in the blessings of the nations as well as in their responsibilities.

Jeremiah 46:21. Egypt's immigrant mercenary soldiers would also flee God's judgment. God would not discriminate in terms of blessing nor in terms of punishment, as principles of equality apply to both the good and the bad.

Jeremiah 50:37. Babylon's downfall would include the flight and death of its foreign mercenary soldiers. They were complicit in Babylon's actions and would answer equally before God as any native born.

Ezekiel 14:7. Yahweh's judgment announcement includes the immigrants in the land as responsible alongside Israel for disobeying Yahweh and involvement in idolatry. Equality of treatment refers to both blessing and responsibility.

Ezekiel 22:7. The righteousness of the people found expression in how they cared for those with the least representation. This was lacking and condemnatory. They were allowing the voiceless to remain unprotected, including the immigrant community.

Ezekiel 22:29. Justice is again defined as caring for the common targets of oppression: poor, needy, and immigrant refugees. This was a common refrain in Israel as well as among other nations of the ancient Near East.

Ezekiel 47:21–22. Land apportionment was to include immigrants who would enjoy the same rights and responsibilities as the Israelites. There was to be one law that would apply in equality to all, without distinction on the basis of immigrant status.

Obadiah 16. God's judgment would fall upon all nations, not only upon Israel. All must answer to Yahweh, regardless of nationality, ethnicity, language, or culture. Before God, they all stood equally with responsibility as well as the possibility of blessing.

Zechariah 7:10. The people are enjoined to care for widows, orphans, poor, and refugees as a counterpoint to evil. This refrain was used as a common rule by which to judge the character of a nation.

Matthew 4:15. Those in the lands of foreigners were also to hear God's announcement along with Israel. God's desire was to announce redemption and inclusion to all, with no distinction among nations.

Matthew 8:10–12. Jesus finds an immigrant whose belief (trust) is greater than that of any in Israel. He declares that other nations would be accepted in the final day ahead of many in Israel. There is no question of equality before God here, only of differences in how we respond to God's call and acceptance.

Matthew 15:21–28. Jesus deals with a foreigner, exclaiming over her faith and using her as an example that it is his will to deal in grace without respect to nationality, standing, or issues of ritual purity. These principles of equality go beyond nationality and immigrant status, entering issues of religious ritual purity as well.

Matthew 25:31–46. The judgment of nations would reflect how they treated the hungry, thirsty, poor, stranger (immigrant/foreigner), unclothed, sick, and imprisoned. Jesus uses the traditional take on justice in regard to the voiceless and powerless, stressing agreement with this very basic definition of justice in treating all with equality of worth.

Matthew 27:7. A field was purchased to bury foreigners or immigrants. Here, there is a sense of provision for all, regardless of their national origin. Immigrants moving to Jerusalem from all over the Roman Empire was a common occurrence, as many Jews wished to live out their last years in Jerusalem awaiting the arrival of the messiah. The community understood a need to provide for those among them who could not care for their burial. There is a reminder here of Abraham buying a field for burying Sarah.

Mark 5:18–20. Jesus' ministry reached outside the bounds of Israel, sending one man here on mission throughout an entire non-Jewish region. There is no respecting of borders. The gospel takes precedence over issues of political boundaries and other related distinctions.

Mark 7:24–28. Jesus' ministry takes him outside the borders of Israel, making a point of ministering to one considered inferior for her status as a non-Jew. Jesus is teaching that grace reaches all with no room for distinction.

Luke 4:16–20. The oppressed (including immigrants) were the essential target of Jesus' preaching of redemption, freedom, and release. These were those who Jesus was most concerned with reaching with the message of God's acceptance.

Luke 4:25–27. Elijah had been sent to care for a foreign widow, not an Israelite. Naaman, a foreigner, had been the only leper in Israel cured by Elisha. Jesus was unconcerned with the fact that these interventions of God had been to foreigners, for he sees them of equal worth to any within Israel. He himself had just healed an immigrant, well knowing the man's status.

Luke 10:33–35. It is the Samaritan foreigner who stopped to help in the parable. He is the answer to the question, "Who is my neighbor that I should love as myself?" Jesus was teaching here that all people are equally worthy of God's love and attention through us.

Acts 13:43. Both Jew and non-Jew converts followed Paul. He preached and ministered to Jews and Gentiles equally, as he considered them of equal worth before God and God had called him to that very same ministry.

1 Corinthians 14:21. God would speak through immigrants and foreigners in unknown languages; even so, God would often be ignored. God was not concerned with issues of nationality, but with announcing the gospel of redemption through grace.

2 Corinthians 11:26. Paul had been in danger from countrymen and foreigners alike. As the gospel was equally available to all, its messengers were also equally targets of oppression from any and all corners.

Ephesians 2:19. Before God, the Ephesians were no longer foreigners, but had come to belong to God's people, the family of God. God had included them in the family of faith in Christ, despite the fact of their status as foreigners to Judaism.

Ephesians 3:6. God called all nations to participate equally in Christ Jesus of the very same inheritance of faith. God offered them inclusion in the promise to and covenant with Abraham, even though they were not of Abrahamic descent.

Immigrants Are Normally Oppressed
(64 Passages)

Immigrant status makes one a natural target for oppression.

This third set of passages demonstrates that being an immigrant makes one an easy and natural target for oppression and abuse. Abraham had no rights among the nations where he sojourned, just as the Hebrews had no rights in Egypt. The implication here would be that for equal treatment to be given to all, special attention would have to be granted to immigrant populations, since the natural inclination or decision processes of society would tend to work against the best interests of immigrant peoples.

While the book of Esther hardly contains any specific terms for immigrants or foreigners, it deals as a whole with this theme of the Jews finding themselves in exile and facing great opposition and oppression due to their immigrant status. As a whole, the book becomes an object lesson for the nation with regard to their own treatment of others who are immigrants within Israel.

In the passage of Acts 6 regarding the election of deacons, we find that the primitive church understood this issue of unequal treatment of immigrants and nationals. It was the immigrant widows who were being inadvertently overlooked by the national residents. The church chose to elect Hellenistic Jewish believers to oversee their entire food distribution program for the community widows, simply because they were the ones who were most aware of the oversight occurring in the daily food dispersal. Equality is difficult to achieve because we are predisposed to mistreat those different from ourselves, whether we mean to do so or not. Often as not, this may simply be due to a lack of awareness of the needs of others who are of a different race, class, language, or culture than our own.

Genesis 4:12–15. Cain fears that his identity as a wanderer will cause anyone who encounters him to want to kill him. He recognizes that simply being an outsider is a naturally dangerous condition, and God steps in to offer him protection, even though he has just murdered his brother.

Genesis 15:2–13. Abram begins the passage despising the fact that a foreigner will inherit his wealth. God answers that he will have his own son, but concludes the passage with the warning that his descendants will be foreigners in some other land, where they will be oppressed.

Genesis 17:3–13. God's pact includes that Abram will be father of many nations (nationalities/peoples). The land in which he lives as an immigrant would one day belong to his descendants. This statement comes as a warning that not all will go well for these descendants.

Genesis 23:4. Abraham recognizes his immigrant status and in humility pleads for rights that would naturally apply only to recognized residents. The status quo was oppressive, as was the cost demanded for the field, for his rights to bargain were limited by his immigrant status.

Genesis 47:9. Jacob speaks of his own life as having begun as the life of a wanderer. There is a sense in this recounting of his life story that living as an immigrant has been a hard life, just as one would expect.

Exodus 20:10. The Sabbath blessing was specifically extended to the immigrants, who would normally have been expected not to enjoy the same freedoms and blessings as the rest of the population. This prohibition against taking advantage of the immigrant, treating such workers as belonging to an inferior class of person with lesser rights, comes in recognition that immigrants would most naturally find themselves as the targets of oppression and enjoying lesser benefits and protections.

Exodus 21:8. We find here a protection for the Israelite women against abuse at the hands of a foreigner. There is plain recognition here that were she to become an immigrant in her husband's homeland, she would likely suffer as an immigrant.

Exodus 22:21. This is a command to respect and not mistreat (oppress) refugees due to their immigrant status. As the Hebrews had experienced oppression as immigrants in Egypt, so they are to understand that the natural tendency to oppress is an abuse they should avoid.

Exodus 23:9. This is a repetition of a command not to oppress or enslave refugees as immigrants on the basis of the empathic experience of the

Hebrews as slaves. There is an underlying motif here that there is reason to consistently remind them not to oppress others.

Leviticus 19:33–34. Refugees and immigrants are to be treated just as well as members of the nation, loved like any other on the basis of empathic experience. As one would desire to be treated as an immigrant or refugee elsewhere, so should one treat others.

Numbers 32:13. The Israelite experience of wandering in the wilderness is viewed here as a punishment, since the life of an immigrant is a difficult one.

Deuteronomy 26:5. "My father was a wandering Aramean" is the oldest known statement of Hebrew identity and faith. This was a core expression of Hebrew origins as an immigrant people. In the context here, there is a reference to how God changed the status of the nation, bringing blessing upon them from these more humble and difficult origins.

Deuteronomy 28:41–44. Beginning with verse 15, we find a series of curses against the people should they disobey God. In particular, their children would become refugees and immigrants in other lands, while immigrants in Israel would become wealthy in the face of Israelite poverty. This passage reflects a clear understanding of the immigrant's plight as easy victims of oppression.

Joshua 14:10. Caleb speaks of the forty years of wilderness wandering as a harsh experience for the Hebrew people, even though God had preserved him during that difficult period of time.

Judges 12:4. Those of Galaad are considered here as mere refugees in Ephraim and Manasseh. This is a pejorative picture of them, which accords them a lesser status as outsiders.

Judges 17:7. A Levite is classed in this text as an immigrant in the land of Judah. There is an understanding here that an immigrant status is oppressive by nature.

Ruth 2:10. "I am only an immigrant." We find here recognition of the secondary standing attributed normally to immigrants. She would be prone to abuse, as she had no one to speak on her behalf. Many read the books of Ruth and Jonah along the lines of parables seeking to counter the attitudes of Ezra 9–10 and Nehemiah 10:30 and 12:23–31 against non-Israelites.[1]

2 Samuel 15:20. Ittai is told to remain behind to keep him from becoming a wanderer with David within Israel as an immigrant, as well as landless. David understands that it will be a difficult enough life as an Israelite to be a wanderer in the land. It would be much worse for an immigrant.

2 Kings 21:8. God promises not to place Israel again in the condition of a wandering immigrant people if they will only obey. There is a clear understanding that such an immigrant or wandering condition would be a difficult one.

2 Samuel 4:1–4. A distinction is made here with regard to some native-born Israelites being considered as immigrants in another part of the nation. The mention stresses the commonly unequal regard given to immigrants.

1 Chronicles 10:4. Saul desires not to die at the hands of idolatrous foreigners for fear of being mocked. There is a sense of this extending to a mockery of God, in the view that victory on the battlefield came from the deities, not the soldiers. It is well understood that a victorious army will not treat the opposition kindly, but as targets for oppression.

1 Chronicles 29:15. David mentions his lack of hope, akin to that of his forefathers who had lived as immigrants. It is common or natural for immigrants to live in a hopeless situation due to oppression.

Job 12:24. God's judgment may cause leaders of the world to become wandering immigrants. The picture here is of God causing a reversal of fortunes from a position of power to a position of becoming powerless and the targets of oppression.

Job 15:23. The immigrants wandering about for food as a result of their evil ways may themselves become food for vultures. An immigrant or errant condition is generally a difficult one, full of uncertainty and insecurity.

Job 38:41. Children are here depicted as needy with the description of their wandering about in search of food. This is the picture of the hunter-gatherer, the landless with no place to belong in security.

Psalm 55:7. The experience of wandering in the wilderness is pictured as a difficult life. It is posited here as an example of great difficulty against which the psalmist measures the calamity he was currently facing.

Psalm 59:15. The enemies of the people were to become wanderers. The condition of being an immigrant is viewed here as a punishment since it is a naturally difficult and oppressive existence.

Psalm 107:4, 40. Wilderness wandering is cast as oppressive and difficult, yet God is cast as ready to rescue the wanderer as needy. At the end, God uses the condition of wandering as chastisement. The immigrant condition is difficult at best.

Psalm 109:10. Being a wanderer is pictured as a condition that is punishment for the wicked since it is a difficult position in which to live.

Psalm 119:176. The psalmist casts himself here as a lost wanderer in need of being rescued. The immigrant condition is a difficult one, as it makes one dependent on power structures that are not designed or used for his protection.

Psalm 137:4. This is an expression of difficulty encountered in worshiping in celebration of God as immigrants under oppression. Immigrant status is oppressive by nature, causing one to be unsure of how to live within the larger society.

Isaiah 8:21. The wanderers would hunger, for the life of an immigrant is difficult and uncertain. Here, becoming an immigrant is the result of a curse upon the idolatrous.

Isaiah 17:2. The text specifically refers to the wandering of flocks in the cities of Aroer, but the context is that the population has become wanderers elsewhere. Becoming wanderers or immigrants is subsequent to the destruction of their nation.

Isaiah 19:14. The wandering of Egypt is used here as a symbol of Egypt's destruction, of having lost its way. Theirs is a situation of powerlessness, resulting according to the norm of life for an immigrant community.

Isaiah 32:20. The cattle here are the ones wandering as part of a larger picture of tranquility for the settled population living in security. This is the antithesis of the standard reality for an immigrant population.

Isaiah 63:17. Wandering here is from the paths of Yahweh, a picture of how living contrary to Yahweh is akin to living the life of a wanderer in need of security.

Jeremiah 2:31. The image of a wanderer is used as God speaks to Israel of being lost and uncared for. The immigrant often faces great difficulty in having his needs met.

Jeremiah 5:19. The reason for the exile was the people having served foreign gods, as a result of which they will serve foreign peoples as an immigrant nation. This punishment is predicated on the understanding that living as an immigrant is difficult.

Jeremiah 22:26–27. Jehoiakim and his mother would live out their days in judgment as immigrants desiring to return to their homeland. They would be removed from their status of power to a position of powerlessness and dependency.

Jeremiah 30:7–8. At the end of the judgment of exile, God's people would never again be oppressed as slaves to foreigners. That is the more natural condition of the immigrant, to live in subservience to the majority population.

Jeremiah 31:19–20. The text speaks of wandering as distancing oneself from Yahweh's provision and protection. Living as immigrants, strangers, or wanderers places one in greater need of protection and security.

Jeremiah 35:7. Judah was to learn a lesson of faithfulness from an errant people, immigrants who were faithful never to settle according to an ancestor's commandment. This was a despised group who Yahweh called Jeremiah to place as an example before Judah.

Jeremiah 50:6. Wandering is contrasted here to having a place of rest, for the immigrant life is difficult. By definition, it is a life that is insecure and vulnerable. Rest is a common Biblical figure of receiving and enjoying the blessings of God. Here the wandering is in contrast to such blessings.

Lamentations 4:14–15. Exile wandering was sent upon Judah in punishment for their unfaithfulness. They would find oppression as the natural companion to an immigrant life.

Lamentations 5:2. Woe is pronounced due to the fact that the land and nation had fallen into foreign hands. There is a basic understanding that this would bring oppression upon the nation as they lost their political independence.

Lamentations 5:18. The wandering of jackals in Zion is contrasted here to the people being scattered away from Jerusalem in exile. As they became immigrants in exile, they would be removed from the security of their own land.

Ezekiel 7:21–22. At Yahweh's abandonment, the land and temple would fall into the hands of foreign thieves. This picture speaks of a loss of security, impending oppression, and powerlessness of the resident population.

Ezekiel 11:9. Judgment would fall at the hands of foreigners given a free reign by God. Their presence and power naturally speak to the expectation of oppression to be visited upon the Israelites.

Ezekiel 20:32–38. Judgment would befall Israel while they were still immigrants in exile. Their immigrant status was fully expected to usher them into a situation of oppression and pain, but Yahweh's judgment would extend even further than their experience of exile and immigration.

Ezekiel 34:6. Israel is cast as a wandering flock without guidance, direction, or safety. This speaks to the common experience of an immigrant people, for normally one does not know the patterns of life in the unknown land.

Hosea 9:17. Wandering among the nations in exile is cast as a punishment of God upon the nation. There is a clear understanding that living as immigrants would be a difficult life.

Amos 8:12. The people would become wanderers in their need to seek God. The category of being landless is cast here as an impending difficulty brought about in judgment and in consequence of an abandonment of Yahweh.

Matthew 17:25–26. It was common practice to charge foreigners tribute, not natives. Tribute was a category of tax specific to acquiescing to the position of a conquering power and the subservience of the people who had been invaded.

Matthew 18:17. Jesus instructs the disciples that they should do all they can to be reconciled with one another. If the other party will have nothing to do with reconciliation after bringing other members of the church into the equation, then they may treat the other as an outcast or Gentile. The underlying motif here is that the outsider is normally treated as irrelevant. Jesus is not so much condoning poor treatment of outsiders as noting that those who do not wish reconciliation cut themselves off from the believing community, a decision that should be respected.

Mark 5:5. The Gerasene demoniac is described as a wanderer, not having a place to which he belongs. He is an outcast who lacks a system of security and support, the easy target for the anger and insecurity of the society around him.

John 8:48. Some Jews used the epithet of "undesired foreigner" for Jesus as an insult. There is ample recognition here that an immigrant or foreigner is granted a lesser status than the resident population.

Acts 7:6. As immigrants, Abraham's descendants would be enslaved and treated harshly. This is a normal expectation for an immigrant people, as they are easy targets with no one to plead on their behalf before the power structures.

Hebrews 11:9. Abraham trusted God enough to live as an immigrant. God was calling him not simply into an unknown territory, but into a life of dependence upon God in the midst of various political structures that would seek to oppress him.

Hebrews 11:13. The cloud of witnesses understood they lived in this world in the status of immigrants. Their sense of belonging could not be defined in accord with political and societal structures, but only with God's provision and protection.

Hebrews 11:38. The cloud of witnesses is here described as wanderers with no place to call home. This condition often made them targets of violence and oppression at the hands of others.

James 5:19. Wandering from the faith speaks to being distanced from the ways of God, God's protection, provision, and belonging. This is the vulnerable condition germane to the immigrant community the world over.

1 Peter 1:1–2. Peter was writing to Jews living as immigrants in the dispersion. He recognized that they were living as outsiders in the various nations of the Roman Empire in which they found themselves. They did not have the protections of living among their own power structures.

1 Peter 2:11–12. Peter was speaking to disciples as though they were immigrants in this world. By implication, the believer is a non-citizen of any political state, due to a prioritized allegiance to the reign of Christ.[2] He takes this beyond a temporary condition for the believers in the dispersion, considering it the norm for all believers, needing to trust God in light of a common condition of being recipients of oppression and persecution.

1 Peter 2:25. The wandering of sheep is used as a symbol of people straying from God's path and will, acting as though they no longer belonged to God. There is a link here between being a wanderer and having difficulty meeting one's needs.

Reminders and Declarations That God's People Have Often Been Immigrants
(45 Passages)

Reminders that the nation of Israel was an immigrant nation and should treat others with empathy in recognition of that history.

An overwhelming array of texts using terms to refer to immigrants or refugees (mainly immigrants) works to remind the nation to treat foreigners as needing justice along the same lines as any other without sufficient voice in Israel, like the poor, the widow, and the orphan. God's care and concern for the voiceless and oppressed is a consistent theme in these texts. The nation should care for immigrants without distinction regarding their resident status. God's blessings and provision should be sufficient to care equally for all.

The immigrant condition in these passages is treated as part of God's plan for the Hebrews, the nation of Israel, and the church. As they were once immigrants, the faithful would often be immigrants in other periods of history. Many would live their lives as immigrants in order to fulfill God's purposes for their lives, like Paul, Jonah, and Abraham. Their past experiences and their future expectations should lead them to treat immigrants and strangers with care and protection.

Genesis 17:3–13. God's pact includes that Abram would be father of many nations (nationalities/peoples). The land in which he lived as an immigrant would one day belong to his descendants. They would at times live as immigrants in other lands, even as he had experienced.

Genesis 20:13–14. Abraham was sent by God to become a wanderer among various lands. He was to be an immigrant with no place to call home, depending along the way upon God's direction, care, provision, and protection.

Genesis 28:4. God's promise for belonging is extended in hope for subsequent generations, along with a reminder of the patriarchs' immigrant status. Isaac extends his concern that Jacob move beyond his immigrant status to become a recognized resident of the land.

Genesis 37:1–2. This passage recognizes and reminds us of Jacob's (Israel's) and Isaac's immigrant status in Canaan. This was part of a consistent series of reminders to Israel that they had not always lived as residents in the land of Israel.

Genesis 37:15. Joseph is found wandering the fields, seemingly lost, though he is in fact seeking his brothers. The text here seems to foreshadow Joseph's being cast out of his own land, becoming an immigrant in a foreign land.

Genesis 47:9. Jacob speaks of his own life as that of a wanderer in a land to which he did not really belong. There is a sense here that living as an immigrant is a hard life. He yearns for belonging, recognizing that being a resident is a wholly different category of experience.

Exodus 2:22. Moses recognized his immigrant status, having left Egypt and living now in Midianite exile. He mentions being "only an immigrant/ foreigner," as such a status placed one in a lesser category, being stripped of certain rights pertaining to others.

Exodus 6:4. God recalls the promise to make the Hebrews owners of the land where they had before only been immigrants. God was changing their condition and status, but in so doing offered one more reminder that their ancestors had also been immigrants and wanderers.

Exodus 18:1–5. Moses' son was named in recognition of God's redeeming him from immigrant oppression. This is part of a passage taking pains to remind the Hebrews once again of their immigrant origins and that of their leaders.

Exodus 22:21. Here is a command to respect and not mistreat (oppress) refugees due to their categorization as immigrants. The basis for protection is related to empathy from the Hebrew experience as oppressed immigrants in Egypt.

Exodus 23:9. This is a repetition of a command not to oppress or enslave refugees as immigrants. The Hebrew experience of slavery was to have provided sufficient grounds for understanding what it means to be oppressed as an immigrant. Empathy should be a motivator not to treat others the same way.

Leviticus 19:33–34. Refugees and immigrants are to be treated just as well as members of the nation, loved as any other on the basis of empathic experience. As one would desire to be treated as an immigrant or refugee elsewhere, so should one treat others.

Numbers 32:13. The Israelite wandering in the wilderness is pictured here as a punishment from God, since the life of a wandering immigrant is difficult in the best of times.

Deuteronomy 10:18–19. God is merciful toward orphans, widows, and refugees, who are the most vulnerable in society. Yahweh sets an example for the people that should serve as a reminder of their having lived as refugees, and later as slaves, in the land of Egypt.

Deuteronomy 23:2–4. A distinction is made here in terms of entrance into the inner part of God's sanctuary. Immigrants are not allowed to enter due to failure to participate in the covenant. Certain nations are specifically disallowed because of their refusal to aid the Hebrews when they were wandering immigrants.

Deuteronomy 24:19–22. The gleanings were to be left in the fields for the benefit of the poor, refugees, orphans, and widows. Remembering that they were once slaves in Egypt was to serve as a sufficient warning of the importance of obeying this commandment of mercy. There is an undercurrent that the land belongs to Yahweh, and the people might be ripped away from the land for not obeying Yahweh's dictates for how they are to treat others.

Deuteronomy 26:5. "My father was a wandering Aramean" is the oldest known statement of Hebrew identity and faith. This was a core expression of Hebrew origins as an immigrant people. It was to serve as a reminder of the needs of immigrants as a whole, as well as to help Israel identify with the plight of the immigrants in their midst.

Deuteronomy 29:16–28. The people were immigrants in Egypt and then spent a generation wandering prior to entering the promised land. God had rescued them from an immigrant and oppressive situation.

Deuteronomy 30:1–5. The people would be taken into exile for abandoning Yahweh. Only after coming to their senses and setting aside their idolatry would they be returned to the land of the promise to Abraham.

Joshua 14:10. Caleb speaks of the forty years of wilderness wandering as having been a difficult experience for the Hebrew people. God had preserved him during that period of time, just as God continues to desire to deal in mercy toward other immigrants.

Ruth 2:10. "I am only an immigrant." Here is recognition of the secondary class standing attributed normally to immigrants. Immigrant status is oppressive by nature. Ruth is a reminder to Israel of David's immigrant roots, specifically as a descendant of Moab.[3]

2 Samuel 15:20. Ittai is told to remain behind to keep from becoming a wanderer with David within Israel as an immigrant, as well as landless. David understands that it will be a difficult enough life as an Israelite, much worse for one who was also an immigrant.

2 Kings 21:8. God promises not to place Israel again in the condition of being a wandering immigrant people, if they would only obey. This is a reminder once again of their history as an immigrant nation.

1 Chronicles 29:15. David prays in memory of his ancestors being foreigners and strangers, living without hope, even as he was experiencing. This serves to remind Israel once again of its immigrant origins.

Job 1:7. God's servant has been traveling the world as a wanderer, not as one who belongs to any particular place. While tradition may cast this servant as Satan, the text posits him as one of God's ministers reporting on a regular basis as standard practice.

Job 2:2. God's servant is once again presented as having been traveling the world as a wanderer, not as belonging to any particular place. There is a sense that the servant sees the entire world, as well as that there is no specific location where he should belong.

Psalm 55:7. The experience of wandering in the wilderness is viewed as a difficult life. This immigrant wandering is here posited as an example of great difficulty, against which the psalmist measures the calamity he faces.

Psalm 114:1. This is a recollection that God brought the people out of other lands where they had lived as immigrants. This speaks of God's protection and provision for immigrants, but it is also a reminder of the plight of the immigrant in general.

Psalm 119:176. The psalmist casts himself as a lost wanderer in need of rescue. There is ample recognition here that the immigrant condition is a difficult one, but also that God is concerned for the immigrant, just as the Israelite should be.

Psalm 137:4. This is an expression of the difficulty to worship in celebration of God as immigrants under oppression. Immigrant status is oppressive by nature, and this carries into worship, here apparently to the nation in exile.

Isaiah 11:12. God would gather the nations and refugees of Israel and Judah from wherever they chanced to be. This is a recognition that once more in exile the people would live as immigrants, but that God was promising another reversal of fortunes for them once they were ready to assume their covenant responsibilities.

Isaiah 17:2. The text specifically refers to the wandering of flocks in the cities of Aroer, but the context is that the resident populace has become wanderers elsewhere. That they have become wanderers or immigrants is subsequent to the destruction of their nation.

Isaiah 52:3–12. The people had sojourned in Egypt but had later been sold freely to Assyria in exile. God would return them, however, to a new reality of freedom. God would overturn their immigrant, enslaved, and oppressed condition into freedom.

Isaiah 63:11–14. The Israelite wandering in the wilderness was under God's care and provision. Yahweh provided for their needs. While it was a troubling and anxious time, God eased the conditions of the wandering experience.

Acts 7:6. As immigrants, Abraham's descendants were to expect to be enslaved and treated harshly. This was a warning from Genesis that Stephen replays as a known theme in Israel in his own day.

Acts 7:29. Stephen reminds his listeners that Moses had lived as an immigrant in the land of Midian. He was using this theme to build up to a declaration of Jesus being the manifestation of God beyond nationalist symbols of the temple.

2 Corinthians 11:26. Paul had been in danger from countrymen and foreigners alike. Part of this danger was due to his living as an immigrant and wanderer throughout the Roman Empire. It was common enough for him to face oppression as an immigrant from other immigrants.

Hebrews 11:9. Abraham trusted God enough to live as an immigrant. This was a life with lesser security, in which he would have to depend more fully on God than on human political structures. The reminder here serves to stress the immigrant character of the faithful through the ages.

Hebrews 11:13. The cloud of witnesses understood that they lived in this world in the status of immigrants. They were immigrants politically, but also in the sense of not truly belonging to this world order.

Hebrews 11:38. The cloud of witnesses is here described as wanderers with no place to call home. This theme of being landless wanderers serves as a reminder to the new generation of landless believers of their faith origins and their relationship to the dispersion experience.

James 5:19. Wandering from the faith speaks to being distanced from the ways of God, God's protection, provision, and a sense of belonging. It speaks to being needy and to the responsibility of the faithful to care for others sharing that same plight.

1 Peter 1:1–2. Peter was writing to Jews living as immigrants in the dispersion. They had been forced out of their land as though in exile once more. This time, however, there is a sense that their future will continually be in the category of landless wanderers.

1 Peter 2:11–12. Peter was speaking to disciples as immigrants in this world, not simply in a particular land. By implication of his words, the believer is a non-citizen of any political state, due to a prioritized allegiance to the reign of Christ.[4]

1 Peter 2:25. The wandering of sheep is used as a symbol of people straying from God's path and will, acting as though they no longer belong to God. There is a link here between being a wanderer and having difficulty meeting one's needs. It is a reminder of the motif of Jewish or Hebrew immigrant experience.

Immigrants, Refugees, Poor, Widows, Orphans, and Strangers Are All of One Class
(42 Passages)

These passages equate immigrants, widows, poor, orphans, strangers, wanderers, and foreigners, placing them into the same class as needy, voiceless, and unprotected.

These passages listed here do not include other similar texts that use alternate lists, omitting terms for immigrants, foreigners, or refugees. If all of those were to be included, the total here would increase to fifty-six passages. These various other texts, however, might well be considered for inclusion alongside these passages, for we should likely consider that those others are simply abbreviated forms of the same basic formula. These passages are basically references to the voiceless or powerless in most any society. The fullest expression of these listings of the vulnerable would include refugees, immigrants, poor, widows, orphans, foreigners, sick, lepers, blind, slaves, homeless, wanderers, travelers, strangers, captives, prisoners, childless, hungry, thirsty, and even the dying. In some cases, lists like these include the Levites or priests, since they were not given a share of land apportionment with the rest of Israel. That was enough reason for considering them vulnerable, as they lived at the mercy of the faithfulness of others.

There is no one text, however, that includes this full list of the voiceless, vulnerable, and powerless. There are, however, several short form variations on this theme. The most common that seem to be repeated on their own are widows and orphans. Alternate to those designations are the poor and strangers. Due to how often these are listed in context with immigrants and other oppressed groups, it would seem most likely that one should apply the concept "the vulnerable" or "the voiceless" to the majority of texts that highlight these terms. Essentially all of these passages extend concerns over the mistreatment of these various groups of vulnerable people.

Genesis 17:3–13. God's pact includes that Abram will be father of many nations (nationalities/peoples). The land in which he is an immigrant will one day belong to his descendants. The pact of circumcision, however, would apply to more than simply the biological descendants of Abram. It would include their slaves and the foreigners (immigrants) in their midst. They would be included in the same category with Abram's descendants, and with them would be recipients of the blessings promised by God. Here, the slaves and foreigners are seen as belonging to one sole class, but this class is placed alongside Abram's legitimate descendants with no distinction.

Exodus 12:14–20. The central Hebrew festival of identity (Passover) was to be celebrated by all as requirement for presence in Israel. No distinction was to be made regarding the resident status of an individual. There was one law that should apply to everyone equally, including the most vulnerable.

Exodus 12:43–49. The foreigner was not to participate in eating the sacrificial lamb if they had not participated in the redemption of the Hebrews from Egypt. In a sense, they were still enslaved with a lesser status, awaiting redemption. If they had become part of the people through circumcision, they were considered part of the people and must participate fully. The only distinction allowed here is one's participation in the redemption process. Otherwise, all are equal before God; nationality itself is negligible. Immigrant residents and Israelites must obey the law alike.

Exodus 20:10. Sabbath was given as a blessing and respite to the Hebrews on the basis of being able to trust Yahweh with sufficient provision for them to take a day to rest. This blessing was to extend to the immigrant, who would normally have been expected not to enjoy the same freedoms and blessing as the rest of the population. Here is a prohibition against taking advantage of the immigrant, treating such workers as belonging to an inferior class of person with lesser rights.

Exodus 22:21–25. Foreigners, widows, orphans, and poor are mentioned in a series of verses regarding legal protections for those most susceptible to abuse. They are all dealt with as being of one essential class.

Exodus 23:6–9. In a section of laws regarding fairness, foreigners and poor are placed side by side as participating in one same class as the most vulnerable. It is this vulnerability that stands behind the need for these laws.

Exodus 23:11–12. The Sabbath laws here are to be of benefit to the poor, slaves, and foreigners, as well as the rest of Israel. These specific groups are mentioned here because of the tendency to shove them aside from God's provision.

Leviticus 19:10. Gleanings are to be left for the poor, including immigrant refugees. Mercy is not to be limited by one's immigrant status, but applied specifically to all those whose life situation makes them vulnerable and in need of mercy.

Leviticus 19:33–34. Refugees and immigrants are to be treated just as well as members of the nation, loved as any other on the basis of empathic experience. As one would desire to be treated as an immigrant or refugee elsewhere, so should one treat others.

Leviticus 23:22. Gleanings are to be left for the vulnerable of the society, both the poor and the immigrants or refugees. They are all of one class and in need of this provision and protection due to their standing as landless.

Leviticus 25:4–7. God would make the seventh year's unplanted harvest sufficient even to care for the slaves, servants, and immigrant refugees. These are the people who would generally be the least able to prepare for the future.

Leviticus 25:35. The poor and the immigrants were both to find economic assistance from the community of Israel. In this text, it is the poor of Israel who are highlighted, as it is assumed that the people know to care for the immigrant populace.

Deuteronomy 1:16–18. The law should operate with equality, showing no preference for rich or poor, native born or immigrant. These social distinctions serve no real purpose except to make the poor and immigrant populations vulnerable, in contrast to the demands of the law.

Deuteronomy 10:18–19. God is merciful toward orphans, widows, and refugees, setting an example for the people in reminder of their living as refugees in Egypt. Each of these categories simply reflects a group with lesser voice and power.

Deuteronomy 14:27–29. Gifts for the care of the Levites should extend to orphans, widows, and refugees. In this passage, it is noteworthy that the Levites are classed as vulnerable since they were not participants in the allotment of land.

Deuteronomy 16:9–11. The harvest feast should be shared with widows, orphans, Levites, and refugees. The land is assumed to belong to Yahweh, as does the land's produce. Its bounty is to be shared, therefore, with all members of the society, including the immigrant community.

Deuteronomy 16:13–15. The feast of tabernacles should be celebrated in the company of families, slaves, orphans, widows, Levites, and refugees. There is an expansion here in the listing we have already seen of the vulnerable peoples of society.

Deuteronomy 24:14–15. Here is another case of the law caring for the most vulnerable of society. The poor must be paid daily with the warning that injustice in this regard will be handled by God's intervention.

Deuteronomy 24:17. One should not mistreat a refugee or an orphan nor ask a widow's cloak as collateral. These people have more glaring needs that must find greater protection by the larger society since they do not have the same voice enjoyed by others.

Deuteronomy 24:19–22. The gleanings were to be left in the fields for the benefit of the poor, immigrant refugees, orphans, and widows. Remembering that the Hebrews had been slaves should serve as sufficient rationale to empathize with the more vulnerable.

Deuteronomy 26:11–14. To this feast of thanksgiving, the people were to invite the priests and refugees living in the land. The triennial tithe would be given to priests, immigrant refugees, orphans, and widows. It is interesting to note that the audience of this command is the landed section of the society, the wealthy.

Deuteronomy 27:14–26. Amid a list of curses toward those mistreating people in need of protection, a curse is called upon those who mistreat immigrant refugees, widows, and orphans. These are the least likely to have someone take up for them.

Deuteronomy 31:12. All are to celebrate the feast of canceling debts, including immigrant refugees. By participating, they should learn to respect and obey Yahweh, recognizing that their own debts were cancelled because of Yahweh's concern for them, just like the rest of the vulnerable.

Job 29:11–16. Protection and defense of the poor and immigrant are cast as signs of righteousness and justice. Both the poor and the immigrant community are among those most vulnerable to injustice.

Job 31:16–32. Job speaks of his righteousness, including actions benefitting the poor, widows, orphans, and strangers. This was a common theme extending beyond Israel in measuring the level of one's righteousness.

Psalm 94:6. Injustice is framed here as killing widows, murdering orphans, and massacring refugees. They are cast as being of the same class due to their vulnerability before the rest of society.

Psalm 109:9–16. The wicked is here cursed with a series of crises in life that equate orphans, widows, immigrants, and poor as being of one singular class. No one desires to become a member of any of these classes, as they are difficult settings for life.

Psalm 146:7–9. God is cast as caring for prisoners, blind, troubled, foreigners, orphans, and widows. The list is not to be considered exhaustive, as it is representative of all those who are vulnerable without God's protection.

Isaiah 14:32. God will be announced as providing refuge for the poorest of the people in Jerusalem. This is a declaration of the character of God's justice and righteousness. God's character is that of caring for the disenfranchised and vulnerable.

Isaiah 58:7. Justice is defined as providing food, refuge, clothing, and other aid. The concern here is not with what we generally define as morality, but is focused much more on material justice, whereby the needs of the most vulnerable are met.

Jeremiah 7:3–7. A major part of repentance is enacting justice on behalf of the oppressed, including refugees, widows, and orphans. We should read this as applying to others sharing their same status of vulnerability. This material focus of justice definitions is standard for prophetic texts in Israel and beyond.

Jeremiah 22:3. God's demands of righteousness are summed up in caring for the oppressed, immigrants, orphans, and widows and protecting the innocent. One's immigrant status places him in the same category of needing protection, just like widows, orphans, and the poor.

Lamentations 5:2–3. Being immigrants, widows, orphans, and homeless is equated as being all aspects of a vulnerable condition. Turning the land over to foreigners is the equivalent of living as immigrants in a foreign land, due to the nature of oppression.

Ezekiel 22:7. The righteousness of the people found expression in their care of those with the least representation. In Israel, this was lacking and condemnatory. They well knew their responsibilities for these underclasses but ignored them.

Ezekiel 22:25. The treatment of foreigners, widows, and the poor is equated as being of the same character. At issue is the vulnerability of these groups who are not represented by the power structures.

Ezekiel 22:29. Justice is again defined as caring for the common targets of oppression: the poor, needy, and immigrant refugees. This is a much greater motif of defining righteousness than the current emphases placed on sexual morality.

Zechariah 7:10. The people are enjoined to care for widows, orphans, poor, and refugees as a counterpoint to evil. The historical context of people struggling for survival should make this a very understandable motif. Their very existence depended on external assistance.

Malachi 3:5. The cheating of workers, widows, orphans, and immigrants is likened to witchcraft, adultery, and lying under oath. As far as Malachi is concerned, the care for the underserved is the most pressing issue in defining righteousness.

Matthew 25:31–46. The judgment of the nations will reflect how they treated the poor, stranger (immigrant/foreigner), prisoner, and sick. What we do in regard to caring for the vulnerable matters, and Jesus places this category of righteousness on a higher plane than current concerns over sexual morality. His definition is about how we treat others, not about the quality of our actions that have to do with our individual care.

Luke 4:16–20. The oppressed (including immigrants) were the essential target of Jesus' preaching of redemption, freedom, and release. We see this in the day-to-day ministry of Jesus, but also in texts like this, in which he uses his efforts to care for others as defining characteristics of his ministry and identity.

Luke 4:25–27. Elijah was sent to the care of and to care for a foreign widow, not an Israelite. Naaman, a foreigner, was the only leper cured in Israel. Jesus posits that God does not make the value distinctions between people according to nationality, but addresses all according to their needs. That is what joins them in receiving God's attention.

Luke 10:33–35. It is the Samaritan foreigner who stops to help the stranger in the parable. He is the answer to the question "Who is my neighbor that I should love as myself?" Neighbor here is equated with any who happen to be in need, with no room for the distinctions we might normally make.

Foreigners and the Immigrant Condition Are Linked to God's Judgment or Punishment
(40 Passages)

These texts link an immigrant or wanderer condition to God's punishment upon a certain people.

Akin to Jesus' words regarding Tyre, Sidon, Korazin, and Bethsaida (Matthew 11:21), these passages mention immigrants or foreign nations as standing in a position of accusers of Israel, due to Israel's infidelity to Yahweh. In effect, they portray that the chosen people often stood on their genealogy while they did not live up to the demands of the covenant with Yahweh.

These texts are a call to faithfulness as the only real measure of being right with God. There is no inherent superiority in belonging to a specific nation. The seemingly only true issue of value and worth for consideration before God is how we treat one another. That is not to say there is nothing more to be said regarding salvation, but at issue in these texts is the question of responding faithfully to God in contrast to making a claim to belong to the chosen people called by God's name.

Numbers 32:13. The Israelite wandering in the wilderness is viewed as a punishment, due to their unwillingness to trust God. In this instance, it is also a case of God's will being to move them into the land promised to Abraham while they were unwilling to cross into the land for fear of the resident peoples.

Deuteronomy 28:41–68. Beginning with verse 15, we find a series of curses against the people should they disobey God. In particular, their children will become refugees and immigrants in other lands, while immigrants in Israel will become wealthy in the face of Israelite poverty. This passage reflects the clear understanding of the immigrant's plight as easy victims of oppression by societies of different cultures, languages, and ethnicities. The bulk of this passage speaks to punishment either in exile or through an occupation by foreigners.

Deuteronomy 29:22–28. Immigrants and other nations will be witnesses to the judgment of God should Israel turn away from following Yahweh in faithfulness. The people would suffer economic distress that would be clearly visible to all, sending them into exile as well.

Deuteronomy 30:1–5. God would return Israel from exile, restoring them to the land after they come to their senses from oppression as immigrants. The exile experience would be the result of their living contrary to their covenant responsibilities.

Joshua 14:10. Caleb speaks of the forty years of wilderness wandering as a difficult experience for the Hebrew people, yet God had preserved him during that period of time. He was ready to move past the period of discipline into God's bounty.

2 Kings 21:8. God promises not to place Israel again in the condition of a wandering immigrant people, if they will only obey. The king of Israel, however, is unwilling to follow Yahweh in faithfulness.

Job 12:24. Amid a series of comments regarding various forms that God's judgment might take, Job mentions that God may cause leaders of the world to become wandering immigrants for their unfaithfulness.

Job 15:23. One of Job's friends argues that the immigrants' wandering about for food is the result of judgment on their evil ways. They may also themselves become food for vultures. The sense here is that it is a difficult life that may be used as punishment. Though Job's friend, Eliphaz, will ultimately be shown to argue against God's positions, there is a sense in which at least in certain circumstances this is the case.

Psalm 59:15. The enemies of the people would become wanderers. The condition of being an immigrant is viewed as punishment by God. The context cries that in their immigrant state they might learn dependence upon Yahweh.

Psalm 107:4, 40. Wilderness wandering is cast as oppressive and difficult, yet God is cast as ready to rescue the wanderer as needy. At the end, God uses the condition of wandering as chastisement upon the ungodly.

Psalm 109:10. Being a wanderer is cast again as a condition that is punishment for the wicked. The condition here is part of a list of curses against the wicked, each one placing them in a position that is at best vulnerable.

Isaiah 8:21. The wanderers will hunger, for the life of an immigrant is difficult and uncertain. This passage is part of a warning of impending calamity upon Israel in punishment for their faithlessness in following after idols and even witchcraft.

Isaiah 17:2. The text specifically refers to the wandering of flocks in the cities of Aroer, but the context is that the population has become wanderers elsewhere. Becoming wanderers or immigrants is subsequent to the destruction of their nation in God's response to their infidelity.

Isaiah 19:14. The wandering of Egypt is a symbol of its destruction, of having lost its way. It is a situation of powerlessness, as is the norm for an immigrant community, here at the hands of Yahweh's intervention.

Isaiah 63:17. Wandering here is from the paths of Yahweh, a picture of how living contrary to Yahweh is akin to living the life of a wanderer in need of security. The wandering becomes its own punishment for straying from Yahweh's patterns for living.

Jeremiah 5:9–19. The reason for the exile was the people's serving foreign gods, for which they would serve foreign nations as an immigrant nation. They would have a difficult life in response for their abandonment of Yahweh.

Jeremiah 22:26–27. Jehoiakim and his mother would live out their days in judgment as immigrants desiring to return to their homeland. They had not followed the requirements of God that would have enabled them to remain in the land.

Jeremiah 30:1–9. At the end of the judgment of exile, God's people would never again be oppressed as slaves to foreigners. Theirs had been a difficult experience of oppression, but God would hear their cries and act in redemption.

Jeremiah 35:7. Judah was to learn a lesson of faithfulness from an errant people, immigrants who were faithful never to settle according to an ancestor's commandment. This was a despised group who Yahweh called Jeremiah to place as an example before Judah.

Lamentations 4:12–22. Exile wandering was sent upon Judah in punishment for their unfaithfulness. Yahweh scattered them in justice to live according to their blindness. This would be a sign for more than simply Israel; it would be a message of judgment that all the nations around would understand.

Lamentations 5:2–22. The prophet here bemoans that the land and nation have fallen into foreign hands. The plight of the nation is dire, but hope is yet posited in Yahweh's vindication after this desperate period of discipline.

Ezekiel 7:21–27. At Yahweh's abandonment, the land and temple would fall into the hands of foreign thieves. This reversal of fortunes for Israel would be in repayment for the way they had neglected to care for others.

Ezekiel 11:7–12. Judgment will fall at the hands of foreigners given a free reign by God. This judgment would include sending Israel to its borders for punishment. Strangers and foreigners would become the tools of Yahweh in executing this judgment.

Ezekiel 20:32–38. Judgment would befall Israel while they were still immigrants in exile. Their immigrant condition was related to God's judgment, even when God's judgment was expected to extend beyond their immigrant exile.

Amos 8:2–14. Amid this series of descriptions of God's judgment upon the people, we find a reference specifically to their becoming a wandering people. Their immigrant plight is linked to judgment for their abandoning God's instructions.

Hosea 9:17. God's pronouncement of judgment upon Israel culminates here in making them wanderers among the nations. This is just the "icing on the cake" of the rest of the descriptions of justice against the people.

Matthew 5:47. The relationship here between foreigners and judgment hinges on their exhibiting a similar level of just actions as the Jews. The righteousness of those who belong to God should be greater than that of those who do not.

Matthew 6:7. Jesus uses the figure of the Gentiles who do not know God as a contrast to the manner in which those who know God should pray. The judgment issue here is one of comparison between those who do and don't know God.

Matthew 6:32. Again, Jesus uses Gentiles as a point of comparison with the standard practice of the Jews. He sees that there is nothing special about Jewish practice, as it is too consistent with standard Gentile religious practice, rather than surpassing it.

Matthew 8:10–12. Jesus finds an immigrant whose belief (trust) is greater than that of any in Israel. Other nations will be accepted in the final days ahead of many in Israel. Others will be accepted on the basis of their faith in God, while many in Israel remain unfaithful.

Matthew 15:21–28. Jesus deals with a foreigner, exclaiming over her faith and using her as an example that it is God's will to deal in grace without respect to nationality, social standing, or issues of ritual purity deemed so important to the Jews.

Matthew 20:19. Jesus anticipates being handed over to Gentiles in league with the Jewish leaders to enact their vengeance upon him. This is not an aspect of God's punishment, but it is God's judgment of both Jews and Gentiles in regard to their unrighteous actions and purposes.

Mark 10:33. Jesus again anticipates being handed over to Gentiles by the religious authorities in Israel. Their actions against him signal God's judgment that they are indeed unrighteous in their attitudes and actions.

Luke 17:18. The foreigner here sets the bar for giving thanks, as the native born were too wrapped up in the protocol demands of legal tradition. Jesus praises him as demonstrating the kind of faithfulness and thankfulness that the Jews should have been demonstrating along with their ritual traditions.

Luke 18:32. The Jewish leaders would hand Jesus over to the Gentiles for punishment, yet they would be found guilty in the eyes of God for acting in unrighteousness and injustice. This turns out to call for judgment upon themselves, even though they consider that Jesus would be the one being condemned.

Luke 21:24. Jesus speaks of the impending destruction of Jerusalem as God's judgment through Gentile forces. This lies in accord with what the Jews understood to be standard practice for Yahweh. God had used foreign powers in the past on various occasions as vehicles for the judgment, punishment, and discipline of Israel.

Romans 2:14. By comparison between Jews and Gentiles, Paul makes note of the fact that righteous actions on the part of Gentiles call judgment upon Jews who are not as righteous. Many of them understand the principles of the law, even if they do not live under its banner.

1 Corinthians 14:21. God would speak through immigrants and foreigners in unknown languages, yet even so would be ignored by those in the direct lineage of Abraham. The acceptance of these foreigners would be itself a statement of judgment against the faithlessness of Israel.

Galatians 2:12–15. The occasion of eating with Gentiles in complete freedom was also reason for Peter to be judged for not acting in accord with the freedom of the gospel of grace. He knew that he had been freed from legalism by the gospel, but was allowing fear of the legalists to keep him from standing for the gospel truth. Judgment here is not directly from or based on the Gentiles themselves, but there is a sense in which the Gentile believers are living in a more righteous manner than some of the Jewish believers.

1 Peter 4:3. Contrast is presented here with the Gentiles beyond the believing community. Their lives are reflected as living outside the parameters and purposes of the gospel, while the believers are called to evidence a higher ethic and purpose in their living.

Concerns over Religious Influence of Immigrants
(19 Passages)

Concerns stated regarding immigrant religious influence over Israel.

This group of passages tends to equate immigrants or foreigners with idolatry and idolatry's negative influence on the life of Israel. Where the Bible makes negative comments concerning immigrants or foreigners, these comments are mainly concerned with issues of idolatry and the national failure to worship Yahweh or only Yahweh due to these external influences. Indeed, this is the sole issue that determines who is and who is not an Israelite or participant in the people of God.

Deuteronomy 17:15. The king of Israel may not be an immigrant. It is important to note that the king represented the people before God and God before the people in the capacity of God's stand-in, similar to the roles of priest and prophet.

1 Samuel 17:25–27. Goliath is classed as an immigrant or foreigner. The import of the statement, however, is that he does not worship Yahweh. He stands in direct opposition to Yahweh, insulting the God of Israel. His challenge and presence stand to cause the Israelites to fear his gods more than they trust Yahweh.

1 Samuel 31:4. Saul refers to enemy soldiers as immigrants or foreigners, with the stress on their idolatry, or lack of worshiping Yahweh. This was both a concern for Israel and a rationale for Saul to write them off as unimportant.

1 Kings 11:1–8. God's warning that intermarriage with foreign wives would dilute Yahweh worship in Israel played out in Solomon's multiple foreign marriages. Due to marriage to these wives, Solomon built temples to their foreign gods.

1 Chronicles 10:4. Saul desires not to die at the hands of idolatrous foreigners for fear of being mocked. There is a sense of this extending to mockery of God, in the view that victory on the battlefield came from the deities, not the soldiers.

2 Chronicles 33:15. The idols of immigrants are removed from the temple. These should never have been allowed in the temple to Yahweh, but due to the religious influence of both immigrants and foreigners never integrated into Israelite Yahwism, the idols had been allowed in the temple.

Ezra 10:11–18, 44. Here is a challenge for the people of Jerusalem to separate themselves from the idolatrous influence of immigrants and their foreign wives. At issue was the impact of the foreign wives on the men's worship of Yahweh.

Nehemiah 9:2. The people separate themselves from the immigrants in their midst as part of their actions to ratify their standing in the covenant with Yahweh. At heart is the issue of religious purity in service to Yahweh.

Nehemiah 10:28–39. The people separated themselves from the immigrant community in recognition of their covenant with Yahweh and their responsibility to follow it. The people renew ratification of the covenant with Yahweh, including aspects pertaining to immigrants. They determine that they will not allow immigrants to lead them astray from serving Yahweh in their commerce or through marriage.

Nehemiah 13:3. The people expelled from their midst those who had mixed themselves in marriage to immigrants in disobedience to Yahweh. The concern here is to establish purity in Yahweh worship to incur God's favor.

Nehemiah 13:25–30. The people recognize that Solomon's greatest sin in departing from Yahweh was due to his marriage to immigrant wives. Intermarriage with immigrants is prohibited in order to protect Israel from falling into the same trap that had led to exile.

Psalm 81:9. The gods of immigrants are not to be worshiped. The immigrants are rather to be taught to worship Yahweh. The Israelites are to keep themselves from succumbing to the influence of these competing forms and targets of worship.

Isaiah 2:6. Israel's error is summed up in a contamination of religious practice by immigrant influences. They should have remained pure in their allegiance to Yahweh, but they failed.

Jeremiah 4:1. God uses the image of a wanderer in reference to Israel turning to idolatry. The concept references that they have lost their way, departing from God's provision, not only the demands of the covenant with God.

Jeremiah 5:19. The reason for the exile was the people's serving foreign gods. Because of this idolatrous failure, they would serve foreign peoples as an immigrant nation. They would need to learn through exile to remain true to Yahweh.

Jeremiah 51:51. The foreigners did not respect the temple, shaming the people as they were mocked. God would turn the tables on Babylon, calling the nation of Judah to return in sincere worship to Yahweh.

Ezekiel 14:7. Yahweh's judgment announcement included the immigrants in the land as responsible alongside those of Israel for disobeying Yahweh and their idolatry. The people should stand up to these foreign influences and be true to Yahweh.

Ezekiel 44:7–9. The people were leaving temple worship of Yahweh in the hands of immigrants who had not assumed the covenant responsibilities with Yahweh. The stress here is on the identification with Yahweh, not immigrant status.

Ephesians 4:17. Paul writes the believers in the midst of the Gentile community in Ephesus to be sure to distance the character of their lives from the attitudes and character of the society around them. They needed to take care to be an influence on their society, rather than being unduly influenced by them.

Being an Immigrant or a Wandering People Is Linked to Losing One's Way
(13 Passages)

These passages speak of wandering as losing one's way in life, or wandering from God's purposes.

There are passages here that refer to Israel or to believers, as well as those making reference to people who still need to enter into relationship with God. The distance from God's purposes is often factored as promoting injustice or idolatry, between which there is some moral link in Hebrew thought. While we might tend to focus on morality in terms of sexuality and violence, the biblical concept would tend to stress issues of economic justice toward the poor and needy, which they also saw in relationship with attitudes of greed and selfishness behind idolatrous fertility cult practices.

Distancing oneself from Yahweh's covenant was seen from the perspective of being lost, without direction, support, or reliance upon God's provision. The import behind this is that the covenant with Yahweh understood that God would provide in bounteous provision for all, while the fertility cult was viewed as stressing provision for the individual at the expense of others in the larger society. This was a distinction between faith and fear as the basic motivation behind both worship and the practical aspects of social relationships and the care of others.

Job 38:41. Children are depicted here as needy with the phrase "wandering about in search of food." This is the picture of the hunter-gatherer, the nomad, or the otherwise landless, with no place to belong and little sense of security.

Isaiah 63:17. This description of wandering is a departure from the paths of Yahweh. This is a picture of how living contrary to Yahweh is akin to living the life of a wanderer in need of security, unsure of where and how to locate the next meal.

Jeremiah 4:1. God uses the image of a wanderer in reference to Israel turning to idolatry. The concept references that they had lost their way, departing from God's provision by seeking after idols, but Yahweh calls them back to faithfulness.

Jeremiah 14:8–10. God is pictured here as a stranger who is not bound to the land. The term for wandering is used here in context with Israel acting as though simply passing through the land as a stranger on holiday. Their actions imply they do not belong to Yahweh, while Yahweh has turned from them due to their unfaithfulness.

Jeremiah 31:19–22. The text speaks of wandering as distancing oneself from Yahweh's provision and protection. The people are called back to Yahweh and the ways of Yahweh in order that they might be restored and find the blessing they have missed.

Jeremiah 50:6–17. Wandering is contrasted to a place of rest under Yahweh's provision and protection. In verse 17, the image shifts to the scattering of a flock, whereby provision and safety are lost in their distance from the shelter of Yahweh's care.

Lamentations 4:14–16. Exile wandering was sent upon Judah as punishment for their unfaithfulness. The text speaks of their blind wandering, as well as of Yahweh scattering them from the land of provision in Israel.

Lamentations 5:2–18. The wandering of jackals in Zion is contrasted to the people being scattered away from Jerusalem in exile. The exile was a result of their straying from the paths of Yahweh. The writer here laments the error of their way.

Ezekiel 34:6–16. Israel is cast as a wandering flock without care, guidance, direction, or safety. This wandering is a picture of the religious distance of the people from Yahweh, akin to the case of an immigrant people in need of redemption and rescue.

Hosea 9:17. Wandering among the nations in exile is cast as a punishment of God upon the nation due to their infidelity. The people had departed from Yahweh's commands, and their wandering comes in consequence of their actions.

Mark 5:5. The Gerasene demoniac is described as a wanderer, not having a place to which he belongs. He has lost his way due to the spiritual oppression under which he lives, which is here pictured in the wandering language used.

James 5:19. Wandering from the faith speaks to being distanced from the ways of God, from God's protection, provision, and care. Distance from the community of faith is emblematic of distance in relation to God.

1 Peter 2:25. The wandering of sheep is used as a symbol of people straying from God's path and will, actions as though they no longer belong to God. There is some connection here with the context in which Peter refers to those who act as enemies of Christ and the wandering of these sheep in need of the shepherd's care.

Failure to Treat Immigrants Appropriately
(8 Passages)

The Israelite reality did not measure up to God's ideal.

These passages demonstrate that the reality of Israelite life remained far from these higher standards of equality established by God. Kings like David and Solomon oppressed immigrant populations by forcing them into slave labor. There are, as well, some laws in the Mosaic code that do not live up to the higher ideals to grant immigrants the same value as the Israelite. Such laws are at odds with the higher ethic portrayed in the multitude of passages we have already seen that call for equality of treatment as a measure of justice.

We should not be surprised that Israel failed to live up to its own received standards, as that is pretty much the case for any society around the world and throughout history. Our political and religious propaganda is one thing, but our practical application of the principles we hold dear is very often a completely different issue. The biggest difference in the Hebrew scriptures is that the prophets were very open in calling Israel out for their failures, as Nathan did with King David.

Leviticus 25:45–46. This is the first instance of an allowance being made for a distinctive treatment of immigrants from the native born. With this relaxing of care to protect immigrants comes a law to protect the native from abuse by an immigrant.

Deuteronomy 14:21. Here is a second exception to a rule applying equally to native and immigrant, pertaining to eating meat from an animal that has died. At issue seems to be a religious distinction based on a covenant relationship lacking in the case of the immigrant.

Deuteronomy 15:1–5. Here is a third exception to the rule of one law applying equally. This time the exception comes in terms of the forgiving of debts every seventh year. This is a practical distinction in terms of justice, unlike the distinction made in terms of ritual purity that would allow for participation in public worship.

Deuteronomy 23:2–4. A distinction is made here in terms of entrance into the inner part of God's sanctuary. Immigrants are not allowed entrance for failure to participate in the covenant. Specifically, certain nations are disallowed because of their refusal to aid the Hebrews when they were immigrants.

Deuteronomy 23:20. As a fifth exception to the rule of one law, interest may be charged to an immigrant, but not to the native born. This is definitely a case of a different definition of justice between the native and the immigrant, which flies in the face of equality issues in so many other texts.

1 Chronicles 22:2–5. David forces the immigrant labor force to gather material for construction of the temple to be built by Solomon. This example flies in the face of principles of treating the immigrant on par with the native born.

2 Chronicles 2:2–18. Solomon places the immigrants in forced labor to build the temple. They are also conscripted to build the temples to foreign gods for Solomon's wives, though that is not mentioned specifically in this text.

Ezekiel 22:7. The righteousness of the people would find visible expression in their care of those with the least degree of representation, specifically including the immigrant populace. This righteousness was lacking and condemnatory to Israel.

Foreign Powers Are Perceived as a Threat
(4 Passages)

Foreign nations are perceived as a military threat.

These texts see other nations as invading forces occupying Israel. There is a mix of commentary among these texts, some categorizing them as servants of Yahweh and others as interfering as a threat to the nation. The concern is the potential threat the nations pose to Israel's security. These passages mention God's protection for Israel in response to the perceived threat.

Isaiah 52:1. The uncircumcised would never again return to attack Jerusalem. Rather, the city would live in peace and freedom. The foreign powers that had threatened them, Egypt and Assyria, would here be vanquished by Yahweh.

Isaiah 60:10–22. God's reversal for Israel will be shown all the more powerful, in that the very foreigners who had oppressed the people would rebuild Jerusalem's walls. Foreign kings would be at Israel's service, paying tribute where once they had waged war and dominance.

Isaiah 62:8–12. God's promise of security to Israel here specifies that foreign enemies would no more despoil it, taking for themselves the agricultural bounty of the land. In contrast to calamity coming from abroad, Yahweh would grant security.

Joel 3:12–17. The future hope of Israel would include the absence of any foreign military presence. God would enact justice and grant protection to the people in security. The threat of foreign powers would be no more.

Other
(4 Passages)

These three uses of immigrant terminology do not fit into larger categories.

These texts are thematically outliers and pretty much irrelevant to our study of attitudes and teaching with regard to immigrants and issues of immigration. They are included here simply because they also utilize terminology specific to immigrants, strangers, foreigners, refugees, or wanderers.

John 2:14. Mention is made here of changing foreign currency into temple currency. This practice was technically allowed by the Mosaic code, but Jesus strikes it down as oppressive toward the poor Israelites who were being charged fees for this service.

Acts 4:24–28. Gentiles and Jews conspire against God's anointed, even though their actions end up effecting God's planned redemption. There is a limited sense here in linking judgment to immigrants and foreigners, but more than anything it is a recognition that Jews and Gentiles together conspired against God's will, even though their purposes could not invalidate God's purposes.

Acts 21:21. Paul is accused of teaching Jews in foreign lands to ignore the Mosaic code. The accusation comes from Jews, but is founded simply on their misunderstanding and misrepresentation of Paul's actual teaching.

1 Corinthians 14:11. Where there is a lack of communication, there may be an assumption of immigrant status. Paul seems to think that speaking in tongues publicly might be akin to the confusion of language between people who have not mastered a language they are using.

Summary Inferences from these Textual Groupings:

Four of the previous categories of passages promote attitudes of equality among people, regardless of their immigrant status. This theme accounts for essentially three-quarters of all biblical passages using terminology for immigrants or foreigners. This is the essential biblical teaching regarding immigrants. We are all alike before God. We should, therefore, treat one another as equals, with no regard to ethnicity, immigration, language, background, or culture.

This is not simply the teaching of the New Testament. It is essential teaching from the Old Testament. Most of the texts cited in the above lists are from the Old Testament. If we accept the common supposition that the ethics of the New Testament writers are of a higher quality and character than that of the Old Testament, there is that much more importance to give to this teaching of equal worth of human life among all nations and categories of people. It was the will of Yahweh that Israel of old learn to treat all people as equal in worth before God. Israel simply failed to rise to the challenge. Unfortunately, our own track record is not so different.

Notes

[1] Paul J. Achtemeier, Harper's Bible Dictionary, 1st ed. (San Francisco: Society of Biblical Literature, Harper & Row, 1985), S. 338.

[2] Ibid., 995 (see Heb 11:13).

[3] Ibid., 338.

[4] Ibid., 995 (see Hebrews 11:13).

SECTION THREE

Other Pertinent Themes and Texts

We have looked at some of the greater overarching themes in the Bible that refer to immigrants and the responsibilities of the nation or believers in their dealings with immigrants or foreigners. We have looked briefly at the biblical passages that use terminology specific to immigrants, foreigners, or refugees. At this point, we turn to a series of secondary passages and themes that may or may not use specific terminology in reference to immigrants, but that have bearing on the biblical imperatives regarding the appropriate treatment and relationship with immigrants, foreigners, and strangers.

The book of Acts will be a central text along these lines, as one of its major themes is the struggle of the Jewish believers to accept Gentile believers as equals with them before God. This was a concept already defined in various Old Testament passages, yet in practice it did not find much application. Just as Jews customarily looked down upon Gentiles, so Jewish believers in Jesus tended to do the same, and Gentile societies looked down on each other and the Jews. The gospel of Jesus turned this attitude on its head, but it took a great deal of soul-searching for believers to accept and adopt the principles of the gospel, even as we still struggle today to allow the character and attitudes of Jesus Christ to find appropriate expression in our own lives.

Acts 10 — Gentile Pentecost

In Acts 10, we find Peter experiencing a vision of animals he has never eaten, along with the command for him to kill and eat. He is taken aback in his vision, as these animals were deemed ritually impure for Jews. While these definitions were connected with a doctrine of purity, the main underlying issue behind them was to keep the Israelites away from the link of these foods with fertility cult practices.

From the days of Moses through the days of Israelite kingship, the nation struggled with the prevalence of fertility cults all around them. Those practices included the use of blood, boiling the young in its mother's milk, and the use of swine as symbols of fertility, life, and power over the forces of life, death, and procreation. Jewish food prohibitions were generally linked to abuses of life from these Gentile fertility cults. The Jews were to honor life as belonging to and on loan from Yahweh. They were not to attempt to grasp on to some life-giving force in a way that dishonored God's gift.

Over the centuries, however, especially upon the return from exile, the Jews had fewer problems with the fertility cults around them. They learned and adapted to consider such as against God's will. They were no longer truly tempted to participate in these practices as an inroad into idolatry. By Peter's day, it was more a question of tradition, culture, and a norm of which foods one ate and which ones were considered nasty, like the difference between eating squirrel and rat. There is little anatomic difference between the two, though one would commonly be deemed noxious while the other edible.

It is in this context, then, that Peter hears the commands to eat what he had heretofore considered nasty or noxious, even while he had heard Jesus declare all foods pure. Jesus had struck down the purity laws in order to reach out to people and call them into God's presence. He abolished definitions of people being worthy or unworthy of God. He simply established that God was willing to love and accept everyone without exception.

The food analogy of the vision was designed to help Peter understand that the same principles Jesus had taught about ritual purity regarding food should apply equally to people. Despite enormous pressure from Jewish tradition to isolate themselves from the Gentiles, God indicated to Peter that not only was this abusive, but it was also in opposition to God's will. God desired that no one be considered unworthy, unclean, or undeserving of God's attention and grace.

To highlight the fact, Luke takes pains not only to record the sheet lowered from heaven three times in the vision, but Peter's relating the vision's message three more times in the passage—to the messengers, to those at Cornelius's house, and to the Jewish believers upon his return. For the Jewish believers, this was a momentous occasion. They were surprised at the extent of God's grace. It was not a message to be missed.

As a result of the vision, Jewish believers travel as immigrants to speak with foreigners, enter a foreign household, eat together with foreigners, and recognize that God has deemed there to be no difference among them. They are all equally covered by God's grace. Since all persons were considered of equal worth by God, the disciples began to recognize that they were responsible to treat all people with equal definitions of worth as well. It meant recognizing that God accepted any and all, and as disciples, we are charged to let go of our distinctions to do the same.

Acts 15 — The Jerusalem Council

The same issue of the place of Gentiles in the gospel from Acts 10 was once again before the Jerusalem church in Acts 15. Paul had begun ministering to the Gentiles without placing conditions on them to force them to become converts to Judaism. At this juncture, the believers considered themselves Jews who had accepted Jesus as Messiah. They did not yet consider themselves "Christians" in the sense of having made a break from Judaism. Cornelius and the others of his household had been viewed as Gentile converts to the Judaism of Jesus. Paul's preaching had taken a new turn, avoiding the issue of conversion to Judaism by focusing simply on Jesus.

For the believers within Judaism, this was much more than simply an issue of witnessing to someone who then joined a church of a different Christian denomination. They were struggling with the very possibility of accepting Jesus beyond the bounds of Judaism, beyond any kind of relationship with Yahweh. The issue and possibility made no sense to them whatsoever, for they could not imagine a relationship with Yahweh apart from their Jewish roots, traditions, and culture of honoring God and the commandments through Moses.

To these Jewish believers, Jewish religious tradition was not simply a foundation upon which Jesus built. It remained for them the basic structure of relationship with God, one that Jesus simply tweaked or explained in a better light. They no longer looked at the Sabbath as a burden, yet they viewed Jewish teaching regarding the Sabbath as a basic expectation of serving God with a more open acceptance of not allowing it to interfere with meeting the needs of others. Circumcision was still an essential element of their covenant agreement with Yahweh, even while they developed a new dependence on faith in Jesus and God's lavish grace and love.

To fully accept Gentiles into a faith relationship with Yahweh without requiring them to adopt Judaism as a whole was more than simply a stretch for them. It meant setting aside a whole series of dos and don'ts that they perceived as integral to a life pleasing to God. The clothing they wore spoke of their allegiance to God's will. The phylacteries they hung on their clothing, the side curls worn by the men, the mezuzahs they hung on the entranceways of their houses and businesses were more than cultural ornaments to them. The foods they avoided, the manner in which they ate, and how they celebrated God's blessings spoke volumes to their personal sense of well-being and identity as a people set apart to serve Yahweh. It was at a minimum difficult for them to accept that Gentiles might enter into relationship with Yahweh through Jesus without adopting these markers of a life devoted to God.

Gentile eating practices seemed noxious to them. Gentile clothing seemed immoral to their perceptions. Gentile ways of eating, customs of travel, vocabulary, and ignorance of the scriptures marked them as immoral, unclean, unworthy, and unsuitable to God's purposes. Peter and Paul called for accepting them simply and purely on the basis of God's demonstrations of love and grace. For most, that was a very difficult pill to swallow. It would require that the Jewish believers take a new and close, hard look at the traditions that had given structure and meaning to their lives before God.

The gospel, however, simply required of both Jews and Gentiles that they accept God's love and grace, not that they become one in culture, language, and tradition. Their unity would not depend on any cultural, ethnic, or national identity. It would have nothing to do with political borders or definitions of citizenship, status, and class. It would depend simply on God's love and acceptance. Whether others were Jews, Romans, Greeks, Egyptians, Ethiopians, or Gauls made no difference, as God demonstrated no such distinction in the offer of grace. Since God accepted and categorized people, such is the example set for our own acceptance and categorization of others. We are all of one class, loved and offered God's full acceptance.

Genesis 20 & 26 — Abraham & Isaac (sister-wives)

"A wandering Aramean was my father" is one of the oldest recorded statements of Hebrew identity. This confession built participation and identity stemming from a tie to Abraham, the forerunner of the people called to belong to Yahweh. This wanderer made his way from Ur of the Chaldeans to the land of Palestine and into Egypt. All along the way he was an immigrant with limited legal rights in the nations in which he lived and journeyed.

Abraham was a nomadic herdsman, a migrant who moved his camp along with the herds of animals under his care. He was a chieftain of a clan, at one point leading a band of some 300-plus armed men. His security in the lands he traversed came from the band who followed in his service and lived in allegiance under him.

It would be expected that at certain times the number of those who followed him may have diminished for some reason or another. One of those times may have been on his entrance into the land of Egypt during a time of famine. It is likely that some determined to part ways with him in a period of famine with a projected move into an established territory such as Egypt.

Genesis records Abraham entering Egypt and surrendering his wife and half-sister, Sarai, into the harem of the pharaoh. This did not mean, as many would presume, that she became wife to Pharaoh. It was an agreement more in keeping with a peace treaty established by a man of importance who entered a land dominated by another man of importance. Allowing Sarai into the harem was a means of maintaining peace between Abraham and his clan and the ruling powers of Egypt.

While Abraham willingly participated in this handing Sarai over into the Egyptian harem, there is equally a sense that he did not feel complete freedom in this action. There was plenty of pressure or threat of violence against him or his clan should he refuse to offer his sister-wife to the harem of Egypt.

In the Genesis narrative, Yahweh intervenes, and Sarai is freed, released back into Abraham's custody. This only happens, however, due to God's intervention by bringing sterility upon the house of Pharaoh. Abraham surrendered Sarai, but without the same voice that would have been granted to one of Egypt's own. He was the immigrant, the foreigner of an unknown tribe who entered foreign territory and had to bow to the pressures of the local political structure.

A few chapters later in Genesis, we read a very similar account of Isaac, Abraham's son, who finds himself in another case of living in the midst of another society as an immigrant. As in the story of Abraham, little is made of the retinue that followed Isaac, but there likely was some band of followers still under his influence after the death of Abraham.

Isaac surrendered his own wife, Rebecca, into the harem of Abimelek, hoping to protect his own life and establish peace between himself and the political structures surrounding him. Again, the ploy is discovered by God's intervention, and Isaac is granted freedom to take his wife, just as Sarai was returned to his father in Egypt.

This is another case of immigrants losing certain rights and voice of equality due to unequal status as being foreign, other, or stranger to the established political structure. Such was the common plight of the immigrant in those days, even as it is today throughout the world. Those outside the halls of power are not treated with the equality or deference granted to those from within. The lowest-ranking segment of society tends to be those whose status is that of immigrant or foreigner. They are the ones with no close ties to those in power, with no one to speak on their behalf or even to understand the situation in which they find themselves.

Abraham and Isaac experienced oppression due to their immigrant status. That is to say nothing of Sarai and Rebecca, who as women were expected to have no voice, regardless of their ethnicity or social class. As women of men who were immigrants, their rights were lessened even further than that of the women of the ruling culture. Among people considered chattel, being attached to a nomad or an immigrant made their position ever more subject to oppression and abuse. The good news is that Yahweh stepped in to provide them with protection and reunite them with family who wished to protect them.

Esther, an Immigrant Queen in Danger

The entire book of Esther is a treatment of what can happen to an immigrant people in exile from their own land. Beyond the narrative of Yahweh's intervention to rescue the chosen people from the oppression they faced, the book is a case study of how easy it is for people to manipulate political forces in an effort to demean and punish a people who are not in their home element.

The story highlights that the Jewish people in exile are misunderstood, due to the fact of the differences in their practices, customs, and religious values. They are viewed through the interpretive lens of the host culture, which places them in a bad light and misreads elements of their identity. Their religious traditions also impede the established process that might give them a path to expressing their concerns and seeking resolution to their plight.

Indeed, some of the oppression they face is purposeful, but a portion, if not a majority, is the result of misunderstandings and misinterpretation of cultural, ethnic, and religious cues. Haman is purposeful in his mistreatment of the Jews, yet the king who allows Haman to act oppressively is seemingly unaware of many of the consequences of Haman's actions and purposes.

Haman took a relationship gone sour with Mordecai and used that as a pretext to exterminate all the Jews throughout the empire. He failed to recognize that Mordecai's actions were not directed at him personally, but reflected a religious position against bowing before any except Yahweh. Haman took exception to Mordecai's actions and projected them upon all of Mordecai's people. It is a cycle we have seen repeated many times over throughout human history.

The outsider, the immigrant, the unknown other tends to be viewed skeptically by the majority population. It is common for a majority group to look down upon another because of their differences in thought, actions, habits, and values. The cultural misunderstandings compound with one bad experience, and it is only natural that we paint the whole of a population with a broad brush, and mostly in a negative light.

Esther paints a difficult scene in which animosity toward an immigrant population is transformed into the makings of genocide. Haman lays the foundation for genocide, though intervention arises through Esther's pleading with the king. Her people are rescued from their impending doom, but there is still conflict between Jewish immigrants and others within the empire.

Haman built his plans for genocide upon prevailing attitudes against the Jews. He did not begin his strategy out of the blue, but built upon the negative views that others shared against this immigrant people who did not conform to all the structures and cultural norms of the larger society.

To conform would have meant a loss of identity to them. To conform would have meant letting go of their identity and the values that gave their lives meaning and structure. It would also have meant the abandonment of Yahweh as the only God for the Jewish people to worship.

We might speak dismissively of a people assimilating into another culture as a matter of course. Reality, however, is that there is much more to cultural assimilation than the external actions we might view as categorizing and identifying culture. Behind each cultural action, attitude, and saying lies a series of values and concepts that will differ from one culture to another.

To Haman, bowing in honor to him spoke of accepting that one was of a lower standing or importance than the one shown the courtesy of a bow. To Mordecai, bowing was a sign of worship and allegiance due to Yahweh alone. For Mordecai, it was Israel and Judah's failure to bow to Yahweh alone that had brought them to their current condition as exiles in a foreign land. They were not immigrants by choice, but as a result of unfaithful relationship with Yahweh.

What to Haman was a simple action to demonstrate respect was something completely different to Mordecai. For Mordecai, the consequences of faithfulness to God were a much greater issue than any consequences in relation to a failure to meet the expectations of Haman. Haman might react against Mordecai, but Mordecai was concerned with God's reaction, one that had sent his entire nation into exile in the first place.

Haman's reaction extended beyond what Mordecai would have expected, yet Mordecai was still focused on a wholly different interpretation not only of the actions and words of each, but also with their larger consequences before Yahweh. On the balance, Haman was concerned with self while Mordecai was concerned with his nation. This tends also to be the essential attitudinal difference between an oppressor and a victim.

When an immigrant community is targeted for some kind of oppressive stance, it is most often that the oppressors are concerned with maintaining positions of power, control, superiority, or sense of worth. The victimized group becomes a focus of the majority population's sense of insecurity. They attempt to increase their security of power, position, or worth at the expense of a group categorized as "other" and therefore unworthy of the benefits enjoyed by the majority in power.

The outside group tends to be much less concerned with issues of power, but with issues of survival and basic security. It is only after those more basic needs are resolved that they can have the luxury of seeking to worry with any sense of dominance. It is dominance, however, with which the majority power tends to be concerned. The lessons from Esther seem to be that our very quest to maintain dominance ushers in the downfall of that position of power. Haman could have avoided a host of problems if he had simply been willing to overlook his own insecurities and not project them onto a people who were already oppressed by their immigrant status within the borders of his nation.

John 4 — Samaritan Woman

John 4 recounts the story of Jesus with the Samaritan woman at the well in Sychar. What we might fail to notice, however, is how Jesus ignores so many social and national taboos in his encounter with this unworthy woman. We most often fail to consider as well that Jesus was an immigrant in the context of this narrative. He had left his home country and crossed through foreign territory, entering a land populated by some the Jews considered responsible for defaming their identity and the name of God by intermarriage with people of other nations.

As far as the Jews were concerned, the intermarriage with idolatrous nations was as grievous an affront to Yahweh as the syncretism they exhibited between a faith based on the Pentateuch and the fertility worship of other lands. The Samaritans were viewed not simply as enemies, but as a people who as a nation had denied Yahweh and given up on their responsibilities to serve Yahweh in purity and sincerity of heart.

Jesus seems all too unconcerned with these issues that were of such great importance to the Jews as a whole. John, in writing his gospel, recognizes a need to explain briefly that Jews and Samaritans did not speak to one another. What he does not get into was that the Jews felt that any contact with a Samaritan would defile a Jew because of the Samaritan abandonment of Yahweh and the traditions of Moses.

When Jesus, obviously a Jew, speaks to the Samaritan woman, she is taken aback that he would stoop to speak to her. She fully expected to be looked down on, ignored, or otherwise demeaned by a Jew in proximity to her. Instead of treating her according to any definition of class, standing, importance, or ritual purity, however, Jesus speaks to her as to an equal. He treats her simply as a person, a human being of dignity in the sight of God.

This was completely unexpected for her. First of all, she was a Samaritan. Secondly, she was a woman. Jews did not speak to unknown women. Jews did not speak to Samaritans. Taking the two issues together, a Jewish man would never deign to speak to a Samaritan who was a woman, especially not without a great attitude of superiority.

As readers of John's Gospel, we are fully aware of Jesus' superiority, but this is no issue for Jesus. He is completely unconcerned with establishing his standing in relation to others, as though his standing might be affected or contaminated by contact with someone of a different class. He soon defends that he is indeed different from what she might expect, but does not use that distinction to put her down in any way.

While Jesus is in the position of an immigrant here, he does not accept that such a status makes him in any way inferior. Neither does he accept the standard Jewish definitions of inferiority and superiority as valid means of classing and treating people. Instead, Jesus goes even further then to send this foreigner, this woman, this woman of ill repute, into the town his disciples have just left as his special envoy regarding the message of God's grace and acceptance of these hated Samaritans.

The disciples had gone into town to seek a source of food, but had ignored that they bore a message of much greater importance than food. They were blinded by the identity of the people of this town. They saw them as detestable Samaritans, unworthy of God and God's grace.

The projected their own loathing as God's loathing for this people. In so doing, they failed in their more important mission as disciples of Jesus to bear witness to their teacher and to call others to heed his teachings. While they failed in their responsibility, this Samaritan woman of ill repute accepted the task before her and ran to fulfill the purpose of sharing God with her people.

Not only were these Jewish disciples blind to the extent of God's grace and acceptance, but their cultural traditions kept them from looking upon others with the same perception of their master. They saw people according to established categories, while Jesus looked beyond those same categories. Jesus treated one and all without distinctions of ethnicity, nationality, language, and culture. In so doing, he set a standard for our own dealings with people of other nations, regardless of where we might find ourselves.

Mark 5 — Gerasene Demoniac

Mark 5 takes us with Jesus to encounter another stranger, a foreigner from outside Israel, with Jesus as the immigrant. This man was an outcast of his own society, plagued by some 2,000 foreign deities (the biblical term demon refers most specifically to the deities of the pagan nations). If anyone could have been considered an outsider to a Jew, this man definitely qualified as such. He was possessed by demons; he was not a Jew; he held no position in his society; he lived among the tombs, a specifically impure place with regard to Jewish concepts of ritual purity.

Jesus entered the area this man inhabited and accepted the encounter with him. The man bowed down at Jesus' feet, and they began to converse, though there is some confusion as to whether it was this man speaking to Jesus or the pagan deities speaking from within him.

Jesus was seemingly untroubled by this encounter. We most certainly would expect the disciples to have been on their guard, to have been unsure as to how to proceed, and to have been very uncomfortable with the contact between Jesus and this seemingly deranged man.

Throughout the course of this encounter, we would do well to remember that these disciples were in the midst of a very uncomfortable experience. Nothing about this encounter was comfortable for them. They were in a foreign land, walking among the tombs of a pagan people, conversing with a man who was under the influence of oppressive spiritual forces.

This scenario did not speak of comfort, ritual purity, or an atmosphere in which one would expect to find people in active worship of Yahweh. That is, however, exactly what we find, counter to any and all expectations. This demonically possessed Gentile man, outcast even from among his own Gentile, pagan society, threw himself down in worship at Jesus' feet.

If this man could be found acceptable and lovable by Jesus, most anyone should be able to qualify. He had no qualities we might consider redemptive. He lived not only a life of impurity, but he lived among a scene of death and corruption. Contact with the dead disqualified a Jew to participate in the religious life of Israel. This man lived among the dead, among the very tombs of a pagan people. Even so, it seems Jesus had come here specifically to seek him out and offer him redemption, rescue, and a new lease on life. Not only that, Jesus then commissioned him to represent what Yahweh had done on his behalf among his own people.

The man departed Jesus' company against his own desires, but embarked upon a mission to witness to Christ in the ten-city region of his people. Jesus accepted him, though he was a foreigner. Then, as an immigrant in this man's territory, he sent this outsider to minister among the very people who had alienated him, treating him as an outcast. It is people like this man, whom society categorized as unfit for service to God, that Jesus seemed to relish bringing into the fold of the new Israel he was creating. He took them and commissioned them as his disciples and emissaries of the reign God was inaugurating through him.

Jesus here took the disciples on a trip through a foreign land, ministered as immigrants to an outsider from among his own people. He then commissioned him to minister to the very people who had cast him out of his society as unworthy of their contact and consideration. In this practical application of God's acceptance and grace, he reached through multiple barriers that societies the world over erect to keep people in distinct categories of worth and inclusion. By example, he taught his disciples to look beyond their prejudices and treat people with a wholly new concept of equality under God's grace.

2 Samuel 11 — Uriah the Hittite

Uriah's place in the story of Israel is a special case study. He was an immigrant, a member of a people considered enemies to Israel. Even so, he enters the muster of warriors serving Israel's political and security needs.

David sees Uriah's wife, who was very likely an immigrant, the daughter of an immigrant, or at least an Israelite who in marriage had stepped outside the boundaries set forth in Israelite law, with its prohibitions against marriage to foreigners. By her name, one would expect that she was an immigrant from the land of Sheba, what today would be considered Ethiopia, since her name means "daughter of Sheba" (it is very likely that this was not her name, so much as a title to identify her as an African immigrant).

In part, it would seem that it is because of her immigrant status that she becomes a target for David's attention and abuse. As the wife of an immigrant, she would not have had the same protections under the law that a native Israelite would have enjoyed.

She should have enjoyed the very same protections as any other. Her husband by right should have had the very same voice as any Israelite male. The problem, however, is that in practice the questions of equality before the law were never truly implemented in the life of Israel, just as the practical application of equality before the law is not a reality for most immigrant communities the world over.

It is very likely that upon returning from the battlefront, Uriah was made aware that something was amiss between his wife and the king. Regardless, Uriah took to heart the established norms in Israel that a warrior was to devote himself fully to the task of war, avoiding intimate contact with his wife or any female as long as the battle ensued. Uriah followed the standard, while David, responsible to lead in the military defense of Israel, did not.

It was the immigrant within Israel who lived according to the standards set by Yahweh, while David, the king and native, was acting against Yahweh's standards.

The outsider of any territory or people generally finds himself in a vulnerable position before the power majority. At times this vulnerability is unimportant and more often a question of potential that is not realized.

At other times, the vulnerability is seen by others as license to oppress, especially since the immigrant is not truly deemed fully to be of a class even with the ruling majority.

It is not difficult to see this principle applied the world over. We can look to the treatment of Jews as scapegoats throughout European history from the Middle Ages onward to Nazi Germany. We can look to other nations around the world who have often oppressed a migrant people, such as the Roma in Europe, Native Americans in the Americas, or even African tribes sold into slavery by warring tribes in their own lands. We might just as easily consider how a nation can dehumanize its own inhabitants, degrading them as simply an enemy faction to be eliminated for some greater purpose. All that is necessary is to class someone as less than human or of less worth than another.

In Uriah's case, the prophet Nathan entered the picture after his murder to call David to account for his error in degrading Uriah, who had lived according to a higher ethic than David himself. David had reacted in response to Uriah's greater morality by having him killed in order to assuage his own guilt. The result was that David simply compounded his own errors, to his own greater shame. He allowed his prejudices against an immigrant to assign himself greater worth and value than this man he categorized as "other."

By the end of the story, David came to recognize that Uriah's and Bathsheba's worth before God was equal to his own. Uriah's widow was then raised to the status of Queen Mother, and it was her son who would become heir to Israel's throne, as though in penance for David's mistreatment of Uriah, the immigrant, and the immigrant's wife he had taken by force due to social position. That Bathsheba was raised to this position was a very loud and strong statement before all of Israel that David had failed in relation to her and her husband on the basis of their immigrant status. Before God, immigrants were not to be abused, though it was easy to do. They were to be protected simply because it was the right or just thing to do.

Joel 2 and Acts 2 — "Upon All Flesh"

Joel 2 was a troubling passage for the Jews of Jesus' day, for generations before Jesus, and even for many today. As a whole, the Jews relished Joel's words, speaking of a coming day when God would lavish his breath upon all of Israel. They looked to this "day of Yahweh" as the ultimate blessing for Israel. The problem was two little phrases in the larger passage. The first spoke of a classless society before the coming of God's blessing. The other phrase applied the blessing not only to a classless Israel, but to immigrants, foreigners, and nations beyond the borders of Israel.

Peter takes up this passage in his explanatory sermon in Acts 2. This is the day of Pentecost, the celebration feast of first fruits, in which the spring harvest was celebrated fifty days after Passover. On this Pentecost, God's breath (spirit) was poured out upon the disciples gathered in Jerusalem, as flames of fire alighting upon them and causing them to speak in languages they had never studied. Peter considered and claimed this event as the fulfillment of Joel's prophecy regarding the day of Yahweh in which God would visit Israel with his presence in disregard of the established social structures.

Jews from all over the known world of the Roman Empire were present in Jerusalem. Most of them had come to Jerusalem on pilgrimage for Passover and stayed for the celebration of Pentecost. Jerusalem's population generally increased in that period from 200,000 to 1,000,000 for these festivals because of religious pilgrimage.

It is among this influx of Jews from all over the world that the Spirit is poured out, and from among them that some 3,000 hear Peter and accept the good news of Jesus. In the months to come, many of these would be returning to the lands of their births, though many would remain in the region of Jerusalem to spend their last days there in anticipation of the messiah's arrival or Jesus' return in glory.

In Peter's sermon, however, what we hear is that Jesus' good news was to be preached to all the peoples. As far as the disciples were concerned, that step was fulfilled in this event of the Spirit's coming, fulfilling all requirements given by Jesus as necessary for his return. The gospel was for all nations, even as the spirit or breath of God was bestowed upon all peoples from all the known nations of the world.

It would be later on that these Jewish disciples would begin to recognize that the gospel applied equally to those who were not and did not become Jews. It would yet be a while before they grasped that Joel's words truly applied across all lines of nationality, ethnicity, and language. At this juncture, however, the heart of the scope of the gospel was clarified, even if Joel's prophecy did not see a complete fulfillment at this point in time. It would be in chapters 10 and 15 that further steps would be taken to address the fact that both Joel's words and Jesus' grace extended beyond identification with Judaism.

Revelation 7 — "A Multitude from Every Nation"

John writing in Revelation speaks in several places of people from all nations gathering around the heavenly throne in worship. This was a troubling yet hope-inspiring concept for the Jews and even Jewish Christianity. For the Gentile church, this was a question of hope and confidence in Yahweh's acceptance without regard to Judaism and Mosaic traditions.

There are other visions represented in Revelation that speak to salvation for Jews, such as the 144,000 gathered from the twelve tribes of Israel. The difficulty in this text, however, is that this number is limited to male, Jewish virgins from a dubious list of twelve tribes. Such a number would exclude the vast majority of believers in the first and second centuries. The Jews at this time were descendants mainly of the tribes of Judah and Benjamin, for the other tribes had formed the nation of Israel after the days of Solomon. Those northern tribes had been racially mixed in the period of the Assyrian exile and return. They had been greatly assimilated into other nations, the main remnant becoming the hated Samaritans.

In John's vision, however, the 144,000 are much more a representation of the pure people of Yahweh who have not been defiled by idolatry. John's terminology and symbolism here function to focus on their religious purity and devotion to Yahweh as the only God. The sexuality mentioned has much more to do with the associations of idolatry with common fertility cult practices of temple prostitution. The numbering of the tribes of Israel takes pains to isolate one tribe known more than most to be idolatrous and unfaithful to Yahweh. The tribe of Joseph figures extra representation, as Joseph is listed along with the name of one of his sons to bring the total back to twelve.

These are not supposed to represent a limitation of God's grace and the extent of the gospel's reach. These numbers are rather a symbolic rendering that indeed God's grace reaches to all those who place their lives in submission to serve God. The number falls in concert with the mention of the numberless multitude from every language and ethnicity on earth, every tribe. It is the representation of the fulfillment of God's promise to Abraham in Genesis, that all the families of the earth would find blessing through him. This is John's higher vision, one of the greatest extensions of inclusion we might find in the Bible. As such, all peoples, languages, ethnicities, tribes, and clans are deemed of equal importance before God. By implication, they should be of equal importance to all who cast their lives in service and submission to the will and call of God.

Matthew 28 — The Great Commission

The final passage of Matthew 28 has often been looked upon as Jesus' great commission. It has been used in missions sermons and texts the world over since at least the days of William Carey and the birth of the modern evangelical missions movement. There is nothing essentially wrong with that application, except for the fact that while Jesus does offer here a commission for his disciples of all generations, it is not a commission necessarily to go.

The imperative verb here is not the traditional "Go ye" of so many sermons. This is one example of a text in which the King James Version of the Bible did not select the best available translation for the underlying Greek text of Matthew. The Greek text expresses the verb to go in a different form. The phrase would be better rendered, "As you are going, therefore, make disciples." Rather than go being the imperative verb, Jesus' command, the imperative here is make disciples. The going is simply to be assumed. It is "as you are going," "wherever you may go," "in going about your routines or travels," or simply "wherever you may find yourself."

The commission to make disciples, then, is not limited to departing on any specific mission or assignment. It is in no way conditioned to departing one's homeland in order to take the good news of Christ Jesus to others. Sure, Jesus speaks specifically of this command being directed at making disciples of all nations, all nationalities, all peoples of the world. There is, however, no sense that this is to occur as missionaries are sent to the remote regions of the world. It is just as much the fact that this is to occur as Christians who have never crossed any national border are to make disciples of those with whom they come in contact, the immigrants, foreigners, and strangers who happen to be in their midst, however that comes to be.

We see this principle play out in Acts 2 at Pentecost with Jews present in Jerusalem on pilgrimage. They are presented the gospel, which they then take back with them to their own lands. We also see this in practice with Philip's encounter with the Ethiopian eunuch, who takes the gospel back to his queen in Ethiopia, Candace, who leads her entire nation to accept the gospel of Jesus Christ. We see this principle alive in Paul's ministry. It matters not where he happened to be headed, what his travel plans were, or how those plans were interrupted. He was on mission for Christ throughout the entirety of his travels, leaving churches behind in places he had never intended to travel or remain. While he was traveling, while he was working, while he was about his business, he was on mission to make disciples of any and all, regardless of their nationality.

Jesus' own ministry demonstrated this same attitude and mission to bring God's message of love, grace, and acceptance to any and all who might cross his path. Occasionally, he went out of his way to make a specific encounter happen. All too often, however, his own path was crossed by someone with a different plan, purpose, or need. He used all of these chance encounters under the banner of the larger mission before him. He reached out to Samaritans, Jews, and Gentiles alike, making disciples along the path set before him.

On one level, our misuse of this text as a missions-sending text does injustice to its message and distracts us from Jesus' actual purpose behind this commission. This is not a text that simply applies to foreign missionaries. If that were the case, every one of Jesus' disciples should take up the call to serve as a foreign missionary, for this commission applies to one and all of Jesus' followers. This is not a command for which we are allowed to make exceptions of ourselves.

We are each to be on mission to make disciples of all nations or peoples. We are not to look at this from the standpoint of "if they happen to be of a different nationality, that is fine." Rather, the command would send us in a very specific direction of making sure that our efforts to make disciples among others do not exclude any group of people. We are commissioned to cross cultural, ethnic, and linguistic barriers to make disciples of all nations, not simply those who are like us.

The commission includes everyone from two perspectives. Each follower or disciple is commissioned. Secondly, we are all under a commission to make disciples of peoples of every nation, with no exception. The most immediate manner in which this commission applies to our lives as individuals is in regard to the immigrant communities within our midst. These are the nations we meet as we go about our daily business and the routines of life. This is where Jesus' great commission begins—right here at home. Sure, it also includes efforts at foreign missions, but it is so much broader a concept than that. It encompasses responsibility for every believer within every nation to reach out with purpose to bear the gospel before all groups of people, with no distinction whatsoever.

Genesis 4 — "Whoever Finds Me Will Kill Me"

We are accustomed to read the narrative of Genesis 4 from a certain perspective, one that treats Cain as an evil man, one whom God punishes and upon whom God casts a curse. This tradition tells us that there is nothing good or worthy in Cain. It tells us that we should hate him, since he is a murderer and is good for nothing else.

If we read the narrative with attention, however, that is not how God treats Cain. Sure, God warns Cain about the consequences of his sinful actions. More than curse him, however, what God does is to place a dose of protection over Cain. God covers him with a sign to tell others that no one should kill Cain.

This sounds rather strange to our ears. The natural human desire would be more coherent with killing Cain, especially because he had murdered his brother. God does not desire to act, nor does God want others to act according to such a manner. God intervenes in Cain's situation with the purpose of offering Cain a certain protection, which was surely necessary. Cain would now be an errant wanderer upon the face of the earth, an immigrant wherever he might chance to go, and that was exactly why it was so necessary that Cain be protected.

The fact that Cain was worried about how he would be treated has a lot to do with his condition as a wanderer and little to nothing to do with his standing as a murderer. At times we lose sight of this, for we are reading the narrative, and his actions to kill his brother Abel are right in front of us. In his condition as a wanderer and immigrant, nobody he encountered would know of his actions in killing his brother. His fear of being killed has nothing to do with revenge for his own actions. It has everything to do with adopting the condition and status of being an immigrant, a wanderer, a stranger, a foreigner, an unknown.

The human tendency is to treat any strange person with a certain dose of scorn and insecurity. We do not know the stranger, and when the other person belongs to some different class, nation, language, ethnicity, or color, we become anxious in regard to them. They do not act according to our norms. They do not dress according to our models. They do not speak with the same meaning, even when they use our same words. Their pronunciation is different. Their values, priorities, and actions tell us we should be on guard against some kind of threat we do not quite understand.

This was the situation into which Cain was entering. This was his fear. He was afraid that whoever might find him would look upon him as a threat. He felt insecure about entering the category of an immigrant and wanderer. He was concerned about this, because the condition of being an immigrant truly makes one vulnerable.

The immigrant is vulnerable because he does not know the rules of the society in which he finds himself. She does not know the norms of interaction with the population. Though he might speak the language, he does so with an accent, not using the words according to the same cultural norms. She does not understand the hidden notions of the language. He cannot distinguish between a joke, a word of praise, and a sarcastic attack. She does not understand when double entendres are being used with hidden motives by others.

An immigrant might learn something of these linguistic issues, but would never be able to fully grasp them along the same lines as the resident population. That is due to the fact that the immigrant does not share the same cultural, social, and philosophical basis of those in whose presence she is found. More than that, he uses a different system of filters through which to interpret the words, actions, and intentions of others.

What is most interesting here, however, is the character of God's actions and attitudes in regard to Cain. As far as God is concerned, it is important to act in order to protect Cain. God recognizes the truth behind Cain's worries over finding himself as an immigrant and a wanderer. God intervenes in order to protect him, even though he knows that Cain is a murderer. Even though Cain has his moral and ethical failures, God is concerned to care for him, specifically because he will find himself in a condition that will tend to make him vulnerable before the resident and established populations. God offers protection to Cain because he will need it.

This seems to be God's greater worry in reference to caring for wandering or immigrant populations. These are the very same concerns he has over the widows, the poor, the refugees, and the orphans. The persons who tend to be ignored by society and treated with some sense of disdain are the persons for whom God tends to offer special protections. These are the most vulnerable, and it is because of this that God requires that they be extended a distinctive level of protection. They are vulnerable, and God requires that they be protected in recognition of that vulnerability.

Matthew 2 — "The Wise Foreigners"

Matthew's Gospel begins with a genealogical list of Jesus' ancestors, interspersed with the names of four women who reflect the presence of Gentiles in Jesus and David's genealogy (Tamar, Rahab, Ruth, and Bathsheba). Having laid a foundation for recognizing that the gospel of Jesus will not only be for the benefit of Jews, Matthew inserts another mention of Gentiles in chapter 2.

Here, it is a group of magi from the East, most likely to be considered as coming from the region of Babylon and reflecting the traditions of the Chaldeans, who were the wise astrologers of the Babylonian court in the period of Jewish exile. Ur was a city in the region of the Chaldeans, the city from which Abraham and his family had begun their migration to the land that would become Israel.

It is likely that Matthew wanted Jewish audiences to make the connection here with Abraham's wandering. It is also likely that he wanted them to see a connection with Babylon and their history of exile. It is also likely that he wanted to remind them of God's use of Cyrus, a king known for oppression of the Jews, who was then used by Yahweh as an instrument to return the Jewish people from exile back to Judah.

In making these connections, Matthew also takes us on what would be an uncomfortable journey for any Jew. We are to understand that Yahweh spoke to these astrologers as they studied the stars for information on the will and actions of their gods. As they proceeded with their pagan rites and worship, Yahweh spoke to them of the birth of Jesus, born to be king of the Jewish nation.

Why would God stoop to speak to pagan astrologers? Why would Yahweh give them information on the coming of Jesus and somehow fail to communicate the same message to the Jewish people themselves? Why would these foreigners be privileged with information about the birth of Messiah when the nation was kept in the dark regarding what God was accomplishing?

Traditionally, we have focused on these magi, treated them as kings, numbered them according to the categories of gifts they presented to Jesus, but we have ignored the religious concerns of God communicating with foreigners and keeping Israel in the dark with regard to the coming of their long-awaited Messiah.

We should be troubled by this passage. Apparently that was Matthew's intent at least. Why would God communicate with a people they counted as enemies? Why would God appear in any form to a pagan, idolatrous band of stargazers who thought the stars in the night sky were deities to be worshiped? As far as Matthew seems to be concerned, however, God is unconcerned with our human categories of who is worthy or unworthy of being influenced by Yahweh. After all, there are many Old Testament passages in which the very same thing happened in Israel's past.

Rahab was a prostitute, likely working with a pagan fertility cult. It was she, however, who communicated to Joshua's spies the message they needed to hear. She was the one who told them that Yahweh would have victory in the impending battle at her city of Jericho. She, the idolatrous, immoral foreigner, knew the truth of Yahweh that Yahweh's own people were unwilling or unprepared to accept.

The same basic story appears in the Elijah narratives. We find in 1 Kings that a widow of Baal's home country has a level of faith in Yahweh that is seemingly nonexistent in Israel. She is willing to trust Yahweh, while Israel's king and his servants are more worried with worshiping Baal. In the balance, she is the one who receives the benefits of Yahweh's attention, while the king of Israel cannot accept or trust Yahweh's blessings.

So here these magi are wise, not so much because of their study of the stars as deities communicating with humanity. Their wisdom is revealed in their actions to follow what God reveals to them, seeking out the one born to be king of the Jewish people. They may still be idolatrous foreigners, immigrants in the land of Israel. They may be outsiders to God's covenant relationship with Abraham and his descendants, yet God has not forgotten them. Neither has God ignored them and cast them aside. Amid their failures and improper ways of worship, God intervened to communicate grace and blessing upon them.

They turn out to be much more holy, worthy, and righteous than Herod, the acting king of Israel. Though Herod is merely a puppet king for Rome, he is much more concerned with protecting his power, prestige, and position than with honoring Yahweh. These foreigners, however, enter Israel to pay homage to Yahweh, not out of any sense of obligation, but in joy at God's communication with them. They worship and celebrate God's gift, concerning themselves with what Yahweh is doing, not with any personal issue of pride, position, or privilege.

As in the case of Rahab and the widow of Zarephath, the foreigners, the strangers, the outsiders to the community of Israel are the ones who demonstrate for those on the inside what a relationship with Yahweh should look like. These wise strangers set the bar for true faith, for truly belonging to God. They show us that God is not concerned with issues of status and standing, but with a heart of dedication, worship, and rejoicing in God's initiatives and actions.

Herod slaughters innocents in Israel to protect what he cannot hold on to. The magi give up worthy possessions to honor one born king of a foreign nation. They demonstrate worthy worship, while Herod can think only of self-protection. While they return home rejoicing, Herod remains worried, preoccupied, and dies unfulfilled and disconnected from God.

Acts 6 — Deacon Election of Immigrants

We have already mentioned that Jerusalem's population swelled annually during the period of Passover to Pentecost. Jews from around the Roman Empire traveled to Jerusalem to celebrate Passover, the most important feast day of the year. Many planned their whole lives to make just such a pilgrimage. Among them, some planned to spend their last years in Jerusalem, hoping they might see the messiah before the time of their deaths. Should they die in Jerusalem, their hope was to be resurrected at the coming of the messiah to participate in the messianic banquet at the restoration of Israel.

Most all Jews, even today, hope to participate in such a celebration. The traditional closing remark on the Passover celebration continues to be "Next year in Jerusalem!" Jews routinely made pilgrimage and migrated to Israel in relation to those hopes. As they died and were buried in Jerusalem, however, many left behind widows in the region, some who had little on which to live out their last days. For the early church, this resulted in a problem.

We know from New Testament writings and from other historical documents that there was a series of droughts in Palestine in the years following Jesus' death and resurrection. Paul speaks of Gentile churches taking up collections to help feed the hungry back in Jerusalem. Acts records that believers in the Jerusalem church also went out of their way to aid the hungry within their community by selling good and lands to purchase food. Yet there were other issues. Some of the widows in the community were being overlooked, as they were unknown to many of the settled resident population.

Those being overlooked were Jewish immigrants to Jerusalem and their widows left behind. They had not grown up and raised their children in Jerusalem. They mostly did not have family to care for them in their old age. They were outsiders, even if they were Jews. Many, if not most of them, spoke different languages from the Palestinian Jews. They spoke Greek, as it was the common tongue of the Roman world, and this caused some separation and distance from the resident Aramaic speaking community in Jerusalem.

The Jerusalem church was not trying to overlook these widows. There was no intent to oppress or slight, but the fact of their being part of an immigrant community meant that they did not have the same facility of connections to get the help they needed. It was an oversight.

When the issue was brought before the apostles, there was some discomfort and concern about the problem before them. The resolution to which the apostles came, however, was rather unusual in its form. What they determined to do was to elect servants (deacons) for the church who would oversee the food distribution in such a way as to be sure that no one was being neglected. That seemed a very reasonable suggestion, as the apostles had other priorities within their own responsibilities. There were plenty of other people who could fulfill the requirements to make sure the food distribution was equitable.

They brought forth names, therefore, to oversee the distribution. Every single one of them was an immigrant Jew. This was nothing like the political definitions used in the United States to respond to issues of civil rights and discrimination. This went several steps beyond. The apostles charged the immigrant community to choose from among themselves seven men of good reputation to oversee the process. They were the ones aware of the injustice being done, though the injustice was not intentional. As the ones aware of the problem, they would also be the ones given responsibility to resolve the oversight, making sure that not only the Hellenistic Jews were not overlooked, but that the Palestinian Jews were not overlooked either.

This was a startling move by the apostles: "We hear you. We recognize that there is a problem. Thank you for bringing it to our attention. We want you, as the people who are most aware of the problem to be the ones responsible for resolving it. You choose from among yourselves people you can trust to oversee the distribution of food. We will commission or ordain them to make sure that the process becomes more just and equitable and that no one is left out or overlooked."

The church as a whole did not seem to have an issue with what the apostles proposed. They saw the wisdom in their response. It is those who suffer injustice who best understand what injustice looks and feels like. They are the ones who should be part of the solution. They are the ones with something at stake in the process. They are the ones who are already aware of the issues. They are the ones who understand the concerns from the inside. As such, they are the ones who most appropriately can be tasked with identifying real solutions.

The church was seemingly not concerned with any concept of reverse discrimination. They were not worried about an immigrant group turning the tables on them. They were not worried about giving power to a group who was experiencing problems as outsiders. Instead, they were concerned about meeting the needs of those who were not being served appropriately. They empowered them as outsiders to become the solution to the issues they recognized and brought to the attention of others.

By giving these outsiders the responsibility and power to correct the issues raised, they brought them into the center of the greater community. The apostles and the rest of the church made the immigrant community of believers equal to the rest of the believing community. They raised them in status from immigrants, foreigners, and strangers to responsible members of the community, just as central to the functioning of the church as any other individual or group.

This is a picture of what it means to include others in the formation of a community. It is a picture of what it means to include strangers, foreigners, and immigrants in the heart of a community, loving and treating our neighbors as ourselves. This is what it means to love as Jesus taught, offering acceptance and grace after the model established by Jesus Christ.

Acts 8 — The Ethiopian Eunuch

Acts 8 tells the story of an immigrant from Ethiopia who was reading a text from Isaiah on his return trip from Jerusalem. This man was a Gentile proselyte to Judaism, having converted, but seeking to better understand his Jewish faith.

As Philip came close to his chariot and recognized that he was reading the Hebrew scriptures, he asked if he understood them. That question opened the door to dialogue about Jesus and the gospel Jesus had proclaimed. Philip took that opportunity to share his faith and understanding with this man.

The result of their conversation is recorded in the book of Acts. As far as Luke is concerned, the man requested to be baptized into faith in Jesus (a rite of conversion like what had made him a proselyte to Judaism) and continued on his way back to Ethiopia, where he served Queen Candace as her steward.

There is, however, more to the story that Luke does not record for us. Luke was perhaps not interested in sharing all the details or did not know of the consequences of that encounter in a deserted region. He may simply have assumed that his audience was already aware of the implications of this story, and he only needed to mention it to help build his case for taking the gospel into Gentile communities all over the world.

Believers in Ethiopia are aware of greater consequences to this story in Acts 8, just as Luke's original audiences may have been aware. This "chance encounter" between Philip and the eunuch had far-reaching effects.

It would seem at first glance that Philip being sent out into the middle of an uncivilized, unpopulated area would be a severe waste of resources. Why take the time to go speak to an isolated individual when there were cities populated with people who also needed to hear the good news of Jesus Christ?

God had a much further-reaching purpose in sending Philip out into this deserted region than Luke records for us. The eunuch in question was a high servant to Queen Candace. As a result of his conversion to Jesus' brand of Judaism, the good news entered the court of Ethiopia, where this eunuch had access to the queen and a position from which to carry great influence among the nation he served.

Candace became a believer as a result of Philip's witness through this eunuch. Not only did she accept Jesus, but she led her entire nation to adopt Christianity to become the first officially Christian nation in the world.

That obviously does not mean that every individual in Ethiopia gave their lives in submission to Christ and entered into a committed relationship with God through Jesus. The impact of this conversion, however, influenced an entire people toward acceptance of the gospel.

The Jews as a nation did not turn to Jesus in acceptance of his place and identity as Messiah. Ethiopia did. More than that, however, traditional history in Ethiopia would claim that the nation was already a center of Judaism from the days of the queen of Sheba's visit to Solomon in Jerusalem. Per that history, the eunuch in Acts 8 was not simply returning to Ethiopia as an individual converted to Judaism and Jesus. He was one of a nation who had accepted Judaism and returned with the complement of accepting Jesus as the promised Messiah.

Eusebius, one of the early fathers of the church, wrote of this eunuch as the first Gentile convert to Christianity and the founder of the church in Ethiopia. There is evidence that some of the rites and traditions of Ethiopian Christianity and Judaism date back to preexilic times, as there is a history of celebrating festivals that date from that early a period. There seems at least to have been some interplay and influence with early Judaism.

Judaism had issues with the conversion of a eunuch, but Luke does not seem concerned at all with such issues. He seems more concerned with the Ethiopian's worship along the lines of Hebraic faith and his acceptance of Yahweh as the one worthy of worship. It is then from this standpoint that Luke speaks of his conversion to Christianity.

Philip does not deal with this eunuch according to the norms of Jewish tradition. He treats him as an equal before God. He speaks to him on the basis of the scriptures being read. He finds no impediment to his baptism in the presence of water. Though he might not have been technically worthy for conversion to Judaism as a eunuch, Philip sees no impediment to baptize him as a believer and follower of Jesus.

The result of this conversion seems to have been not only Luke's literary foreshadowing of the gospel coming to Cornelius. It also prefigures Paul's ministry before kings and authorities the world over. Before Paul can begin his Gentile ministry, Philip, one of the Hellenistic deacons of Jerusalem, is responsible for the presentation of the gospel on its way to Ethiopia, considered the most remote of lands as far as the Jews and Romans were concerned.

Here we find a Hellenistic Jewish immigrant communicating the gospel to an immigrant from a different land. This man with a questionable conversion to Judaism finds full acceptance in the gospel of Christ. It is through acceptance of this immigrant passing through Israel that the mission established by Jesus in Acts 1:8 will become fulfilled in the land of Ethiopia, "the uttermost parts of the earth" in the minds of Luke's readers. Not only does this immigrant receive the gospel for himself, but apparently takes it back to others, assuming the full responsibility of discipleship. An immigrant here is transformed into an emissary of the gospel to another immigrant, who takes the same gospel to his home country.

Paul, the Jewish Immigrant Apostle

Paul himself is an interesting character in terms of his status as an immigrant. He was a Roman citizen and a Jew, yet he was born in Tarsus, outside the land of Palestine. As a Roman, he was a citizen of the world power. As the son of Jews, he was Jewish from the standpoint of ethnicity, religion, and education. Being born outside of Palestine, however, made him an immigrant in Jerusalem, though he grew up in Jerusalem as an outsider who spoke Greek as much as Aramaic, along the lines of deacons like Philip.

Despite those considerations, Paul managed to enter the power structure of Jerusalem in his early efforts to squelch the rise of popularity of Jesus' followers. At the same time, his ministry as a Jew and later as a Christian took him mainly to other lands, where he was classed as an outsider, either due to his birth and identity as a Jew or as having been born outside of Palestine.

This identification with Judaism classed him as an outsider throughout the Roman Empire. His Roman citizenship placed him in an outsider class among Jews. His work and life among Gentile nations created a sense of his having abandoned his Jewish roots, creating growing animosity from Jews and Jewish believers. Both his birth and the character of his ministry made him an outsider among Romans, Greeks, Jews, and even the Christian converts with whom he worked.

He was an outsider in Jerusalem and notably did not hold a position in the Jerusalem council. There, it is Peter who speaks with authority, along with James. Though Paul may be credited with writing the majority of the New Testament, he did so as an outsider, an immigrant working among many populations, yet always as one who did not belong in religious, cultural, political, ethnic, or national terms. At times his immigrant standing was beneficial to his ministry, yet it mainly cost him personally and physically, as it placed him in the position of an easy scapegoat for any perceived threat upon a growth in the believing community.

Paul was seen as a threat to Judaism by the Jewish populations around the world, but most notably upon his return to Jerusalem after significant missionary enterprise. Here, the accusation is that he has brought Gentiles into the temple courts where they were not allowed to enter. In Gentile lands, Paul was looked upon as an outsider, guilty of turning the world upside down. He was seen as an anarchist and antisocial, as he did not participate in the norms of idolatry.

As an outsider, he was an easy target for abuse, ranging from prison, beatings, floggings, and being dragged out of town for stoning. He was routinely chased out of town by the local authorities, even when they were the ones who had broken with Roman law and ignored Paul's rights as a citizen of the empire.

It is this outsider and immigrant in many lands who is credited as the greatest single influence in the growth of Christianity in the first century. As we treat immigrants, strangers, and outsiders, so are we likely to be treating the likes of Paul, for he would have been among those we consider as beyond the definitions of belonging to the resident, established population.

It was his ministry to Christ that took him to so many places and cast him as an outsider. He was an outsider to Jews, Athenians, Corinthians, Romans, Ephesians, and Philippians. It was these peoples, however, who both mistreated him due to their fear and uncertainty of his outsider status and on the flip side gave heed to his words and accepted God's call to rest upon the grace and love of God portrayed in Christ Jesus. It was his outsider status that enabled him to see how the gospel might change the people to whom he preached. It was also his outsider status that both granted him a hearing by some and caused others to seek ways to silence him forever.

Ultimately, however, it was those who ran Paul out of their towns who were most responsible for the growth of the gospel. That is not to say that Paul did not minster and share the gospel message effectively. It is simply that as he was forced to leave first one town then another, others were called upon to step into positions of leadership within the fledgling community of believers. Had Paul remained present for much longer, it is likely that their leadership and growth in responsible ministry would never have gained the same traction. In being forced to accept responsibility to give continuity to what Paul had begun among them, the community grew in a way it may never have grown otherwise.

Galatians 3 — "Neither Jew nor Greek"

Paul has famously written that in Christ there are no distinctions between Jews and Greeks, males and females, slaves and free. These are striking words, yet they sound somewhat trite to modern, Western ears. While we may accept these words at face value, our practical application of them across the centuries has been less than stellar. We have claimed equality for ourselves, yet most often have rejected equality for others. We desire the rights and benefits such words might accrue to ourselves, yet are loathe to allow others the same benefits, as though God's grace were of insufficient substance to go around and benefit all to the same degree.

For Paul, these were not simply words. There was much importance behind the phrases he penned for the churches with whom he communicated. In many ways, these equality concepts were earth-shattering. Not only that, he also applied these words in ways that shook the communities of the faithful. This was part of the issue he faced with the Judaizers who seemed to dog his steps from town to town.

These Judaizers were emphatic about the distinctive superiority not simply of the gospel, but of their standing before God as Jews. To them, the identity issue was much more than a cultural or ethnic identity. It spoke to them of their importance before God. It was a source of pride to them that they were Jewish. Beyond that, however, their Judaism distinguished them from the rest of the world population. It made them holy. It made them acceptable to God. It was almost a substitute for any reliance upon grace. Indeed, that is Paul's major criticism of the whole issue brought by the Judaizing community. If one relies on one's Jewishness, there is no room left for grace.

As a result, Paul determined that there is no intrinsic value difference between those who are or are not Jews. Before God, there is no difference whatsoever. His argument in Romans is that all are sinful and that our best efforts at righteousness are as filthy rags before God. The Mosaic code may have shown a better way to live, a higher ethic by which to conduct ourselves, but it does not and cannot make us more deserving of God's attention, care, and love.

Once we accept salvation and redemption through grace, we must recognize that we are not coming to God on the basis of any personal qualifications, worth, or deserving. We simply come to God on the basis of God's qualities of grace, love, mercy, and forgiveness. As this is all that is necessary for a life in God's presence, there is immediately no distinction among us along the lines of worth or importance. There are no ethnic, cultural, linguistic, or national designations to make any one group superior or inferior to another.

As a matter of fact, Paul extends the concept beyond the bounds of ethnic, linguistic, and religious identification. He applies the same principles to distinctions of gender and social standing. He says there is neither Jew nor Greek, male or female, slave or free. Such words cut at the very heart of the social structure of the world in which he lived. If taken at face value, they would be sufficient not only to destroy the social fabric of Israel, but of the whole Roman Empire as well.

Women, slaves, and foreigners were not deemed according to the same value as the men of the power structure. For Paul to simply wipe out these distinctions from within the gospel of Christ was a radically disruptive message. It was more than simply revolutionary, as for many it would be deemed an attack on the basic structures of society. In a very real sense, that is exactly what Paul's words of equality meant. They determined that there was no difference of worth according to any of the categories in use by the cultures of the day.

Religiously, perhaps the distinction between Jew and Greek was the most obviously important distinction, but Paul does not leave the issue there. He speaks to the whole of division between categories or classes of people. He obliterates the whole definition of insider and outsider, power broker and oppressed. within the bounds of the gospel of Christ Jesus.

If this is as important an issue in the gospel as Paul claims it to be, there is no reasonable rationale to continue to make any distinction between classes or castes of people on any basis whatsoever. One's standing as an immigrant, stranger, or foreigner becomes less than a non-issue before the gospel. They become irrelevant labels being applied where, by rights, they no longer exist. They become definitions that struggle against the very purposes of the gospel of God's grace in Christ. They become attacks on God's initiatives to fashion one people out of all nations, classes, and categories.

There can be no such distinctions within the church in accord with the claim of Jesus Christ as Lord, for the purposes of God are to make us one, casting aside any and all categories of distinction or worth. Any discussions of nationality, ethnicity, gender, or social standing in regard to worth or importance become more than simply discussions outside realm of the gospel. They effectively become discussions that run counter to the gospel. They are in opposition to the gospel categories of grace, under which no one has greater merit than another. Merit, worth, and status are completely alien categories to this equality, which originates with the grace of God in Christ Jesus.

John 17 — Jesus' Prayer for Unity

In this chapter of John's Gospel, we find Jesus at prayer for his disciples. He prays both for those disciples before him as well as his disciples throughout the ages. He expresses a desire that his disciples be united as one body, but also calls upon God to fashion his disciples into that one body.

We are well familiar with this theme of unity as a central category of New Testament teaching, but what we may overlook is the degree of unity to which Christ Jesus would call his followers throughout the ages. We have traditionally looked at unity in so many terms, yet most all of them tend to fall by the wayside when we look at concerns of practice, as well as the degree of unity to which we aspire.

There are many calling for unity through doctrinal conformity. They would have us believe the same things, accept a core set of truths, and apply the gospel in a coordinated way to our understanding of God and concerns of doctrine and theology. There is a problem with this category of unity. It begins and ends with questions of thought patterns. It never moves beyond those things that can be memorized, categorized, or systematized. It does not have the inherent flexibility needed to adapt to new contexts of life, new situations that were never before imagined, and the experiences of life that take us by surprise. It leaves no room for learning.

Others call for unity in terms of an organizational structure. They want all believers around the world to enter into membership into one institution, which will then be the one unique representation of God and the gospel of Jesus Christ. The problem here is first that Jesus never established any institutional framework for the church. He established a multifaceted, living, organic community of faith. He also spoke of sheep of other folds that were yet to be gathered. He spoke of faith outside the borders of Israel and commissioned individuals to share their witness of God's mercy far from the center of faith in Jerusalem, detached from communication with any hierarchical structure. The other major problem with this kind of unity is that it depends on some kind of political reality, whereby individuals or groups are making decisions that must be carried out on the ground in situations unknown to the decision-makers. Jesus never accepted this kind of power structure. He rather commissioned individuals to depend upon God for direction as they applied the principle of relaying to others what God had done for them, with no system of oversight in place.

Others call for unity in terms of procedure and identifiable process. They look to groups like the Jehovah's Witnesses, who utilized a worldwide strategy for evangelism and education. They desire to take one model and have everyone unite in the application and use of this product. When we look at Jesus' ministry in John, however, we find that his conversation with people changes considerably at every event and with every person. He speaks the good news in terms of living water, transforming water into wine, rebirth, shepherding, bread, and a host of other presentations that respond to issues his audience was dealing with. He does not employ any single strategic method to be applied across the board, other than meeting people at their point of need and couching his message within their context of life.

These three concepts of unity fail to join believers the world over, as well as in the depth of unity to which Jesus calls us. These are all superficial answers to much deeper questions. They are the response of those who want a simple answer, a quick definition with which to work. They fail to grasp the deeper issues that impact unity, and they disregard Jesus' words about the quality of unity to which we are called.

Jesus prays here in John 17 that we might be one in the same manner in which Jesus and the Father are one. That calls for a very different take on the character of unity to which we must aspire. It calls us to unite in terms of purpose, character, desire, vision, and focus. It calls us to set aside any sense of personal worth, ambition, value, and comfort in order to grasp a unity along the lines of Paul's declared purpose in Philippians, discounting all else that we might gain the ever upward call of God in Christ Jesus.

It would seem that the unity to which Jesus calls us has much more to do with character and purpose. It is about uniting our lives to God's purpose, allowing God to live through us, both individually and corporately. Due to the intrinsic variability and diversity of God's creation, we would not expect this unity to be an external element visible in an institutional structure, a methodology, or a groupthink. Rather, it would be a unity of purpose and character, a unity based on God's love. It is a unity that would draw us together in seeking to implement the principles of the good news of a relationship with God and with one another. It is a unity that would take us beyond our boundaries of nation, ethnicity, culture, language, gender, status, wealth, influence, and power. It would bind us together in caring for those around us.

This is the character of unity that Jesus portrayed in speaking and living the will and purposes of the Father all throughout his ministry. He applied the principles of this unity with God and others in many ways, in many places, and in a multitude of situations. It brought him to speak of acceptance and living water to the Samaritan woman at the well. It led him to speak with Nicodemus of a new birth, which did not rely on any system of legalism or ancestry, but that would radically transform his living from the inside out. Jesus did not organize and publish a unified code of doctrinal analysis that we might memorize and quote upon request. He established no organizational structure we might rely upon. Rather, he called us to unity in dependence upon God. This dependence would cast aside all our categories by which we isolate ourselves from others and claim some kind of superiority over those who do not meet our definitions.

At heart, that is what is at the basis of these contrary definitions of unity through one or another system. It is a way to categorize ourselves as the "in" group and label all others as outsiders. Nothing could be much further from the purposes of God in Christ Jesus. He casts no one aside, except for the religious hypocrite who claims to be something he is not. Even to these he offers acceptance, if they would first let go of their self-importance. It is the same issue for our categories of keeping people out by considering our discomfort with them somehow reflective of God's discomfort and lack of acceptance. Jesus' call to unity, however, would destroy such claims completely. No one is more or less deserving. The gospel, after all, is a message of grace, a message that casts out all categories of acceptability, worth, dignity, and superiority.

This is a call to unity under the grace of God, a unity that abolishes any sense of superiority. It places us all on an equal basis before God, accepted due to love, not due to special standing. It is this acceptance, grace, and love that should unite us, regardless of our instinctual means of categorizing people to make ourselves feel somehow superior to others. We are to join God's purposes of grace and love, reflecting God's purposes of grace toward all, just as evidenced in the life of Jesus. This is our model of unity, accepting the Samaritan woman at the well, the lepers, the Canaanite woman, the blind man, the Gerasene demoniac, fishermen, tax collectors, Pharisees, and poor alike. In that light, our definitions to divide us become worthless and work counter to the gospel we claim to uphold.

Matthew 8 — The Centurion's Servant

In this passage, the story of Jesus is surprising in a way we might not expect. In this case, it is the Jewish community that comes to Jesus to beg his intervention on behalf of a Roman centurion and his servant. Jesus does not begin to teach acceptance of an outsider, a Gentile. In fact, we see a community of Jews who recognize in this foreigner, who represents foreign occupation, a man who is worthy of God's mercy.

The Jews in question seem to have good reason to see in the example of this man one worthy of Jesus' attention. At the same time, their definitions of his worthiness are based on his help of the community to build its synagogue. The centurion in question has taken all the initiative to draw near to the Jewish community. The Jews themselves had seemingly done nothing to warrant his positive attention and assistance. They have recognized in his actions and attitudes, however, that he is not like other Gentiles, or at least not like their prejudiced concept regarding a Gentile, and specifically a Roman soldier.

This is often the case, as we are wont to categorize others in accord with a prejudiced view of an entire culture. Our ideas of cultures have some validity, as they help us understand what to expect of other members of the same culture. Yet as we get to know an individual from within the larger culture or society, we see that the individual is not identical to our prejudiced concept of the larger group. Our stereotypes fall as we take a closer look at individuals belonging to the larger group we class as one. If we invest enough energy into the process, we often find our original prejudices are meaningless.

Jesus never met this centurion in the entirety of this narrative. He is first of all met with Jews who tell him of the man's need and share their concept of his worthiness to have Jesus grant him an audience. The next encounter, however, is with a group of servants who then come out to meet Jesus en route and turn him back. Their message is that there is no need for Jesus to come in person. All he needs to do is send word for the healing of the man's servant. He believes that the authority of Jesus' word would be sufficient, with no greater need to trouble Jesus with a trip to see him.

It is at this point that Jesus becomes impressed with the centurion. Jesus was not impressed with the man's good works in donating money toward the construction of a Jewish synagogue. Jesus was seemingly not impressed that Jews were begging Jesus to pay attention to this man's need. Jesus did not seem to be impressed with the coming of servants from this man as an envoy to request his intervention. What he is impressed with is the character of this man's faith.

What is significant about that? The fact that the man is a Gentile is of seemingly no concern to Jesus. It should have bothered him, as is evidenced by the attitudes of the Jews who come to meet him and request his intervention. They feel they must justify their request on the basis of this man's actions, which run counter to his position in representing the occupation force from Rome. The man was a Gentile. The man was not a convert to Judaism as far as we know. The man was officially an enemy of the nation of Israel, for he represented Rome. The man was part of the force of Roman oppression under which the Jews were struggling. He was most likely idolatrous, worshiping his Roman deities after the customs of Rome. Regardless, Jesus is impressed with him due to the character of his faith and his faith alone.

Those other issues seem to have been secondary to Jesus. Sure, Jesus did not promote idolatry and the worship of pagan deities. Jesus did not encourage the oppression of anyone. Jesus did not represent the priorities of Rome, but Jesus did understand and give value to the character of this man's confidence in Jesus.

This foreigner, an emblem of oppression and enmity, saw in Jesus an authority that in some ways was similar to his own. He understood that if Jesus could heal up close on the basis of his authority and dependence upon Yahweh, he would be able to do the same at a distance. Jesus would not be limited by geography as we might normally believe, but could simply ask God to intervene with no concern over distance.

Jesus did not seem to care about the man being a Gentile, a foreigner, a member of an oppression force in Israel. All those categories that marked the centurion as an outsider are seemingly of no concern for Jesus. He was concerned instead with the man's faith and used it as an example for the Jews. While they were focused on how the centurion did not belong to the people of Israel, Jesus was concerned with showing the Jews how this outsider demonstrated qualities in which they themselves were lacking. His was the character of faith they themselves needed to obtain.

The fact that this man was a foreigner, an official representative of a military occupation, did not qualify to Jesus as important. These are categories that seem to be insignificant to him. While they may speak volumes to us, as they obviously did to the Jews around Jesus, they made little impact on the character of his response toward this man. Neither should they have made a difference to them or to us. The only thing that stands out to Jesus is the fact that this man's faith displays a higher quality than what he had encountered among the Jews themselves. If being an officer of a foreign military presence is inconsequential to Jesus, how much less should one's immigrant or foreign national status mean to us?

John 1:46 — "Can Anything Good Come Out of Nazareth?"

When Andrew was introduced to Jesus, he went to find Philip and invited him to come meet Jesus. Philip's response is one that displays just how little Nazareth was considered as an important town in the area: "Can anything good come out of Nazareth?"

There was plenty of geographic prejudice in Judah, even among the people of its own borders and nationality. The Jews were obviously prejudiced against Samaritans, Canaanites, and Romans, as well as other foreigners. Yet inside their own borders and among people of their shared ethnic, cultural, and linguistic background, they maintained other prejudices as well.

There were the attitudes that looked down on the poor, the blind, the lame, the lepers, the mendicants of the day. There were the attitudes against people from certain towns or regions, like that of Nazareth. Philip could not believe that Nazareth was special enough to warrant any position as the birthplace or launching pad of anyone with any kind of importance. It seems to have been in his mind a place with a history of uneducated, uncivilized people with no special standing or any prominence to mention.

Jesus lived with this class of stigma. His disciples were mainly Galileans, deemed uncultured locals with no special standing. It was a stigma with which he began his ministry, and one he countered in the way he addressed issues of position, status, power, and importance. It colored the way he treated people, as well as guided the patterns he used even to select people to become his disciples and envoys.

It would seem that Jesus even went out of his way to call as disciples people who would fall into the same questionable class as he himself was placed by Philip. There were questions about the disciples in the beginning chapters of Acts, specifically because they did not have the right background and education. There was a recognition, however, that they had been with Jesus.

As far as Jewish society was concerned, there was nothing special at all about Nazareth. There was nothing special in Jesus' background and home life to usher him into the limelight of Israelite society. He did not study under the recognized rabbis of the day. He did not come from the connected families. He was not born or reared in the right towns, the right neighborhoods, the right circles.

His origins placed him as an outsider, a misfit, one who was ill prepared to enter the political, social, and religious scene of Judah with anything approaching importance or validity. Despite his meager social origins, however, some like Andrew recognized something special in him.

Philip had to set aside his prejudiced views of Nazareth to take a closer look at Jesus. He had to put his expectations on hold in order that he might look at Jesus according to his own identity, rather than according to the social definition of a class to which he belonged. He was not prepared for what he was to find in Jesus, but he would have missed it completely had he not set aside his prejudiced understandings and taken steps to meet Jesus and hear him with his own ears.

These are often the same issues we face in our encounters with people from different traditions, cultures, and places. The less we know of them personally, the more our stereotypes seem to fit. As we listen to their stories and get to know them personally, however, we find that our social prejudices tend to fall away. We begin to see them as persons, not as a class.

It requires some initiative, openness, and investment, however. We must open ourselves to truly hear them and get to know them. It is not often that a quick encounter such as Philip's with Jesus will be sufficient to break through those barriers that have been constructed by years of prejudiced attitudes. What we find in those from other backgrounds may end up being the completely unexpected, just like Philip found in Jesus.

Jesus did not seemingly fault Phllip for his initial reaction to Andrew's invitation. After all, it was a question of being a rather expected reaction. He did, however, call him to recognize that there would be plenty of other surprises in store for him in a life of following Jesus. It would be a life of being introduced to a series of unexpected realizations about God, about other people, and about who was truly worthy of redemption.

Philip would begin a journey with Jesus that would dash all of his received expectations about people in categories of worth. Recognizing Jesus as something good out of Nazareth was, for Philip, just a beginning. Jesus would teach him to throw away all those categories and even the whole question of worth.

Jesus was not in the business of classifying people according to categories of worth. He was in the business of calling people beyond those categories into a life of dependence upon and trust in God. He would teach them to discard issues of earning God's good will and cast their lives upon God's grace instead. Grace does not consider merit and worth. It focuses on the quality of love being offered instead.

Rather than wonder if anything good can come from one of those categories of people we would brush aside as worthless, we should consider that Jesus himself came from one of those same categories and ministered mostly to people likewise considered of questionable value to society. If Christ Jesus loved them enough to redeem them, we have no standing to do any less and claim service to Christ.

Acts 26 — "Except for These Chains"

After Paul's missionary journeys and eventual return to Jerusalem, he was arrested and held until a tumult revolving around him might be investigated. On hearing of a plot against his life, Paul appealed to have his case heard before Caesar to avoid being released into an ambush. In the course of waiting to be sent to Rome, he had the opportunity on multiple occasions to speak with Roman officials. On one such occasion, he shared his faith in Jesus Christ, such that he was charged with wanting all to become like himself. His response was, "Yes, except for these chains."

Paul was unconcerned with questions of nationality, politics, status, ethnicity, language, or background. He accepted the accusation of desiring that the entire court be transformed as he himself had experienced transformation. He treated all in accord with the same perspective and purpose. It was his mission to share the message of Christ Jesus with all, making no kind of distinction among his listeners.

What we might overlook here is that in preaching the gospel of grace, love, and acceptance, Paul left aside any concern over condemnation of others. That had indeed been central to his background in Judaism. Upon accepting the message of Jesus, however, he turned his back on those traditions he had followed that placed people under definitions of condemnation.

Paul could have looked here upon the Roman officials who kept him in chains as though they were enemies. In fact, they were his jailers, even if they were bound by law to send him to Rome while desiring to release him. He lived in chains, even when his jailers did not view him as any threat. They were more concerned with the political repercussions of sending Paul to Caesar when they had no accusation to warrant even his arrest.

Luke does not speak to the issue of why Paul never spoke to his jailers of the threat against his life. It should have been an issue of import to Rome to protect any citizen against such a conspiracy. At some unmentioned point, however, one of the Roman power brokers was perhaps in league with those seeking Paul's life. Regardless of the possibility of such collusion against Paul and against the purposes of Roman law, Paul still did not look upon them as enemies, but as people who simply needed to hear and respond to the grace of God freely offered in Jesus.

Enemies were to Paul simply more people with whom to share God's love. He held no such category by which he wrote people off as unworthy of the message he had to proclaim. Sure, he spoke harshly of the Judaizers who would force Gentiles to first become Jew and legalist before accepting faith in Jesus. He was adamant in his opposition to this doctrine as contrary to the very heart of the gospel. Even so, he did not allow his disagreement with them to grant him standing to write them off before the grace and mercy of God.

The Roman officials who held him captive were likewise simply potential disciples of Christ Jesus in Paul's eyes. They were no different from him, and he wished that they be no different, except for the chains that bound him. It was his desire that they become like him in his relationship to and dependence upon God. He would exclude no one and call everyone into the unity and grace he had found in the gospel. Even those who were responsible for his imprisonment, he was unwilling to write off.

He considered these officials representing an oppressing force of empire throughout the world as equal to himself in having a claim upon the gospel. He considered them loved by God in no way different from the love and grace he had himself experienced from God in Christ Jesus. Not only was he willing to share the gospel with them, but to make no demands on them outside of giving them the opportunity to respond freely to the grace of God in Christ Jesus.

Except for the condition of his imprisonment, Paul saw all as equal to himself. After all, he did not consider himself as anything special, except insofar as he made Christ Jesus visible in his words, attitudes, and actions. He refused to place himself above or before any, but worked to bring all to the status before God that he himself enjoyed, based on a simple acceptance of what God freely offered in grace.

Humanly speaking, Paul had every reason to view those around him as enemies, foreigners, strangers, and occupiers, but he refused to look at them as anything other than individuals God desired to redeem. In that light, they were simply equals, and that called him to treat them as such, regardless of the circumstances of his imprisonment.

Romans 12:13 — "Bring Strangers into Your Homes"

The term used here in Romans 12:13 is philoxenia. As discussed earlier, it has as its root meaning the love of strangers. The New Century Version translates this phrase as "Bring strangers into your homes." We most normally consider it a term for hospitality, but the sense of this term goes beyond simple hospitality, both here and in Hebrews 13. It is hospitality on a deeper level.

The xenia is the traveler, the stranger, the other, the unknown person. This is about welcoming those who are unknown to us, bringing them into our homes as an expression of God's love and care for one and all. This verse is followed immediately by Paul's comment about doing good to those who would bring us harm. That sets the phrase into a context of reaching beyond a simple hospitality to people we already know, trust, and love. This is about expanding our circle of love and acceptance to include people we might even fear, offering them a share in the bounty God has placed into our care.

Paul was well acquainted with philoxenia, as he had been received into many homes along the course of his missionary endeavors. We know of his entering the home of Lydia in Philippi as an honored guest, as well as his being brought into the jailer's home in the same manner and in the same town. We don't know much about most other places he had traveled, but we get some sense that he had been on the receiving end of philoxenia on more than one occasion, more often than simply in Philippi.

Luke speaks in Acts 28 of Paul being on the receiving end of the hospitality of Publius, though he uses a different term for hospitality in that instance. That is a more general term with the sense of a loving or kindly attitude toward others. In Romans 12 and Hebrews 13, however, the term used is more distinctive. Xenia itself is the modern Greek term for hospitality, related back to ancient concepts of Zeus as the Greek god of travelers and caring for those far from home.

The Roman world of Paul's day would have been familiar with the concepts of hospitality toward strangers as a motif of righteousness associated with religious responsibility. These concepts had already been in circulation throughout the Greek-speaking world since at least the days of Homer, some 1,000 years prior to Paul's ministry. The motif expressed here in Romans 12 and in Hebrews 13 meshes perfectly with this principle already in existence throughout the Gentile religious landscape. Paul takes this theme and builds on it here in relation to one's responsibility toward God in caring not only for the needs of believers, but also for strangers, foreigners, travelers, and immigrants.

Love and care for strangers fits well into the context of Paul's comments here in Romans 12. The concept relates to Paul's command to do good to those who would mistreat us, being friendly toward all, not to mistreat any, and to make friends with ordinary people. This is a social component to the gospel that compels us to become positive contributors to the society in which we live. We are never to become so heavenly minded that we lose sight of our responsibility for doing earthly good. On the contrary, as far as Paul is concerned here, offering our lives as living sacrifices to Christ Jesus entails becoming servants of God who reach out in love, grace, and blessing to the benefit of everyone all around us.

1 Timothy 2 — "God's Will That All Be Saved"

As Paul writes Titus, he is very specific about the reach of God's desire to offer salvation. God does not distinguish among people in classes of being worthy or unworthy, acceptable or unacceptable. The very concept of salvation through grace argues directly against any such understanding of salvation as being limited by God to a certain class of people.

Human beings have long-established systems of placing people in categories along lines of worth. We have determined who belongs or does not belong to families, tribes, clans, communities, cities, societies, nations, ethnic groups, social classes, and even castes.

God's purpose of reconciliation in Christ Jesus, however, does not utilize these categories. God does not place people in boxes, sorting them according to merit and value. The message of the gospel is that God loves the entirety of creation, not only humanity, but animals and plants as well.

While we may yearn to place ourselves in the category of insiders, God has no such category, for under God's plan of redemption, there is but one category in which to place humanity. All are acceptable to God, for God's will is that all would be redeemed and enter into a relationship of confidence in God.

That was the whole purpose of Jesus coming to Israel in the first place. They had been picked as an unimportant people with nothing to give them any source of pride of position and importance. God had taken that rag-tag bunch of escaped slaves and formed them into a nation. God had lowered himself to the status of a human being in Christ Jesus to display before all the lengths to which God was willing to go to rescue, redeem, and restore a people who had abandoned God's purposes.

Now in the New Testament, God had to remind the Jewish believers that the same purposes of God in fashioning them into a nation were at play in God's renewed purposes to redeem all of humanity. God still considered them no better than others, and no worse either. Even so, God was just as willing to take both Jews and Gentiles and make one nation out of them. Out of them all, God would fashion a new people beyond the limits and boundaries of political definitions, territories, ethnicities, citizenship, language, and culture. Out of all nations, God would create a people, bringing them into existence despite any and all distinctions, for it was and is God's will to redeem all.

If that is God's purpose, any action of ours that would run counter to establishing that character of unity is an action against God's purposes to which we have been called. Furthermore, it is upon these very purposes of God that we base our own saving relationship with God. To exclude another is to cast aside God's purpose of redemption.

1 Peter — Disciples in Dispersion

Peter wrote his letters to the disciples in the dispersion. This was seemingly after the destruction of Jerusalem in AD 70, though there is some scholarly debate about the dating of the text. The Jews stopped offering annual sacrifices to Yahweh on behalf of Caesar in June of AD 66, part of their negotiated treaty with Rome to relieve them of having to make sacrifices directly to the Roman gods. When the Roman general Titus marched into the temple to sacrifice a pig to the Roman gods on Yahweh's altar four years later, the Jews reacted to this desecration of Yahweh's temple by torching it and beginning to tear it down. In the ensuing chaos and confusion, Jerusalem was utterly destroyed, and the Jews clashed with the Roman forces.

Jerusalem and the surrounding region were vacated by the Romans, and Jews were expelled from Rome, as well. The center of Judaism shifted to Babylon, where some Jews had been living since the exile. Jews and Christians alike were scattered all over the Roman Empire and beyond, as they fled the violence in Judea and sought tranquility. Shattered along with the destruction of Jerusalem were Jewish dreams of the messiah coming to establish the messianic reign in the Jerusalem they knew. They still clung to the dream, but recognized that any coming of the messiah would be delayed.

When Peter wrote the believers in the dispersion, it was the flight from Judea to which he referred. By definition, these believers were all immigrants or refugees, having fled war and destruction in Palestine. None of them could live anymore in their home country. Jews had been kicked out of Rome, as well as the other major cities of the empire, and Jerusalem was no more.

Christians at this time were still considered little more than a sect within Judaism, thus Jews as far as the Roman world was concerned. As Jews or Christians, they were not simply immigrants in foreign lands; they were refugees in exile. They were fleeing war, oppression, conflict, and all manner of prejudice. The Christians faced a second layer of persecution as well, this from Jews who did not like the Christians' inclusion among their ranks.

Peter spoke to them in language and pictures reminiscent of the exodus, when God took a band of escaped slaves and began fashioning them into a nation. This time, however, Peter contended that their status as a people was not defined by any earthly citizenship, but by participation in the reign of Jesus Christ. It was among this scattered population who lived as refugees across the Roman Empire that God would work to build a new reality, to fashion them into a people quite apart from their political status or historic nationality.

Peter took his words a step further, including Gentiles into the mix as a formative part of this new nation God was forming. The believers were refugees, but their ranks would swell from the peoples among whom they lived. God would take them all, regardless of their racial, ethnic, national, or political backgrounds, and create out of them a completely new people with an identity beyond that of nationhood.

In many ways, that may have been the point of the establishing of Israel as well, though the ideal never materialized. Apparently, many enslaved people left Egypt along with descendants of Abraham. Moses led the twelve tribes out of Egypt, but it would seem that many others actually left along with them in this bid for freedom. Gentiles like Rahab, Ruth, and Uriah made their way into the nation of Israel in days long past, begin assimilated into the life of Israel. This seems to have been part of God's purpose all along, even as God promised Abraham that all the families of the earth would be blessed in him.

Even so, Israel never really measured up to the quality of such ideals, just as the church has so often failed to measure up, as well. Peter, however, had no qualms in holding such an ideal out before believers scattered across the Roman Empire as refugees in this dispersion. They were not a people. They had lost any protections they had due to a national identity. Politically, they were rejects, refugees from war, with little to no rights or hopes for a bright future. Yet God looked upon them as worthy of grace, love, mercy, and being fashioned into the center of this new people God called into existence.

"You who once were not a people" is part of Peter's theme. They had lost their identity, but God was now working to give them a new identity, one that reached beyond the bounds of nationality, politics, and nationhood. In their condition as refugees, they were commissioned to become a kingdom of priests to Yahweh, a nation set apart for a special mission from God. For a second time, this is God working to take a people who were the rejects of society, trampled on by those in power, and transform them into a new reality far beyond the limitations and definitions of political realities and categories. In a way, this was a first divine step toward a globalization concept regarding God's reign.

It is this same principle that should guide our own attitudes toward those who are immigrants, refugees, foreigners, or strangers. God cares enough for those we might cast aside to honor them with inclusion in the reign of Christ Jesus, then to commission them as ministers and priests of this new reign so that all might know God. The categories we might use to discard some to the trash heap of humanity are the same categories from which God has acted at least twice to fashion a people for him from among the nations of the world.

Revelation — Distinguishing Allegiance to Caesar and God

The book of Revelation has inspired a host of imaginative interpretations across the centuries. We have seen predictions of the end of the world time after time, beginning at least as far back as 1,000 years ago. More recently, we have seen interpretations of the likes of Hal Lindsey, who tried to use it to predict political realities and the return of Christ Jesus. Like others, he recognized problems with his interpretation after the fact and published a new accounting of his failed interpretation.

John's letter, however, is much more straightforward in so many ways than these inventive interpretations, which attempt to use it to predict future events. John had much more important concepts to communicate than to offer believers an account of how God would end the world thousands of years after John had died. In effect, his message was directed to the churches of his own day, the readers and listeners of his narrative visions who were facing real issues in their daily application of faith to life.

We would do well to remember that most of this kind of interpretation of Revelation today is based on failed models from the past. Thousands have attempted to use the book within the framework understanding that prophecy is about revealing the future before it comes to pass. Biblically, however, prophecy is much more about communicating God's message to the people of the prophet's day and age. This message may have a future component, but almost ninety percent of the time it is about the present or immediate future of the prophet's audience. Moses, after all, was considered by the Jews as the greatest of the prophets along with Elijah. Their prophetic ministries had little to do with the future. They were not concerned with predicting future events, but with communicating God's will to the people of their day. This is the heritage from which John speaks and writes, as well.

John's major concern is about how believers in Christ Jesus should respond and live in the context of Roman religious expectations of the day. We like to speak of persecution, and there was some of that. The bulk of famed Roman persecution of Christians, however, was from periods of time that are inconsistent with the period of John's writing. Instead of outright, systematic persecution, Christians faced a wholly different issue: prejudiced misunderstanding.

If we return to the discussion of the destruction of Jerusalem in AD 70, we will recall that the Jews revolted against Rome, and the Christian community was caught up in the net of accusation leveled against the Jews. On the other side of the equation, believers were suffering the brunt of Jews who did not like that Christians were being classed as Jews. After all, they had accepted Jesus as their Messiah, and the rest of Judaism could not accept such a claim.

Traditionally, the Romans had recognized that the Jews did not make idols or participate in sacrifices before idols. That had been allowed as long as they made sacrifices to Yahweh on behalf of Caesar. As far as the Romans were concerned, the basic security of the Roman Empire depended on keeping their gods happy with the population. If a group of people stopped participating in the sacrifices and offerings, they feared the gods might punish the whole of the Roman Empire. Atheism or failure to offer sacrifices was considered sedition.

Hence the problem faced by Christian believers. They should not participate in the ritual sacrifices, but the Jews also claimed they were not part of Judaism. At some points, there were accusations that the title "Christian" was equivalent to being antisocial in the sense that their existence and practices were structured to undermine the very fabric of society, causing the gods to be enraged with the society of which they were part. On the other hand, there were accusations that in celebrating the Lord's Supper, they were eating human flesh and drinking human blood, therefore being cannibals and child murderers. If a Jew were to level an accusation against someone of being a Christian, it was not simply a question of their being part of a different religious group. It was an accusation of working against the established order of society, being a threat to the empire.

John sets out possible responses a Christian might make to the accusations leveled against one. First of all, one could die. If one refused to participate in the Roman sacrifices, then one would be considered guilty as charged and executed. Secondly, one might lie and pretend not to be a believer. In such a case, one would be forced to denounce Christ and offer the appropriate sacrifices before Roman officials in proof of their participation in the rites to secure the stability of the empire.

As far as John is concerned, only being faithful unto death was the appropriate response for the faithful Christian. Pretending not to be a

Christian was to be unfaithful. Taking the stance that Rome simply did not understand and going through the motions to please the officials was unfaithfulness to God. John wrote that in order to be faithful, one must submit to Christ Jesus and stand in opposition to Rome, trusting oneself to the mercy and grace of God. If one died as a result, John proclaimed one as having become victorious over Rome. After all, Rome had no authority or power beyond putting one to death.

The call to faithfulness for John, then, was to proclaim the gospel and to follow its indications, regardless of where it might lead. If it forced one to walk in a manner that opposed the dictates of the state, one had a higher allegiance to follow. One might die as a result of faithfulness to God, but the promise of the risen Christ was of a life over which Caesar had no power whatsoever. The victory that awaited the faithful could never be lost. It could only be surrendered or abandoned by becoming unfaithful to God.

The believers lived under threat from Rome. They lived under threat as foreigners, strangers, immigrants, refugees, and a misunderstood people. Life was uncertain for them. In some areas of the Roman Empire, life was smoother. In other areas there was greater unrest. They had no voice or vote in Roman politics, for they were mainly outsiders. Rising up in revolution against Rome ran counter to the peace to which Jesus had called them. It ran counter to the principles of loving one's enemies and doing good to those who might offer persecution.

As a persecuted people, they were called by this prophet to suffer their persecution according to the same manner they had seen in the example of Jesus. They were to be confident that the real victory would be theirs due to God's faithfulness. They were to live their lives in faith and leave the results to God. All the while, they were to follow God's directions and purposes, even when it led them to live in defiance of the state.

They were under a higher law than that of Rome. Sure, they were to obey the laws in general. When those laws called on them to live contrary to the demands of the gospel of Christ, however, they were to stand firm for Christ and accept whatever consequences came their way. In such a manner, they would give faithful witness to the sufficiency of God in Christ Jesus, claiming that ultimate power and victory did not belong to Caesar, but to God in Christ Jesus.

He who is faithful to the end will receive the prize. He who gives his witness through death will enter life. He who dies for his faith in Christ Jesus will not lose the victory that only God can offer. This is the message John has for us. We are called to this higher faithfulness. We are called to live according to the reality of John's heavenly vision of God's supreme authority. We are called to live out the demands of the gospel, even when they run counter to the laws of the state, and willingly accept the consequences of being faithful to Christ Jesus. After all, there is but one to whom we should give complete allegiance and submission. To do less is to turn our backs on God and the example of Jesus Christ, who gave his life on our behalf.

We live in a different reality from John. We live in a reality in which people often have a voice in the establishment of laws. We have voice, vote, and representation. We have political power that was denied the early church. With that power comes responsibility. While we have the ability to influence our legal systems, working for more ethical and just laws, we also have the responsibility before God to be faithful to the principles of the gospel, even when they might call us to action that is deemed unlawful.

With responsibility, power, and opportunity, however, also comes the burden to bear the consequences of one's actions. John would call us to be faithful to Christ Jesus above any allegiance to political authorities. He would call us always to respond in concert with the principles of the gospel, yet always be ready to bear the responsibility for our actions should they run counter to the laws of the land. The higher authority is that of God, not that of any state.

Luke 14 — "Compel Them to Come in"

Jesus did not always preach easy words that were comforting for his audiences. He often caused them discomfort instead. He spoke a challenge and established new parameters for living and interacting that made the established society around him uncomfortable. This was especially true in relation to the religious establishment in Israel. One motif within these more uncomfortable aspects of Jesus' message had to do with those he was willing to accept and include in an offer of God's grace, mercy, love, and forgiveness.

One parable on this topic referred to in Luke 14 was not at all comfortable for polite Jewish society. Jesus shared the story of a king who invited all the rich and powerful of the land to a feast. Each invited guest refused with one reason or another. They may have been politically and socially acceptable reasons, but they were nonetheless excuses designed to keep them from attending the feast. In response, the king determined that none of them would be allowed into the feast after all. On the other hand, the king wanted the feast to go on and his hall to be full. He then sent out his servants once more, this time with invitations for the rank and file of the population. When the feasting hall was still not full, he sent them out again with the charge to compel the outcasts of society to join in the celebration.

There is a striking tone to this latter commission. Jesus' words are "compel them to come in." This is no longer simply an invitation. This is an order from the king that the larger population join in the festivities.

The implications of Jesus' words here are multiple, but we will look at three of them. First of all, established society often has competing allegiances and priorities that are in conflict with those of God. God would have them participate in the life of salvation, but God's invitation is often refused by the powerful and wealthy. They are more consumed with themselves. Their priorities are often not in line with God's priorities. Consequently, they do not always enjoy or relate to God's purposes. While the invitation is available, God respects their excuses and decisions not to accept the invitation, even if it does not please God.

Secondly, God is willing to fill the celebration hall with those polite society would all too easily brush off as unworthy or unimportant. God's priorities are different, for what God is after is the filling of the hall for the planned celebration. Our participation in or acceptance of God's invitation is of much greater importance to God than so many other issues that would claim our attention. Though we might be the socially unworthy, God is not concerned with such definitions.

Thirdly, God issues a strong invitation through his servants. It is almost a demand, if not fully one, that those deemed unworthy be pressed to attend, even if against their own will. The targets of this invitation are specifically those we would most want to keep out of the king's celebration halls. These are, however, expressly invited to attend, even when their desires and normal occupations might run counter to fellowship with God.

As far as the Jews were concerned, the people with whom Jesus was ministering often fit in this category. They were the sludge of society as far as the religious leaders were concerned. It is to these that Jesus tended to focus his message, specifically because the status quo proclamation was leaving them out.

They were not the educated. They were not the connected. They were not the ones with a history of purity, status, importance, and pedigree. As far as most were concerned, they were the Jews who were living under God's condemnation. They had made themselves believe that God blessed with power and riches those who pleased God, but punished the unworthy with illness and poverty. It was these reportedly undeserving, reportedly under God's curse and condemnation, to whom Jesus gave the greatest attention.

In most societies, these are the foreigners, strangers, poor, immigrants, homeless, or ill. Yet it is these we shrug off or fail even to notice to whom Jesus turned the bulk of his attention. He called them specifically because society tended to ignore them. Consequently, they were the ones who most needed to hear God's invitation to fellowship.

Likewise, those on the outside or margin of society most need to be pressed to inclusion. They feel the separation from the acceptable nobility most strongly. They are the one who need the compelling voice calling them into the midst of God's celebration. They have so often already been cast out by the social elite that they would be the least likely to take initiative to join in God's celebration.

It is likely that this is the best rationale for this stronger version of the king's invitation to the outcasts in Jesus' story. This invitation would need to overcome a larger degree of prejudice than any other, a prejudice already internalized by those on the bottom rung of society's ladder. They have "learned their place," and it requires greater energy and a committed conveyance of acceptance for them to accept a message so contrary to what society has repeatedly told them.

Jesus is not less concerned with these outcasts than with the elite. Nor is he less concerned for the elite. The difference is that his words of acceptance and invitation to "the least of these" have to overcome greater barriers erected by the social structures than is the case for any other class of people. They are used to being ignored. They are used to being brushed aside. They are used to being stepped on, forgotten, and neglected. Such a systemic issue requires a greater dedication of resources to overcome. The elite and powerful already consider themselves acceptable, worthy, and the obvious recipients of the king's invitation. It is the underclass or the fringe who must overcome the force of social barriers that have far too long kept them as outsiders to the rest of society.

While Jesus' words here are not directed specifically to the immigrant community, they apply to them because they are the ones who most often find themselves beyond the reach of social care and concern. They are the neglected and invisible, just as the homeless, poor, and disabled are so often relegated to less visible segments of society, treated as a drain on the resources of others rather than as full participants in the benefits society has to share.

1 John 4 — "He Who Loves God Cannot Hate a Brother"

John's first epistle dealt with issues the church as a whole was facing from a quarter of Gnostic influence. At issue was dissociation between the spiritual and the material spheres of life. The Gnostics wanted to teach that Jesus could not have been truly human, since by their concept God could have nothing to do with the material realm of life. Hence, Jesus would not have bothered with healing people of their physical infirmities, touching people, or caring about their needs for food, shelter, clothing, etc. For them, God as spirit would have no direct contact with the material world. Rather, humanity needed to escape the physical realm in order to enter the spiritual realm inhabited by God. There, they believed, one could truly enjoy God's immediate presence, but only in dissociation from all things physical.

John begins his epistle stressing the very physical, earthly nature of Jesus. He speaks of him as living in a visible, audible, physical manner among the disciples. He speaks to issues of life in the physical realm, amid relationships with people as things that matter. He speaks to the issues in which the Gnostics not only wanted to escape the physical reality, but also wanted to ignore the realities of sin and its impact on life and relationship with God and others. While they tried to say that only the body was involved in sin and that sin was of no consequence, John called the bluff.

He spoke to the very physical, material application of the gospel to our daily interactions with others.

Seemingly, the biggest issue for him was how our living impacts the lives of others in demonstration of God's love entering our daily existence and relationships. One cannot claim a love for God while failing to love another human being. He simply did not allow for creating a false distinction between one's spiritual life and one's relationships with others. If one is truly spiritual, as claimed the Gnostics, one's spirituality had to alter the way one interacted with the people among whom Jesus lived and demonstrated God's love.

John's message went beyond its direct application to Gnostic tendencies within a segment of the church. His was a very practical address of how God's love manifest in Jesus Christ should transform our lives in accordance with the pattern established and taught by Jesus. As Jesus lived, preached, and interacted, so John was attempting in his letter to extend Jesus' presence and message, applying Jesus' own application of the good news to our interactions with one another. If we claim to love God, it should be visible in our attitudes and interactions with others.

There is no room in the gospel of Christ for loving God and ignoring the needs of those around us. There is no room in the gospel for loving those who are most like ourselves and those we place in some category to excuse our responsibility to apply the same measure of love we might share with any other.

Love for God, claims John, works itself out in our dealings and relationships with other human beings on the same pattern that Jesus established for us. Loving God requires caring about the issues with which God is concerned. It requires joining our lives and purposes to the life and purpose of God. There is, therefore, no room for defining any class of people as unworthy of our love and attention when Christ has come equally for one and all without distinction.

Matthew 5 — "You Are the Salt of the Earth"

The traditional take on Jesus' words in Matthew 5 is that they were directed at the disciples, as though to set the disciples, and by implication the church, apart from the rest of the world. What we find, however, is that Jesus was teaching not simply the disciples, but a multitude as well.

His words were not directed to the in group, but were broadcast to the entire population within earshot. Every one of them was being told that they were the salt of the earth and the light of the world.

At the beginning of the sermon, Jesus laid out standards that would define those who are indeed blessed in God's eyes. When he got to his comments on being salt of the earth and light of the world, however, his comments became descriptive of reality and applied equally to all of his hearers. We would understand that all kinds of people were present for the occasion. We apply these same words to all people today. That's the rub. That's where this text begins to cause some discomfort for the church.

We are accustomed to reading these words as though they applied simply to the church, the insiders, those like us who have accepted Jesus as Lord, Savior, etc. We have used the terms to make distinctions between ourselves and others. We have used the text to give ourselves greater value or importance than those on the outside. These words on Jesus' lips, however, apply equally to one and all, with no special distinction for the church. Jesus was calling everyone in his audience the salt of the earth and the light of the world. He made no distinction with this definition!

Each of Jesus' hearers had the same potential for fulfilling the purposes of God. Each of them was in essence light and salt to make a difference in their environment. They were, every one of them, filled with the potential to make a lasting difference, a positive impact according to God's purposes. The question Jesus raises with these words, however, applies to what we do with the potential God has placed within us. That is the only place a distinction might now matter.

If we fulfill our purpose, others should see the distinctive nature of God's presence and action in our lives. They should awaken to the same spark of light that resides within themselves as well. They should glorify or reveal God as they see us living in such a way that the purposes of God become reality in our living.

We are called to shine for others, even as lights are designed to do. We are called to fulfill our mission and purpose before others, not because we are better, but because we accept the purposes and mission God has placed upon us all.

Inherently, we are all of equal worth before God. The question is what we will do with that standing of worth. What will we do with the light of the world (not our own) that is placed within us? It is not for our personal benefit so much as for the benefit of those around us. It is together that we are called to shine before others until they take up the same purpose to light the world for all. It is only in fulfilling this mission set before us that there is any real distinction between ourselves and others. In terms of inherent value and worth, we are all identical.

Luke 10 — "Who Is My Neighbor?"

Perhaps this story of Jesus and the lawyer who sought to justify himself is truly the central text of our responsibilities toward immigrants, foreigners, and strangers. Jesus had just answered one question regarding the greatest commandment of God. Then Jesus answered this follow-up question on which the real issue of following God's commandments impinged. "Who is my neighbor?" was supposed to be a question of identifying limits to the definition of those we are charged by God to love. It was supposed to offer relief and justification for unequal treatment of people once categories of worth might be defined and defended. Jesus' answer, however, destroyed the entire foundation for the question itself.

Jesus turned to the man seeking self-justification and forced him to deal with a definition of neighbor that was much more expansive than any definition he had ever before accepted, most likely more expansive than he had ever heard.

The parable of the good Samaritan brought new parameters for defining a neighbor than Judaism had ever seriously considered. A hated enemy with whom Jews would not stoop to speak finds himself in the story as the hero who cares for a Jew who was neglected by Jews over concerns of ritual purity. This enemy who would never qualify as ritually pure enters the picture to act according to grace and fulfill the command just defined as one of the two greatest commandments.

The Samaritan here was an outsider. He was an immigrant. He was ritually impure. He was verifiably beyond the boundaries that were comfortable for Jewish religious society. He was, however, the embodiment of what Jesus sought as establishing the model for interaction with others.

The point here was multiple. Issues of ritual purity so important in Jewish life were cast aside not simply as irrelevant, but as operating contrary to the greater importance of God's instructions and commands regarding love of others. Secondly, Jesus places this hated immigrant in the position of fulfilling the greatest of God's commandments, becoming the embodiment of God's will and purpose.

Any rationale for discarding classes of people as beyond the bounds of personal responsibility before God are here wiped away. Before God, there is no definition as sought by the lawyer of someone who lies beyond the definition of the question "Who is my neighbor?" Jesus could not have been much clearer than he was in this encounter. Everyone is my neighbor. Everyone is included in God's commands for me to love. Everyone is of equal worth before God. Any actions I might take to define the issues otherwise make me guilty of ignoring God's commandments and purposes.

The immigrant, the foreigner, the stranger are equally my neighbor under Jesus' definitions. The command to love my neighbor knows and respects no borders or definitions of culture, ethnicity, language, or origin. As Christ Jesus has come to love all, so are we called to love all without distinction.

SUMMARY CONCLUSIONS

John's visions in Revelation reference multitudes from every nation, language, and tribe at the feet of the risen Christ. This is perhaps the end goal of life in Christ Jesus. In this vision and perspective, there are no boundaries or borders to cross. Under the banner of Christ, we are one without distinction. It is in this quality of diversity that Jesus calls us to essential unity in John 17. Despite our differences and distinctions, we are charged to join together to corporately become the people of God.

National borders and immigration policy are the concerns of politics, human quests for power, influence, and control. The concerns of God regarding immigrants throughout the Bible are wholly other. They are the concerns of justice, treating one another with dignity, respect, equality, and love. They are the concerns of bringing others into the realm of God's reign, whether that of Israel or of the Spirit, beyond concerns of nationality, ethnicity, or language. Human concerns with immigration are those of exclusion, while God's are of inclusion and equality.

The standards of justice set forth, especially by Jesus, go far beyond limited human concepts of justice for "those who are like us." They embrace "the other" as being just as important as those within our own group, class, tribe, language, and nation.

As John puts it, "For God so loved the world." God does not so much love me and mine, as God loves the entire world, far beyond our definitions of nationality, ethnicity, language, status, and origin. We are all loved by God and called to love one another as kindred sons and daughters of the Most High, without distinction.

—Christopher B. Harbin

FOR FURTHER READING

There are many available texts that deal with issues of concern regarding immigration. Below are a few texts I have found helpful in better understanding what it means to be and live as an immigrant. It is often a life filled with challenges and requiring a large measure of grit.

My own experiences as an immigrant fail to grasp what it means to most, since while I have been an immigrant, it has been as a citizen of a first-world nation amid populations of developing nations. Becoming an immigrant in a world superpower, while coming from a developing nation, is a completely different experience from my own. It is at best difficult to grasp what it means to live as an immigrant when one identifies with the dominant culture. It is a challenge we must take up if we are to truly love one another as Christ Jesus has loved us.

Marina Budos. *Ask Me No Questions.* New York: Scholastic, 2007.
Sonia Nazario. *Enrique's Journey.* New York: Random House, 2007.
Linda Sue Park. *A Long Walk to Water: Based on a True Story.* Boston: Clarion Books, 2010.

ABOUT THE AUTHOR

Christopher B. Harbin, born in South Carolina, has lived half of his life as an immigrant. He was raised by missionary parents in Brasil before returning to the United States for college and seminary. He studied modern languages at Mississippi College and then graduated with an M.Div. from Southern Seminary in Louisville, where he served as ethnic liaison for Long Run Baptist Association. Chris and his wife, Karen, served as missionaries in Mexico and Brasil, where they worked in church planting, taught seminary, and Chris developed and coordinated a seminary extension program in Rio Grande do Sul. Since returning to the United States, Chris has pastored two churches in Virginia, where he also worked with Latino congregations of the local Baptist associations. He now serves as associate pastor for Latino ministries at First Baptist Church in Huntersville, North Carolina. He lives in Davidson, North Carolina, with his wife and two immigrant sons born in Brasil. Chris was recognized as the 2014–15 Distinguished Alumnus of the Year from the Department of Modern Languages at Mississippi College, has written extensively for his seminary students and churches, and publishes weekly sermons on sermonsearch.com.

www.theotrek.org — An online journey of faith in God…

PALABRAS INICIALES REFERENTES A LA INMIGRACIÓN

El tema de inmigración es un tema antiguo. Es también un tema actual en la política de los Estados Unidos de América, así como alrededor del mundo, desde Europa hasta América Latina, África, Australia y Asia. Desde tiempos inmemoriales, es un tema acerca de cómo tratamos y nos relacionamos con gente de algún otro grupo étnico, identidad, u origen que entran en la esfera de nuestra vida. Los hebreos y más tarde los judíos, tuvieron una historia con el concepto de inmigración, una historia específicamente relacionada a sus comienzos en la persona y experiencia de Abraham, su antepasado eminente, el patriarca de la fe y de la nación hebrea. Su clasificación como inmigrante, extranjero y errante, quedó establecida en la más antigua declaración de fe e identidad en las Escrituras: "Un arameo errante era mi padre…." Esta fue la declaración base para su autocomprensión como nación y su posición entre las demás naciones de su mundo de su tiempo.

Este documento no pretende tratar con las políticas de inmigración en el ámbito nacional o internacional. Sin embargo, es pertinente realizar cómo algunos temas y discusiones bíblicas afectan la escena política, pero se enfocará esencialmente en la relevancia del texto bíblico referente al tema de inmigración desde una perspectiva más personal. Mientras que haya aplicaciones bíblicas a políticas nacionales, el énfasis se dará a lo que la Biblia tiene que decir a la iglesia y a aquellos que la componen. ¿Qué dice la Biblia referente a nuestras interacciones, actitudes y reacciones a la inmigración y hacia los inmigrantes?

La discusión bíblica referente a la inmigración se aplica igualmente a preocupaciones del racismo y a las relaciones interraciales. Desde una perspectiva política, la inmigración tiene que ver con la muy indeseada presencia del "otro;" tiene que ver con la forma de cómo tratamos a aquellos que son de una raza, religión, fondo, región, idioma, cultura o etnia distinta.

En los Estados Unidos de América, esta discusión ha tenido históricamente una relación con las naciones nativas del continente, los franceses, los españoles, los aliados a la corona británica, los esclavos, los irlandeses, los católicos, los italianos, los judíos, los chinos, los comunistas, los japoneses, los hispanos, los norteños habitando en el sur, los africanos, los yanquis, los rebeldes del sur, los incultos, los montañeses, los musulmanes, los árabes y así sucesivamente. La preocupación no ha sido nunca la naturaleza específica del grupo bajo observación, sino más bien las cosas que marcan una diferencia y que de alguna forma se perciben como una amenaza. En casi todos los casos, hemos elaborado términos para los inmigrantes que los denigran, colocándolos en una categoría de no ser queridos, de no encajar, de no ser deseados.

Ésta, generalmente, ha sido la condición del inmigrante, tanto aquí como alrededor del mundo. Para calificar como un inmigrante, uno no necesita cruzar una frontera, ni entrar a un país diferente ni hablar un idioma diferente; basta simplemente con ser ajeno a un grupo de personas que se ven y se consideran diferentes. Uno puede ser extranjero, o ajeno al entorno, o simplemente desconocido.

En la mayoría de los casos, la iglesia ha mantenido silencio en relación al trato que se le da a los grupos minoritarios que la sociedad ha tratado de excluir o colocar en alguna categoría subordinada.

Antes de tratar con los textos bíblicos específicos que usan la terminología relacionada a inmigrantes, extranjeros o refugiados, miraremos algunos temas generales en la Biblia relacionados con éstos. Algunos de los textos no utilizan la terminología específica, pero se aplican de igual forma a temas relacionados con la inmigración.

PARTE UNO

Temas y Pasajes Especiales Referentes a Inmigrantes

Este libro se divide en tres secciones. La primera trata de algunos temas bíblicos sobresalientes referentes a inmigrantes, extranjeros y desconocidos. La segunda nos muestra los pasajes bíblicos que usan una terminología específica referente a inmigrantes, extranjeros, refugiados, errantes, naciones y desconocidos. Estos serán categorizados temáticamente. Finalmente, en la tercera sección, veremos una serie de historias, textos y personajes cuyas vidas y el trato que se les dio, tienen implicaciones en la forma como nosotros nos relacionamos con ellos, en la comprensión que tenemos de ellos y cómo Dios quiere que los tratemos.

El tema de inmigrantes, extranjeros y desconocidos es muy extenso. Este libro es simplemente una introducción al tema tratado a lo largo de la Biblia.

"Recuerden Que Ustedes Eran Esclavos en Egipto"

Este dicho, "Recuerden que ustedes eran esclavos en Egipto," fue hecho como un recuerdo constante a los hebreos en su trato con los extranjeros en medio de Israel. La gente debería recordar cómo sus propios antepasados fueron maltratados y cuánto les hubiera gustado que los hubieran tratado de forma diferente. Este dicho llamó a la nación a una ética más elevada de empatía para con los de afuera, quienes eran naturalmente impotentes en medio de una sociedad a la cual no pertenecían. Esto recordatorio frecuente era un llamar consistente para colocarse en los zapatos de aquellos a quienes consideraban "el otro".

Los hebreos deberían recordar que habían pertenecido a la misma categoría de inmigrantes o extraños; de hecho, el propio término "hebreo" parece haber significado "esclavo," lo cual indicaba que fueron reducidos a la categoría de una propiedad material o mercancía sin la completa autonomía de ser considerados personas. Era el ser considerado menos que los demás. En conjunto con la degradación de su persona, la esclavitud, categorizó al individuo con menor valor que los demás, lo cual es la esencia de nuestra definición de ser "el otro" o "el extraño."

Fue luego de escapar de Egipto que la gente que se transformó en la nación hebrea. No fueron más que un bando de harapientos, de esclavos que huyeron y que, ante los ojos del mundo, su valor personal e identidad comunitaria fue categorizada como inferior a las demás naciones. Fue en su liberación por la intervención de Yahvé, por medio de Moisés, que ellos se transformaron en algo semejante a una nación con soberanía. Cuando aun eran esclavos se les consideró como menos que seres humanos. Gracias a la intervención de Yahvé todo cambió. Dios tomó ese grupo estimado sin valor y los transformó en una nación con una nueva identidad, la gente perteneciente a Yahvé.

Como fue al inicio una nación de ex-esclavos debió reconocer que una persona realmente no es mejor que otra; ante Yahvé, todos deben arrodillarse por igual como esclavos y siervos. Ellos fueron especiales, solamente por causa de la gracia de la intervención de Yahvé en su beneficio. Por el contrario, ellos hubieron continuado siendo esclavos en Egipto. Fue principalmente por causa de su estatus inexistente que Yahvé los escuchó y redimió. Ellos no tuvieron un estatus especial para reclamar, a no ser, el de pertenecer a la descendencia de Abraham, un errante, un inmigrante, un nómada que no pudo reclamar un título por la tierra, pero a quien Dios le había prometido una bendición.

En cuanto escaparon de Egipto como esclavos, entraron a una tierra que no fue suya por derecho de ley o herencia; hasta las Escrituras definieron que la tierra no les pertenecería; ellos simplemente entraron a la tierra que le pertenecía a Yahvé, y sirvieron como mayordomos de esa tierra prometida con Su bendición. Desde esta posición ellos miraron a los demás; al final, si alguna clase de gente debió ser menospreciada, era la clase esclava, de la cual ellos eran parte desde el inicio de su éxodo.

"Debe Haber Una Sola Ley"

La ley mosaica no fue diseñada para favorecer a aquellos con poder, riqueza, tierra o estatus; su intención fue la de tratar a todos por igual. La frase "Debe haber una sola ley," fue usada para indicar la necesidad de tratar con el mismo grado de respeto y valor a cualquier individuo.

La ley en casi todos los países puede crearse para alcanzar altos ideales; sin embargo, en muy pocas ocasiones se logra. Si mencionamos la Declaración de la Independencia de los Estados Unidos de América, donde se proclama la igualdad; Jefferson, quien la formuló, mantuvo a hombres y mujeres como sus esclavos. Con una mano escribía sobre la igualdad entre todos, mientras que en la práctica mantuvo una clasificación de jerarquías con la cual trató a los demás.

En los escritos de Jefferson, el conflicto entre sus ideales y la práctica de estos en su vida, tuvo que ver también, por ejemplo, con el trato a las mujeres, a quienes las consideró como personas de segunda clase. Él no fue diferente a los demás fundadores. Se formularon leyes que defendían la igualdad, pero jamás alcanzaron sus propios ideales, porque nunca comprendieron la igualdad plenamente.

El código legal hebreo no fue diferente. Aunque hay muchos textos que apuntan hacia los ideales más elevados de igualdad bajo la ley, fallan al alcanzarla. Debería existir una ley donde el trato debería ser igual para todos, pero la naturaleza humana interfiere en conjunto con la comprensión cultural y social de cómo se aplican estos ideales en la práctica diaria. Aun así, la igualdad es el ideal mayor defendido en las Escrituras que debiera llamar nuestra atención. Debemos estar conscientes de nuestras fallas para que podamos alcanzar la completa voluntad de Dios.

"¿Qué Requiere Yahvé de Ti?"

El llamado a justicia por Miqueas fue un recordatorio para Israel de que la adoración y el culto comprendían mucho más que sacrificios, ofrendas y alabanzas; comprendían la forma en cómo se trataban los unos a los otros, dando especial atención a los oprimidos, a los sin voz en la sociedad, tales como las viudas, los huérfanos, los pobres y los inmigrantes.

Este llamado no se ve solamente en Miqueas. Debió ser el patrón y el propósito con los cuales Israel en su totalidad debió haber alcanzado justicia. Esta fue la condición suprema que faltó entre una población de esclavos oprimidos por los egipcios. La falta de justicia entre las naciones fue declarada en las narrativas de Abraham en lo tocante a Sodoma y al trato a los extranjeros. La justicia se definió en cómo hacer lo que es correcto, a pesar de no estar contemplado en la ley.

Bajo definiciones legales, un extranjero, como los visitantes que llegaron donde Abraham y a Sodoma, no tenían derechos. Ellos estaban completamente a la merced de la gente que encontraran, tanto por ley como por costumbre. Las tradiciones de Génesis colocaron a Abraham como un ser justo, recto en su trato a los extranjeros, ya que él vigiló por sus necesidades. Les dio comida y abrigo, sin dar importancia a su posición o estatus. Simplemente atendió a sus necesidades. En contraste, Sodoma sacó ventaja de su condición de extranjeros debido a la falta de restricciones legales.

El denominador común entre las naciones fue el concepto de que la justicia se reflejaba en la forma por la cual se trataba a los extranjeros, huérfanos, viudas y pobres. Esta fue la preocupación básica de Miqueas, como también la fue del narrador de Génesis y los eticistas de las culturas babilónicas y ugaríticas. Desafortunadamente, así como en Israel, muy pocos vivieron conforme a los ideales de justicia que promovieron. Fue esta falla la que motivó a profetas como Miqueas a llamar a Israel de regreso a los patrones de Yahvé.

"Entregue a Dios lo Que de Dios"

Este dicho específico en el griego contiene la noción de que Jesús habló sobre las orígenes de todo. Lo que viene de Dios o pertenece a Dios es lo que debemos de regresarle a Dios. Podemos pensar aquí en preocupaciones referentes a la vida y a la espiritualidad, pero para la mente judía, las palabras de Jesús, contienen un sentido mucho más amplio y hondo. Comprenden tanto lo que consideramos espiritual, como lo que consideramos material. Para los judíos del primer siglo, mucho de lo que nosotros describimos como físico, ellos lo consideraron espiritual, como por ejemplo, el aliento. Para ellos, el respirar era un préstamo divino de vida, una conexión directa con Dios.

Jesús nos llama a entregar respetuosamente nuestro todo a Dios, aún mientras cumplimos con nuestras obligaciones ante el gobierno. A la vez, Él hace hincapié en mirar más allá de nuestros derechos y bendiciones personales, hacia una responsabilidad para con los demás. Nuestras obligaciones con Dios, hacia los demás, no deben ser suspendidas por cualquier autoridad en conflicto, sin importar cuál sea esa autoridad.

La base de las palabras de Jesús, es la comprensión de que todo pertenece a Dios. Él nos llama a colocar todo lo que tiene origen en Dios en sujeción a su voluntad y sus propósitos. En lo tocante a la ley judía, incluso la tierra le pertenecía a Dios. La comida cosechada de los campos vino de Dios, quien envió las lluvias, fue dueño de la tierra, causó la germinación de las semillas, su crecimiento y la producción del fruto. El ganado y las manadas daban crías dada a la iniciativa y creación divina. El respirar de cada uno dependía de que Dios concediera la vida y el aliento para poder hacerlo.

Considerando esto, no hay nada que uno puede reclamar como propiedad personal, pues todo depende del regalo divino de la vida y todo lo que la sostiene. Si nosotros sólo somos nada más que mayordomos de los regalos de Dios, no tenemos nada que sea nuestro para proteger y guardar; al contrario, todo lo que está a nuestra disposición tiene su inicio en Dios y se queda para los cuidados y dirección de Dios.

"Entregue al César lo que de César"

La moneda, que fue discusión de Jesús para pagar el tributo a Roma, llevaba la imagen del César, pues fue elaborada bajo su autoridad. La moneda fue instituida para facilitar el comercio con un patrón de precios, pesos y medidas. Las palabras de Jesús aquí, dan eco al concepto de que lo que el César ha providenciado u originado, al final de cuentas, a él le pertenece. Si el César exigió tributo en moneda romana, entregarlo no era más que regresarle lo que vino del César. Aquellos que le preguntaban a Jesús sobre esta práctica tenían la atención captada por el término "tributo." Desde la perspectiva romana, eso era un reconocimiento de la legitimidad del poder de Roma y que su dominio reflejaba la importancia y supremacia de los dioses de Roma.

Desde la perspectiva religiosa, la moneda del tributo no debería haber circulado en Israel, dado el mandamiento en contra de imágenes grabadas, por lo tanto debería haber sido regresado a Roma sin preguntar. Lo importante, no era la dignidad o rectitud de Roma, sino el hecho de que el judío tenía una lealtad mayor a Yahvé que a la riqueza monetaria o al hacedor de monedas.

A los judíos del primer siglo, les dolía obedecer estas exigencias de la ocupación romana, pues les recordaba el poder de Roma sobre ellos, tal como Roma lo deseaba. Jesús reconoció que mientras que Roma oprimía a los judíos, también les proveía ciertos beneficios. Él vio más allá de la opresión, porque Él comprendió que los judíos no tenían el poder para cambiar las estructuras políticas bajo las cuales vivían. Jesús no estaba tan preocupado como los demás judíos con las estructuras políticas ni como nosotros también nos acostumbramos estar.

En un sistema de gobierno democrático, uno debe reconocer que el ciudadano tiene una responsabilidad ante el gobierno, como también una responsabilidad por el gobierno. No hubo ningún patrón semejante para los oyentes de Jesús. Aunque hubo uno en Roma, los judíos fueron aislados de tal proceso. Jesús hizo referencia a un gobierno que era comúnmente visto como opresivo, sin embargo, las palabras de Jesús siempre instaron a obedecerlo, aún, a un costo personal, haciendo hincapié en mantener la lealtad a Dios. Roma, o cualquier otra estructura gubernamental, quedaban en un segundo lugar, aunque se exigiera un tributo.

Si una ley es justa o injusta, al individuo se le exige cumplir con ella o de lo contrario debe pagar las consecuencias. En el contexto de la enseñanza de Jesús, hubo una conexión entre las autoridades humanas y la divina; hay muchas instancias donde las exigencias de Dios andan en contra de las exigencias del estado. En tales casos, el creyente es llamado a vivir en sumisión a Dios teniendo en cuenta el ejemplo de Jesús, el de los apóstoles y el de la iglesia primitiva.

Acabando con la Opresión

Es responsabilidad del creyente ante Dios, trabajar para acabar con la opresión hacia los demás, aunque debe aceptar la opresión que él experimenta. Aunque esta opresión puede que no sea definida y declarada como tal, es responsabilidad del creyente aceptarla. Vemos este principio aplicado a la vida de Pablo, donde él llega a negarse ciertos privilegios y derechos legales solamente por el hecho de servirle a Dios y trabajar para el bienestar de otros. Lo vemos también en las acciones de Pedro y Juan, quienes fueron arrestados en el templo después de haber sanado a un hombre cojo bajo la autoridad y el nombre de Jesús. Lo más importante, lo vemos en el ejemplo de Jesús.

Pablo escribió una carta donde intervino a favor de un esclavo que se había escapado, indicando a un hermano en Cristo a tratar al esclavo no como propiedad, sino como un ser igual. Él entonces aceptó completa responsabilidad económica por cualquier daño que el dueño hubiera sufrido a causa del esclavo que se había escapado. Pablo libremente aceptó cierta injusticia a sí mismo con la intención de realizar la liberación del otro que sufría opresión. Su intención no era derribar toda una estructura social, sino que él quiso incentivar un plano de interacción más elevado entre los creyentes.

En el ejemplo de su propia vida, él aceptó castigos que fueron opresivos. Pedro y Juan con alegría hicieron lo mismo, tomando su experiencia como una oportunidad para compartir los sufrimientos de Jesucristo. A la vez, los apóstoles trabajaron para crear dentro de la comunidad de creyentes una ética más elevada que generaría un fundamento firme para un modelo nuevo de comportamiento.

Pablo escribió que en Cristo no existen distinciones sociales como en el mundo. Así, no hay base para justificar la opresión a los demás. La nueva comunidad de los creyentes en Hechos se reunió bajo parámetros radicalmente diferentes. Esto no dejó espacio para la opresión, ni adentro, ni afuera de su comunidad. Inicialmente, la opresión cesó, y gracias a la influencia de la iglesia, fue a partir de allí que las acciones y estructuras cambiaron también en la sociedad mayor.

Trabajando por la Justicia

Bíblicamente, la justicia tiene que ver con la igualdad y la provisión para aquellos quienes son más fácilmente oprimidos bajo cualquier sistema de poder. Aquellos sin recursos y sin voz son aquellos a los que estamos llamados a proteger al máximo. La justicia divina nos da a entender que Dios es suficiente para proveer recursos abundantes y para atender cualquier necesidad de uno.

Cuando los hebreos se convirtieron en una nación en la tierra de Yahvé, la justicia incluyó cambiar las normas establecidas por las sociedades que encontraron. Ellos debieron actuar de forma diferente, sin pretender ser los dueños de la tierra. Debieron actuar como mayordomos de la abundancia de Dios. La producción de la tierra debió atender las necesidades de todos: de los que no poseían tierra, voz, poder o amparo. Esta fue la característica central de la justicia que ellos deberían defender.

La sociedad hebrea debía vigilar por las necesidades de sus miembros más frágiles o los más impotentes. Debía dar atención especial a aquellos que no pertenecían a la comunidad. Los hebreos no debían convertirse en la nueva ola de poderosos que actuaban para oprimir a otros. Deberían establecer una comunidad completamente nueva, basada en principios totalmente diferentes.

Ellos no alcanzaron esto altos ideales, pero fueron estos mismos ideales los que encontraron expresión en su ley y en la boca de sus profetas. El rey debió actuar como campeón de la causa de los débiles y oprimidos, así como Natán llamó a David para que respondiera por sus malas acciones. La nación debió depender de Yahvé para atender sus necesidades, no crear estructuras que fortalecieran la avaricia y la generación de alas de poder. Su seguridad debía estar basada en el cuidado de los débiles y la dependencia en la suficiencia de Yahvé para cuidar a la nación, mientras que sirvieran de defensores de la causa de justicia para todos.

Amando la Misericordia:

El amar la misericordia debe ser la regla de medir para los fieles, junto con el concepto de la justicia y de la igualdad. La misericordia es el patrón por medio del cual se mide la ley, y es uno de los ideales más elevados que se ha establecido para el comportamiento del cristiano. Miqueas trató la justicia y la misericordia como trabajando de mano en mano, más allá de las limitaciones de cualquier prescripción legal. Esta es también la forma con la cual Jesús implementó el cuidado a los necesitados. Nuestras acciones y actitudes deben ser guiadas por la misericordia y por la justicia.

Shakespeare nombró la misericordia como el llamado más sublime de un rey en "El Mercader de Venecia." Las palabras no vinieron de la Biblia, pero sus conceptos se encuentran asociados con varios pasajes bíblicos. Lo más notable es el texto de 2ª Reyes 6, donde Eliseo llevó un ejército enemigo ciego hasta Samaria y lo entregó en las manos del rey de Israel. Restaurándoles la vista, le ordenó al rey que se les diera de comer y que fueran liberados para regresar a sus casas. El resultado fue treinta años de paz para la nación.

Una vez más, podemos observar la misericordia en la actitud que tomó Pablo en lo tocante a la persecución que él enfrentó sin hacer ninguna recriminación o maldición desafiante. Al contrario, él ofreció la salvación y el perdón a su carcelero en Filipos. La justicia, la gracia y el perdón, todos se encuentran atados a la misericordia como parte integral del mensaje del evangelio referente al amor por todos.

Vimos a Jesús aplicando principios de misericordia al liberar a muchos de la opresión. Colocó de lado los prejuicios judíos en contra de los pueblos diferentes. Él ofreció gracia a una mujer sirofenicia y a una judía con un flujo de sangre, devolvió la vista a los ciegos y sanó a un leproso samaritano. Su demostración de misericordia no conoció ningún límite de nacionalidad o definición religiosa de dignidad, valor o mérito.

"Ama a Tu Prójimo"

El término "prójimo" o "vecino" normalmente no hacía referencia a un extranjero, pero así es exactamente como Jesús lo interpretó en su parábola del buen samaritano. Él hablo de la responsabilidad que se tiene de atender las necesidades del inmigrante, enemigo, desconocido, de la misma forma como se atienden las necesidades de un hijo, una esposa o un padre. El amor no se preocupa por consideraciones del valor del otro antes de ayudarlo.

La interpretación tradicional del mandamiento a amar al vecino se limitaba a los de la propia nación. La intención de Jesús con esta parábola, entretanto, fue distinta. Discriminaban en contra de los inmigrantes, extranjeros, desconocidos, y miembros de la comunidad que consideraban como de segunda categoría. Lo más triste es que ha sucedido lo mismo en comunidades y sociedades alrededor de todo el mundo hasta la época actual.

Nuestro uso establecido del concepto de vecino no simplemente limita la definición del término, sino que también limita la forma por la cual nos relacionamos con los demás. Buscamos a aquellos que más se nos parecen como nuestros familiares o amigos, mientras que miramos a los ajenos con desprecio. Este es el tema de la parábola del buen samaritano. Nuestro amor debería incluir a todos, no simplemente aquellos cuya identidad y estilo de vida se asemejan a nuestros valores personales, así confirmando nuestro sentido de bienestar.

Para complicar aun más las cosas, Jesús colocó en el papel de buen vecino al enemigo odiado por los judíos, el samaritano, quien había mezclado el judaísmo con otras tradiciones religiosas y se había casado con naciones ajenas a la promesa de Dios a Abraham. Ellos fueron vistos no simplemente como personas impuras que no eran fieles a Dios, sino también como traidores a las tradiciones de Abraham y Moisés. Sin embargo, es esa misma clase de gente sin mérito y sin valor a la cual Jesús colocó en una posición enaltecida para enseñar un amor al que todos estamos llamados a imitar.

Igualdad en Cristo

En Jesucristo, no hay distinción de estatus, posición o preeminencia, a no ser en sentido de servicio. Pablo fue muy claro cuando declaró ésto en Gálatas, como lo fue Lucas al escribir Hechos. Hasta Mateo empezó su evangelio elaborando este tema del Mesías que vino por medio de una genealogía cuestionable que incluyó a extranjeros como Diná, Rahab, Rut y Betsabé. Para completar, el anuncio del nacimiento de Jesús comunicado fue a astrólogos paganos de tierras orientales, aparentemente de la región de Babilonia.

Este concepto de igualdad se construyó en base a un tema empezado en el Antiguo Testamento con la benevolencia de Dios hacia extranjeros, desconocidos y a aquellos rechazados por la sociedad. Todos tienen un valor igual en Jesucristo. Lo vimos dirigiéndose a los rechazados de la sociedad israelita, como también a personas más allá de Israel.

Hubo soldados romanos, samaritanos y sirofenicios quienes recibieron la misma misericordia y cuidado que aquellos de adentro de los límites del judaísmo.

Jesús habló de ovejas de otros rediles, aparentemente de aquellos que no eran judíos, pero que necesitaban acceso a las buenas nuevas de la aceptación de Dios. Jesús incluyó a mujeres en su círculo interior de discípulos, como se evidencia en su conversación con Marta y María en la casa de Lázaro. Él incluyó a pescadores, cobradores de impuestos y mujeres en el mismo grupo de discípulos, entregándoles los detalles íntimos de las buenas nuevas para ser compartidas. Él incluyó en la lista de discípulos, a judíos palestinos y judíos helénicos. No simplemente ignoró las distinciones sociales, sino que las eliminó. Jesús concedió a todos, no una simple tolerancia o aceptación, sino la plena gracia y misericordia de Dios.

Lo que Jesús predicó y vivió, Pedro y Pablo usaron como base para la construcción de la vida de la iglesia a lo largo de Hechos. Pedro aprendió a admitir que todos los gentiles eran aceptables a Dios, sin importar las exigencias de la circuncisión. Pablo batalló con muchos que velaban con celo por distinciones en base a la circuncisión. Él fue más allá de eso, defendiendo contra hacer distinciones en base de idioma, cultura y hasta género. Proclamó que estas distinciones ya no tenían sentido bajo la luz del carácter abundante de la gracia de Dios.

Génesis 18-19

La visita que se hizo a Abraham en este pasaje contiene temas de justicia de acuerdo con las definiciones ya establecidas en su época. Se pensaba que era posible medir la rectitud o justicia de las personas al mirar su trato con categorías específicas de personas: inmigrantes, desconocidos, viudas, niños y pobres. Esto era un concepto mantenido comúnmente entre judíos y la mayoría de las demás naciones a su alrededor. Semejante a hoy día, las culturas de todo el mundo acostumbran a expresar cierto orgullo de ser una cultura hospitalaria.

Los visitantes que llegaron adonde estaba Abraham eran extraños, inmigrantes de alguna categoría superior, probablemente viajando con un grupo mayor de siervos que no fueron mencionados en el texto. Selos recibió con honor, presentando una mesa generosa ante ellos y colocándose a sí mismo en la categoría de siervo para atender a sus necesidades. La gente de Sodoma, en contraste, interfirió con los intentos de Lot por ofrecer hospitalidad. Intentaron abusar de los extraños que habían llegado en la ciudad. El punto importante en la narrativa parece ser el contraste entre la hospitalidad hacia un extraño con el abuso al impotente, estableciendo una medida visible de rectitud, y justicia e iniquidad.

Hay también muchos otros pasajes bíblicos que tratan este mismo tema. El Nuevo Testamento retomó el concepto de la hospitalidad hacia desconocidos (probablemente debería leerse extranjeros o inmigrantes) en referencia a este mismo pasaje donde Abraham hospedó a los mensajeros de Yahvé sin reconocer quienes eran. También describió a Jesús tratando de forma positiva a extraños, extranjeros e inmigrantes, sin condenarlos, sino atendiendo a sus necesidades.

Los babilonios y otras naciones entendieron que el nivel de la hospitalidad de alguien refleja el carácter de su justicia y rectitud. Ugarit, una ciudad en la costa norteña de Palestina, dejó atrás textos que utilizan el refrán de tratar a las viudas, los huérfanos, los extraños y los pobres como una forma de medir la justicia y rectitud. Este concepto fue reconocido en todos los territorios del Medio Oriente Antiguo, no solamente entre los hebreos. Sin embargo, las mismas naciones no vivieron de acuerdo a estos patrones establecidos comúnmente, aunque siempre comprendieron que la forma en que se trataba al extraño demostraba la realidad de su carácter e integridad, mucho más que seguir una serie de leyes y reglas.

Como se ha mencionado anteriormente, la medida de un hombre no es como él trata a sus superiores, sino como él trata a los otros que considera ser sus inferiores. De esa forma, Abraham y Lot pasaron el examen sin problema, aunque Sodoma y Gomorra lo reprobaron por completo.

Filoxenia

Hay una palabra que surge en dos pasajes del Nuevo Testamento, Romanos 12:13 y Hebreos 13:2. Esta palabra normalmente se traduce por hospitalidad, pero su sentido es un tanto distinto a una simple la hospitalidad. Es una unión de dos palabras griegas, una para amor y la otra para extraño. Aunque el concepto aquí es de una hospitalidad, es específicamente una hospitalidad hacia un desconocido.

Pablo, escribiendo en Romanos habla de la necesidad de servir al desconocido con acciones y actitudes de hospitalidad. Para Pablo, esto es parte integral al servicio que el cristiano debería de aplicar a su vida por motivo de haber entregado su vida en sacrificio vivo a Jesucristo.

El autor de Hebreos habla de forma semejante, mencionando que otros personajes habían ofrecido hospitalidad a desconocidos y sin saber habían recibido ángeles como sus huéspedes. Obviamente, el pasaje hace referencia a Abraham y Lot, pero también hace referencia a las viudas que recibieron a Elías y Eliseo, quienes eran mensajeros de Dios (la palabra ángel tiene ese sentido de mensajero en ambos el hebreo y el griego).

No es en todo caso que se traduce la palabra hospitalidad que hay este fondo en el griego, como en 1ª Pedro 4:9. En la mayoría de los casos, la hospitalidad se trata por ejemplo, no por el término específico. En 1ª Pedro, el texto refleja la idea de extender la hospitalidad entre integrantes de la iglesia. Es en Romanos y Hebreos que se trata específicamente de hospitalidad hacia gente desconocida.

Para Pablo y el autor de Hebreos, no es lo suficiente que el creyente acepte al inmigrante, que le trate con amistad, o que le trate con justicia. El cristiano tiene también la responsabilidad de extender su hospitalidad al inmigrante que esté pasando alguna necesidad. No hay espacio aquí para indagar por su dignidad, su estatus migratorio o su forma de conducta. La responsabilidad queda de parte del cristiano como si serviera a Cristo, sin depender de la calidad del individuo pasando necesidad.

Séfora

Moisés no simplemente tomó una esposa de la tierra de Madián, sino que se unió a la familia de un profeta fuera de las categorías conocidas por los descendientes de Abraham. Jetro, su suegro, aparentemente sirvió al mismo Dios de Abraham, aunque no era del mismo linaje. Él aceptó a Moisés como hebreo refugiado de Egipto. Moisés entonces creó lazos de parentesco con este sacerdote de Madián, casándose con su hija y viviendo con él como inmigrante. Más adelante en Éxodo, él recibió a su suegro cuando éste lo visitaba y aceptó su orientación en lo que correspondía a la organización administrativa de la nación. Vemos a Jetro como un modelo de cómo se trata a un inmigrante y cómo también Moisés actuó recíprocamente, poniendo en práctica las lecciones aprendidas de su suegro quien le cuidó sin hacer caso de distinciones de linaje y cultura.

Es notable que Moisés se casara con Séfora por el hecho que el texto la menciona por nombre. No sabemos nada de la esposa de Josué, ni de Aaron, Samuel 0 Elí. Parece que tenemos el nombre de la esposa de Moisés, por causa de su estatus extranjera. Encontramos otro nombre para la esposa de Moisés en el texto de Éxodo, probablemente indicando que tuvo más de una esposa. La Biblia hace más mención de ésta extranjera viviendo en medio de la nación que se formaba entre los descendientes de Jacob.

Hay varios textos que hablan de la necesidad que tenía la nación de Israel de mantenerse separada y pura en el matrimonio, sin embargo, hay varias mujeres de origen extranjero que figuran de forma prominente en las crónicas de personajes sobresalientes en la historia de Israel. Séfora fue una de ellas, pero definitivamente no es la única. Lo que pudo distinguirla de las demás es que ella vino de una familia que sirvió a Yahvé como el único Dios verdadero. Ella fue hija de Jetro, sacerdote del Dios Más Alto. Fue esa su relación con Yahvé que se la dio mayor valor entre la nueva nación que se formaba en esos lugares desérticos.

Rahab

En Josué 2, encontramos la historia de Rahab, quien no fue precisamente una inmigrante, aunque se encontraba fuera de los límites de la gente de Yahvé. Ella eligió identificarse con el pueblo hebreo que estaba al punto de conquistar el territorio. Al tratar de forma misericordiosa a los dos espías de Josué, ella imploró ser incluida en la nación de Yahvé. El hecho de que ella fue incluida ignoró su oficio como prostituta en una religión pagana, así como también su origen. A ella le fue concedida la oportunidad de hacerse parte de la gente de Yahvé. No fue solamente aceptada por los espías, sino que llegó a ser un ancestral del Rey David.

El nombre de Rahab se encuentra también en el evangelio de Mateo, en la lista genealógica de Jesús. Él hizo hincapié para señalar que esta mujer era extraña al linaje de Abraham y debió haber sido condenada a muerte por su estilo y forma de vida, pero que sin embargo encontró gracia y participación dentro de Israel.

Aunque fue una extranjera, fue incluida como parte de la nueva nación, simplemente por reconocer el valor y la soberanía de Yahvé, por encima de su propia gente y sus dioses. Ella pidió participación en la nación formante y tomó pasos para ayudar a los espías de Josué en su huida del rey de Jericó. No fue juzgada por su raza, sino por sus acciones, por los cuales ella buscó pertenecer a la nación de Israel y presentó su vida al servicio de Yahvé.

Si la inclusión de cualquier personaje del Antiguo Testamento debería causarnos un choque, sería Rahab. Ella era extranjera, pagana, idólatra y prostituta trabajando a servicio de los dioses de fertilidad de su nación. A pesar de eso, ella encontró que la gracia de Yahvé fue suficiente para tomarla desde el punto de su necesidad y darle una nueva oportunidad de vida.

Rut

El libro de Rut es una crítica explícita al desprecio de la sociedad israelita al extranjero. Rut fue descrita como una extranjera quien aceptó ser leal al Dios de Israel. En el curso de su historia, ella no solamente demostró ser más digna que muchos, sino fue más digna que la mayoría de los israelitas. Luego, ella fue caracterizada como un vehículo por medio del cual nació el abuelo de uno de los renombrados siervos de Dios, el rey David, quien fue su biznieto.

Rut no solamente fue extranjera, sino que vino de la tierra de Moab, nación considerada como uno de los peores enemigos de Israel. Su gente había negado al bando de esclavos hebreos que pasaran por su tierra en el peregrinaje por las tierras desérticas, al huir de Egipto. Moab no debía ser perdonada por su oposición hacia los hebreos. Aún así, fue del carácter de esta mujer joven que Israel aprendió algo importante referente a su propia infidelidad hacia Yahvé.

Rut se unió a su suegra al regresar a Israel con un grado de lealtad que pocos alcanzaron. Ella unió su vida y futuro con Noemí, aunque Yahvé aparentemente no había prestado mucha atención a esa pobre viuda cuyos hijos habían muerto. Rut juró quedarse con Noemí y cuidar de ella en su regreso a Israel. Colocó de lado sus necesidades propias para cuidar de su suegra inmigrante, y por su vez se convirtió en inmigrante en la tierra de Israel.

Requiere valor para que uno se torne inmigrante, dejando atrás todo lo que conoce. Para hacerlo como una viuda atada a otra viuda, lleva aun otro nivel de valor y fe en un Dios que no había demostrado mucho de la calidad de fidelidad que nos gustaría ver. Así, Rut demostró una calidad de fe y confianza que era virtualmente desconocida en Israel. Es ella , mujer, inmigrante y moabita, quien establece el patrón para la fe israelita en Yahvé.

Betsabé

La viuda de Urías el hitita, Betsabé, fue tomada como esposa por el Rey David después de su arrepentimiento y la muerte de su hijo ilegítimo. Ella luego vino a ser madre del heredero de David, el Rey Salomón. Técnicamente, ella no debería haber recibido tal aceptación, dado a ciertas leyes de Israel. Aun así, ella entró en el linaje de los antepasados de Jesús, según la descripción de Mateo.

Betsabé era una inmigrante o ella había por lo menos sometido a casarse con un inmigrante en contra de las expectativas y prescripciones legales de Israel. Como en los casos de Rut y Rahab, estas inmigrantes encontraron un sitio en la gracia de Dios. Parece haber aquí algún progreso en la revelación de Dios en cómo Él trabaja más allá de las limitaciones de ciertas nociones de la sociedad y ley de Israel.

El hecho del Rey David tomar a Betsabé como una de sus esposas era una cosa. Él tenía muchas esposas y concubinas. Lo que es más notable aquí es que ella fue elevada a ser madre del futuro rey de Israel. No llegó a esta posición por ser la madre del hijo mayor de David. David ya tenía muchos otros hijos mayores. David la colocó en esa posición, aparentemente en compensación por haber abusado de ella mientras estaba casada con el inmigrante Urías.

El profeta Natán estuvo de acuerdo en darle tal bendición. Aunque su estatus inmigratorio debería habérselo negado, Yahvé no parece preocuparse por estos motivos que eran de preocupación entre las estructuras legales de Israel. Las leyes supuestamente provenían de Yahvé, pero parece que Yahvé no da tanto énfasis al código legal, como al conceder libertad para extender la participación y su bendición para otros en el acuerdo y la promesa a Abraham. Después de todo, la promesa era que todas las familias de la tierra serían bendecidas en Abraham. Esto se extendía a incluir a todos los gentiles, extranjeros, extraños e inmigrantes.

Naamán

En 2ª Reyes 5, Eliseo sanó a un enemigo que había llegado a Israel en busca de sanidad. El hombre era un extranjero y siervo de un rey que era un enemigo declarado de Israel. Dios eligió sanar a Naamán por medio de la intervención de Eliseo, demostrando la gracia y el poder de Yahvé. Mientras el rey israelita no demostraba confianza en Yahvé. Este extranjero aprendió y aceptó por fe la intervención del profeta de Yahvé.

Jesús señaló esta historia como un ejemplo de la gracia de Dios abundantemente concedida sobre algunos que técnicamente no pertenecían a la gente elegida. Él hizo referencia a esto en respuesta a su propia acción de sanar a algunos fuera de los límites de la sociedad judía. Él utilizó la historia para demostrar que él estaba no solamente dentro de la voluntad de Yahvé para ministrar a aquellos fuera del judaísmo. Él estaba siguiendo los propios patrones que Yahvé había establecido de traer a otros dentro del redil de la gente nombrada por Dios como sus elegidos.

El rey de Israel miró la llegada de Naamán para sanación de su lepra como una amenaza velada. Lo entendía como estrategia para ganar una justificación para declarar guerra contra Israel. Eliseo miraba a Naamán no como una amenaza, sino como una persona con una necesidad que Yahvé podía atender. Mientras que el rey miraba la situación desde una perspectiva de miedo e incertidumbre, Eliseo la miraba como una oportunidad para demostrar que Yahvé es digno del título de Dios de Israel, tanto para Israel como también para todas las naciones del mundo.

Desde la historia en 2ª Reyes, encontramos que Naamán jamás fue una amenaza, aunque muchos así lo consideraban. Él era un hombre necesitado, procurando una solución improbable para sus problemas. Como en el caso de muchos inmigrantes modernos, él estaba simplemente buscando una salida del dilema en el que la vida le había puesto. Eliseo estaba confiado que Yahvé podría proveer la solución y le buscó desde una posición de confianza que Dios fue fiel en respaldar.

Jonás

Jonás es entre todos los profetas aquél que es llamado específicamente para ser un inmigrante en tierras de los enemigos de Israel. Para su mal, Jonás no quiso cumplir con los propósitos de Dios, aunque Dios le obligó a hacerlo.

El libro de Jonás responde a actitudes y prejuicios a inmigrantes, extranjeros y otras naciones. El mensaje responde a ciertas actitudes judías en contra de naciones enemigas al describirles por contraste desde la perspectiva del amor de Yahvé por toda la creación, incluyendo a naciones, plantas y animales. El deseo de Dios es que el amor, la misericordia y el perdón reinen sin los estorbos de determinar quién se puede considerar digno o indigno. Es un mensaje del valor igualitario que tienen ante Dios todas las nacionalidades y etnias, no obstante a cualquier circunstancia atenuante.

Jonás no compartía el concepto de igualdad de las gentes. Aunque era profeta de Yahvé, su actitud no estaba de acuerdo con la de su propio Dios. Desde el inicio de la llamada de Dios enviándole a Nínive, él se encontró en oposición a los propósitos de Yahvé. Él Huyó, no por no creer que Dios amaba a los ninivitas, sino por temer que Yahvé sí les amara.

Fue enviado a predicar arrepentimiento a Nínive, aunque cuando él llegó, estructuró su mensaje en los moldes de una condenación y ruina inminente. En el siguiente capítulo vemos que durante el trascurso de su experiencia él ya sabía que la misericordia de Dios era parte integral del mensaje. Había oportunidad para el arrepentimiento y el perdón. Había un mensaje inherente de gracia tras su mensaje de condenación.

Mientras que Jonás deseaba la condenación de Nínive, Yahvé estaba interesado en su restauración. Jonás se sintió justificado por su actitud en contra de los habitantes de Nínive, ya que eran conocidos por una crueldad extrema contra los propios israelitas y sus demás enemigos. Dios, entretanto, no estaba dispuesto a dejar que tales actitudes fueran impuestas contra otros. Jonás reconocía esto. Él simplemente no quiso aceptar las implicaciones de tal conocimiento. Una cosa era que Dios les amaba, pero otra era dejar que el amor de Dios fluyera por medio de él. A despecho de nuestras justificaciones para colocar gente en categorías de indignos de gracia y misericordia, Dios no utiliza tales categorías, ni acepta que nosotros tengamos tales actitudes.

Fuga a Egipto

La fuga de Jesús a Egipto en su infancia le coloca en la condición de inmigrante, lo que hoy día se llamaría de inmigrante indocumentado. Aunque que la legislación referente a la inmigración era mucho más fluida en la época, cuando Jesús llegó a Egipto con su familia sería tratado como alguien que era dependiente de la misericordia de la población local.

Ellos no trababan con visas y verificaciones para cruzar fronteras como se hace en el mundo de hoy. Lo que sí hacían era definir la ciudadanía más o menos en conformidad con los conceptos griegos de que uno naciera en las familias correctas dentro de una ciudad o región. En conjunto con esas categorías de ciudadanía, hay que comprender que aquellos quienes no eran ciudadanos tenían pocas o ningunas protecciones legales. El extraño quedaba a la misericordia de aquellos quienes tenían las protecciones legales.

Siguiendo las huellas de los visitantes de Abraham que siguieron su camino hacia Sodoma, los que no eran miembros de la sociedad local no podían contar con ningún sistema de derechos o protecciones que la población local no decidiera conceder.

El Imperio Romano no entraba en disputas de ese tipo, a no ser en lo tocante a sus propios ciudadanos. Un judío podía haber nacido en territorio controlado por el Imperio, pero eso no era suficiente para garantizarle los derechos de ciudadanía. A pesar de esto, había muchos grados de importancia que se le concedía a la gente de acuerdo con su origen o etnicidad, como por el sitio en donde se encontraban. Jesús en Egipto vivía privado de muchas protecciones que pudiera haber gozado en Judea, aunque Herodes decidiera ordenar su muerte. Como un inmigrante en tierra ajena, su existencia, sus derechos y sus libertades estaban limitados a los de una persona de segunda o tercera clase, aunque no se encontraba al nivel de un esclavo.

La Mujer Cananea

El capítulo completo de Mateo 8 se dedica al tema del trato de Jesús con inmigrantes, extranjeros y otros designados indignos por Israel. Esta categoría de "impuro" de acuerdo con las leyes de purificación es uno de los temas más significantes que Jesús trata aquí. La pureza en este sentido tiene que ver con el estado ritual de uno para la participación en el culto y adoración en el templo o la sinagoga. Mateo capítulo 9 continúa tratando el tema con una mujer que tenía un flujo de sangre, con "pecadores" y con un leproso.

Es en el capítulo 15 que Jesús viaja afuera de Israel. Él anda en busca de una mujer cananea por medio de quien mostrará a los discípulos el ejemplo de cómo la gracia de Dios es suficiente para extenderse más allá de los límites de la sociedad judía. Él se extiende hacia aquellos que un judío habría normalmente ignorado por indignos de atención y extraños a la gracia de Dios.

Jesús había dicho a los discípulos que la limpieza real o pureza ritual no tenía nada que ver con comer las comidas correctas o seguir ciertas instrucciones del código de Moisés. La pureza real tenía mucho más que ver con asuntos del corazón (el centro de las decisiones que uno hace.) Fue cuando ellos no podían comprender sus palabras referentes a comidas puras e impuras, gente pura e impura, que dejó la región para entrar en una tierra en donde todas las personas serían categorizadas por los judíos como ritualmente impuros y repugnantes.

Fue allí (como inmigrante o extranjero) que Jesús se encontró con la mujer cananea que no tenía ninguna reclamación legítima desde la perspectiva judía para reivindicar la misericordia o la intervención de Dios para sanarle. Ella le rogó por su intervención, y Jesús primeramente le ofreció la respuesta tradicional judía: de que sólo existe gracia y misericordia para aquellos que quedan adentro de los confines establecidos por el judaísmo. Si ella se hiciera pura e ingresara al redil, entonces quizás pudiera ser digna de pedirle algo a Dios.

Su respuesta es anotada para el bien de los discípulos y para nosotros los lectores. La gracia de Dios es suficiente para que haya migajas en cantidad para que se las compartan con aquellos definidos como indignos.

Jesús tomó esta respuesta y la reformuló en relación a su propia enseñanza a los discípulos. Su fe interior no tenía nada que ver con las preocupaciones exteriores de las leyes y reglas de pureza y purificación ritual. Tenía que ver con cosas que quedaban más allá de lo que el Judaísmo podía categorizar. Aunque ella era parte de una nación impura, la gracia de Dios libremente la alcanzó y la miró como digna de la atención de Dios en misericordia y amor.

Filemón

Pablo no hizo campaña contra la institución de la esclavitud. Lo que sí hizo, fue más bien definir una categoría para la institución de la esclavitud en su carta a Filemón de una forma muy diferente de aquella de la norma de ese tiempo. Él animó a Filemón a que tratara a su esclavo como una persona de igual valor ante Cristo Jesús, y no de acuerdo con los patrones socio-políticos del día. Él le pidió que ignorara sus derechos legales para que la gracia de Jesucristo tomara cuenta de sus actitudes y acciones en lo tocante al esclavo escapado que se le regresaba. Tales actitudes promovidas por Pablo actuaban en contra de la manera en que la sociedad y los códigos legales de entonces respondían a los individuos, sus derechos y su valor inherente.

La esclavitud de aquellos días era una institución diferente a la del comercio transatlántico de esclavos de hace poco. No se daba un trato humano a la gente y colocaba a muchos de estos en la categoría de propiedad o mercancía. A la vez, dejaba que un individuo se vendiera como esclavo para cubrir sus necesidades físicas y económicas en momentos de desesperación. El esclavo aun era propiedad, pero tenía ciertos derechos limitados y no era considerados menos que humano.

Pablo, entretanto, establece en esta carta corta una perspectiva completamente nueva con referencia a la persona del esclavo. El esclavo aquí debería ser comprendido y tratado como un hermano en Cristo, una persona igual en valor y dignidad. Pablo interpreta que la forma en la cual Filemón trata a su esclavo es un reflejo de su trato de Jesucristo, quien habita en la persona de su esclavo. No hay aquí un simple concepto de propiedad, aunque Pablo reconoce que el esclavo escapado de alguna forma hizo daño económico a su amo. Su persona y posición en Cristo debería superar cualquier preocupación económica de su amo. Pablo llega a pedir que cualquier daño económico sea colocado a su propia cuenta, una que Filemón difícilmente podría cobrar.

Pablo recuerda a Filemón que él mismo le debía una deuda que no tenía como pagar, así como tenía una deuda para con Jesucristo. Es en esta estructura que Filemón es dirigido a mirar a su esclavo ahora: una persona por quien Cristo murió y en quien Jesucristo ahora vive. Esto sería causa suficiente para considerar a todos y a cada uno del mismo valor que nosotros, a diferencia de la categoría en la que nuestra sociedad quisiera colocarles.

"Multiplíquense y Llenen la Tierra"

Hay otra serie de textos, específicamente empezando en Génesis, que tratan con una categoría completamente distinta. En esta, el inmigrante llega a ser central a los propósitos de Dios. Repetidas veces, Dios ordena a la humanidad para multiplicarse, esparcirse y llenar la tierra. Al hacerlo, la humanidad cumple con el propósito de Dios para que la creación esté rebosando de vida, incluyendo a la vida humana alrededor de todo el mundo.

Abraham es llamado a emigrar a una nueva tierra que le es desconocida. De forma parecida, Felipe, Bernabé, Silas y Pablo son llamados a nuevas tierras en misión por Cristo. En textos como Mateo 23, los discípulos son alertados de la destrucción venidera de Jerusalén, momento en lo cual deberían esparcirse por todo el mundo con este evangelio. Convertirse en inmigrante era comúnmente asociado con cumplir con la voluntad de Dios. Convertirse en misionero requiere que uno tome pasos a tornarse inmigrante en alguna otra sociedad.

Mirando a otros inmigrantes en nuestro medio, debemos también mirar aquellas ocasiones en que nosotros somos también llamados a vivir como inmigrantes en otras tierras o a apoyar aquellos enviados por Dios hacia otras tierras como inmigrantes y misioneros. Desafortunadamente, muchas veces estamos demasiado ansiosos con los extranjeros para mirarles con las mismas actitudes con las cuales queremos que los demás nos miren a nosotros cuando se invierte la situación.

Felipe, Pablo, Silas, Pedro, Bernabé, Lucas, Juan Marcos y muchos otros fueron enviados como emisarios del evangelio a otras tierras. Jesús también llevó y envió a sus discípulos a regiones afuera de Israel, sanando al demoníaco de Gadara en Marcos 5 y enviándole a otra región para compartir el testimonio de la actuación de Dios en su vida. En Mateo 28 y Hechos 1, los discípulos son encargados de llevar el mensaje de Dios a todas las naciones, haciendo discípulos de ellos. Para que esto sucediera, tendrían que tornarse a su vez en inmigrantes o peregrinos como lo fue Abraham.

Nosotros somos el producto de la gente que como estos discípulos dejaron una tierra por otra. Los europeos embarcaron para las costas del Nuevo Mundo, los africanos salieron de sus costas para Europa y los asiáticos han salido de sus tierras hacia otras tierras. Aunque esas migraciones durantes los siglos no han sido necesariamente estimuladas por decreto divino, ellas son consistentes con el mensaje de Dios por todo el Pentateuco, de que la humanidad debe llenar toda la tierra, multiplicándose y esparciéndose en nuevas maneras. Quiera o no, los inmigrantes en nuestro medio están cumpliendo con este mandamiento de Dios.

PARTE DOS

Pasajes que utilizan términos específicos para inmigrantes, extranjeros, errantes o refugiados

En esta segunda sección, miraremos el ámbito de los pasajes bíblicos que utilizan terminología específica para inmigrantes, extranjeros o refugiados. Como se ha mencionado, hay otros pasajes que están relacionados al tópico, aunque no utilican esas palabras específicas. Por ejemplo, Mateo 15 habla de la mujer cananea, pero en esta situación son Jesús y sus discípulos que se encuentran en la categoría de extranjeros, aunque no se utiliza ningún término específico para tal.

He compilado una lista de pasajes que utilizan la terminología específica y los he organizado de acuerdo a sus temas. He organizado estos temas en orden decreciente en cuanto al número de veces que cada tema aparece. Para cada pasaje, he colocado las referencias bíblicas, seguido por una declaración resumida de la importancia de estos pasajes en lo tocante al tema referente a la inmigración.

Algunos de estos pasajes referidos caen a veces bajo más que un grupo temático. Por lo tanto, estos serán incluidos otra vez conforme sus temas variados. En total, son 182 pasajes en la Biblia que utilizan la terminología específica que se traduce como inmigrante, extranjero, refugiado, desconocido o errante. Menciono, por ejemplo, a Génesis 17:3-13 como un solo pasaje, aunque los términos en cuestión pueden aparecer más de una vez en este rango de versículos. Si el mismo pasaje trata más que un solo tema, también será mencionado bajo más de una categoría.

Las Bendiciones de Dios Son para Todas las Gentes
(91 Pasajes)

Las bendiciones de Dios están al alcance de todas las personas sin ninguna distinción nacional o étnica.

Este grupo de textos mira más allá de preocupaciones de nacionalismo, reconociendo que Dios quiere incluir a todas las personas dentro de los lazos de amor, gracia, aceptación y bendición. Este mensaje se aclarará en el Nuevo Testamento más de lo que se ve en el Antiguo, pero definitivamente tiene sus orígenes en el Antiguo Testamento. Estas voces simplemente eran muchas veces aplacadas por otras voces clamando con preocupaciones de una superioridad nacionalista.

Dios extiende su gracia más allá de las fronteras de Israel o sus definiciones de nacionalidad. Algunos de estos textos como Hechos 2 harán referencia a judíos viviendo alrededor del mundo conocido durante el Imperio Romano. Otros demostrarán como la gente de Dios han sido siempre definidos por categorías más amplias que las definiciones comunes utilizados por la sociedad de Israel. Esto se hace claro tanto en la promesa a Abram de que Dios desea bendecir a las naciones como en la inclusión de varios extranjeros dentro de la identidad central de la nación de Israel, quisás más notable en las descripciones del linaje de David.

Génesis 17:3-13. La promesa de Dios incluye el hecho de que Abram sería el padre de muchas naciones. La tierra en la cual él vivía como inmigrante pertenecería un día a sus descendientes. Todas las familias de la tierra encontrarían bendición en lo que Dios planeaba hacer por medio de Abram.

Éxodo 12:43-49. El extranjero no debería participar en comer el cordero pascual si antes no había participado en la redención de los hebreos desde Egipto. Si los extranjeros se habían hecho partícipes de la nación por medio de la circuncisión, eran considerados completamente parte de la nación y deberían participar de forma completa de la pascua. La única distinción que se dejaba aquí se basaba en la participación de uno en el proceso de redención. De otra forma, todos eran iguales ante Dios y la nacionalidad en si llegaba a perder significado. A los inmigrantes que no participaban en la alianza, se les permitía participar en otros elementos de la celebración, como también en las bendiciones de Dios que les alcanzaban también a ellos.

Éxodo 20:10. El sábado fue dado como un día de bendición y descanso a los hebreos. Se entiende que podían confiar que Yahvé haría provisión suficiente de alimentos para que ellos tomaran un día para descansar a cada siete. Esta bendición debería ser extendida a los inmigrantes, quienes normalmente no habrían esperado gozar de las mismas libertades como lo demás de la población. En lugar de ser una categoría de gente inferior, a quienes Dios no deseaba bendecir, ellos reciben protección aquí en la ley con base en la provisión de Dios que se extiende a ellos.

Éxodo 23:12. No se debería colocar a los trabajadores inmigrantes en una categoría inferior a los animales de carga. Ellos reciben la misma categoría de protección y bendición que se le da a los residentes nacionales. Mientras que hay un reconocimiento que los inmigrantes son normalmente víctimas de opresión, ni ellos, ni los animales deben sufrir trabajo forzado más que aquellos gozando la protección de pertenecer a la tierra. Son los designios de Dios bendecir y protegerles igualmente a todos.

Levítico 17:8-16. Se hace una distinción entre vivir en la tierra y pertenecer al pueblo de Dios. No hay aquí ningún sentido bajo cual el inmigrante no se le dejara participar plenamente en el pueblo de Dios, pero la conversión debería ocurrir antes de gozar plenamente de la alianza con Dios. Las protecciones de la alianza aún se extienden como exigencias éticas y restricciones legales que se aplicarían a todos.

Levítico 19:10. La rebusca (la parte de la cosecha que se queda atrás en el campo) se debe dejar a los pobres, incluyendo a los inmigrantes refugiados. Esto hace parte de la provisión abundante de Dios para atender a las necesidades de todos, sin consideración de su estatus.

Levítico 23:22. Otra vez, la rebusca se debe dejar en el campo para el consumo de los pobres, incluyendo a los refugiados inmigrantes. El enfoque aquí por la repetición refuerza el hecho que Dios planea proveer por las necesidades de todos, sin distinción.

Levítico 24:22. Hay no más una sola ley que se debe aplicar igualmente a todos, los nativos e inmigrantes por igual. La ley es para el beneficio de toda la sociedad. Los inmigrantes deben encontrar redención, rescate y provisión juntamente con todos los demás.

Levítico 25:4-7. La cosecha no plantada del séptimo año debería ser lo suficiente para cuidar de los esclavos, los siervos, y los refugiados inmigrantes. La provisión de Dios se planeaba para cuidar de las necesidades de todos, incluyendo no únicamente los considerados de más valor por la sociedad.

Levítico 25:35. Un israelita que llegara a la pobreza debería ser tratado con la misma misericordia que se le concediera a cualquier otro refugiado inmigrante. No se hace aquí una distinción, aunque parezca raro que el texto espera un buen trato para el inmigrante en comparación al pobre. Queda subentendido que naturalmente se trataría mejor al inmigrante que al pobre.

Números 9:14. Los inmigrantes deberían celebrar la Pascua en conjunto con los israelitas. El mensaje y las bendiciones asociadas con la Pascua estaban al alcance de todos, sin distinción con respecto a los orígenes étnicos, culturales o nacionales. Lo importante del éxodo era que Dios tomó un grupo de esclavos para de ellos formar una nueva nación.

Deuteronomio 5:14. Hasta los inmigrantes deberían participar en el día de descanso sabático, junto con los nativos y los animales de carga. Esto era definido como una bendición con origen en la provisión de Dios e incluía aquí a todos en Israel.

Deuteronomio 10:18-19. Dios es misericordioso hacia huérfanos, viudas y refugiados inmigrantes, poniéndolo como un ejemplo para la gente en memoria de que habían vivido como refugiados y esclavos en Egipto. Las bendiciones y las protecciones de Dios aquí son para todos.

Deuteronomio 14:27-29. Las ofrendas para aprovisionar los levitas deberían también suplir las necesidades de huérfanos, viudas e inmigrantes refugiados. Esto es uno de los usos de las ofrendas exigidas por Dios para cuidar de las personas fuera de los límites de la identidad nacional.

Deuteronomio 16:9-11. La fiesta de la cosecha debería ser compartida con viudas, huérfanos, levitas y refugiados inmigrantes. Todos deberían compartir de las bendiciones de la abundancia de Dios, sin hacer referencia a su origen nacional.

Deuteronomio 16:13-15. La fiesta de tabernáculos debería ser celebrada en compañía de las familias, los esclavos, los huérfanos, las viudas, los levitas y los inmigrantes refugiados. La fiesta debería ser un recordatorio de su vida errante en lugares desérticos. Los inmigrantes aquí son animados a participar de esta celebración de la provisión de Dios.

Deuteronomio 24:14-15. Habría aquí una repetición de la regla de igualdad entre el nativo y el inmigrante. Los pobres debían recibir su salario diariamente, con la observación de que la injusticia en lo tocante a esto sería juzgado por Dios. Dios quería proveer para todos.

Deuteronomio 24:17. Uno no debería maltratar a un inmigrante refugiado, ni pedir el abrigo de una viuda como garantía. Las protecciones de Dios en contra de la discriminación y la opresión cubrían igualmente a todos los miembros de la comunidad, incluso a los extranjeros.

Deuteronomio 24:19-22. Otra vez se instruye la gente que se debe de dejar la rebusca en las huertas para los pobres, los inmigrantes refugiados, los huérfanos y las viudas. Todos los vulnerables deberían ser recipientes de la abundancia y las bendiciones de Dios, aunque no habían entrado al acuerdo de la alianza con Yahvé.

Deuteronomio 26:11-14. A la fiesta de acciones de gracias, se debería invitar a los sacerdotes y los refugiados viviendo en la tierra. El diezmo de cada tercer año debería ser dado a los sacerdotes, los refugiados inmigrantes, los huérfanos y las viudas. La instrucción aquí es para que los dueños de las tierras compartieran con los vulnerables sin tierras.

Deuteronomio 27:14-26. En medio a una lista de maldiciones en contra de quienes maltratan a los que carecen de protección, una maldición se nombra en contra de quienes maltratan a los refugiados inmigrantes, a las viudas y a los huérfanos. Esta maldición viene de Dios, puesto que Dios quiere que la abundancia y la justicia de la tierra sean compartidas con todos.

Deuteronomio 29:11. Todos estaban reunidos para ratificar la alianza con Dios, incluyendo a los trabajadores inmigrantes, quienes hacían trabajo forzoso en beneficio de la nación. Aunque haya alguna inconsistencia aquí en estas acciones, hay un principio básico que las bendiciones de la alianza eran para todos.

Deuteronomio 31:12. Todos deberían celebrar la fiesta, incluyendo a los refugiados inmigrantes, para que ellos también pudieran aprender a respetar y a obedecer a Dios. Era el deseo de Dios que todos llegaran a ser participantes en la alianza y recipientes de sus bendiciones.

Josué 8:33-35. Los inmigrantes fueron incluidos en la convocación de Israel para la bendición sacerdotal ante el Arca de la Alianza. La participación de los inmigrantes era en parte para enseñarles las normas de Yahvé, pero también para incentivarles integrarse en la participación plena de la misma.

Josué 20:9. La creación de ciudades de refugio se aplicaría para la protección de los inmigrantes tanto como para la de los nativos. Hay una sola ley para todos, aplicando por igual sus protecciones y sus responsabilidades sin cualquier sentido de discriminación.

1ª Reyes 8:41-43. Salomón clama ante Dios que utilice el templo para alcanzar a todas las naciones desde el impacto del templo en la vida de los inmigrantes viviendo en Israel. Está de acuerdo con la voluntad declarada de Dios para bendecir a todas las naciones.

2ª Crónicas 6:32-33. Se le pide a Dios para que atienda a las oraciones de los inmigrantes que oraran en el templo, contestándoles para llevar a la fe en Yahvé hacia las naciones del mundo.

2ª Crónicas 30:25. La celebración de la Pascua se extendió por más una semana, porque la celebración fue levantada con alegría por todos, incluyendo a la población inmigrante. Dios quedó contento con su participación en esta celebración de las bendiciones de la alianza.

Job 29:16. La protección y defensa de los pobres e inmigrantes es definida aquí como señal de la rectitud y la justicia. La justicia real no discrimina entre categorías de personas y sus supuestos niveles de dignidad y valor.

Salmo 18:43-45. Esta es una reiteración del reconocimiento de David que Dios le había colocado en una posición de respeto ante la gente inmigrante. Era la voluntad de Dios ser conocido entre todas las naciones, sin importar las distinciones que podamos considerar como importantes.

Salmo 94:6. La injusticia aquí se define como matar a viudas, asesinar a huérfanos y masacrar a inmigrantes refugiados. No hay nada más injusto que discriminar en contra de alguna gente en base de alguna categoría u otra. La injusticia es aun siempre injusticia.

Salmo 107:4, 40. El vagar de los hebreos por el desierto aquí se designa opresivo y difícil, pero se retrata a Dios como listo para rescatar al errante necesitado. Dios utilizó la condición de errante para disciplinar a la gente, preparándoles para su futuro. El único criterio aquí para la ayuda de Dios es clamar en necesidad.

Isaías 14:1. En la restauración de Israel, Dios haría que muchos inmigrantes llegaran como refugiados para unirse a la nación en formación. Dios les ofrecería aceptación, así como muchos otros inmigrantes habían encontrado aceptación bajo las bendiciones de la alianza con Yahvé.

Isaías 56:3-7. Aquí hay una promesa de seguridad para los inmigrantes que vienen adorar a Yahvé. Dios desea que el templo sea un lugar de oración para todas las naciones, no solamente para aquellos de la descendencia biológica de Abraham.

Jeremías 7:3-7. Una gran parte del arrepentimiento incluye establecer justicia para los oprimidos, incluyendo a los inmigrantes refugiados, las viudas y los huérfanos. Es hacer lo que es correcto por los vulnerables de la sociedad de acuerdo a las definiciones divinas de justicia y rectitud.

Jeremías 22:3. Las exigencias de Yahvé referente a la rectitud se resumen en el cuidado de los oprimidos, los inmigrantes, los huérfanos, las viudas y la protección de los inocentes. Los inmigrantes son específicamente incluidos por estar bajo la extensión de la protección de Dios.

Ezequiel 14:7. El anuncio del juicio de Yahvé incluye a los inmigrantes en la tierra como responsables en conjunto con Israel por desobedecerle a

Yahvé y por su idolatría. Ellos quedan bajo los cuidados de Dios, quien les mantiene responsables por prestar cuentas igualmente con Israel.

Ezequiel 44:7-9. La nación estaba dejando la adoración en el templo en manos de inmigrantes quienes no habían asumido las responsabilidades de la alianza con Yahvé. El énfasis aquí es en la identificación con Yahvé, no el estatus migratorio. Las bendiciones de Dios estaban accesibles a todos, pero había responsabilidades atadas a esas bendiciones.

Ezequiel 47:21-22. La repartición de la tierra debería incluir a los hijos nacidos a los inmigrantes. Ellos deberían gozar de los mismos derechos que cualquier otro israelita, especialmente incluyendo la repartición de tierras en una base igual a cualquier otro individuo.

Mateo 4:15. Aquellos en tierras lejanas también deberían escuchar el anuncio de Dios en conjunto con Israel. El deseo de Dios era que el mensaje y las bendiciones de las buenas nuevas llegaran a todas las naciones igualmente, sin cualquier distinción nacional.

Mateo 8:10-12. Jesús encuentra a un inmigrante cuya creencia (confianza) es mayor que la de muchos en Israel. Él menciona que otras naciones serían aceptadas adelante de muchos en Israel en el último día, ya que ser nativo no era tan importante como ingresar a una vida de fe en Dios.

Mateo 10:18. Jesús alertó a los discípulos que ellos sufrirían persecución y peligro desde judíos como de extranjeros. Ellos tendrían que dar testimonio a Jesús ante todos. El propio motivo por lo cual irían ante las autoridades desde la perspectiva de Dios era para que comunicaran el evangelio.

Mateo 12:18-21. Aquí se le llama el siervo de Dios para proclamar la justicia de Dios a todas las naciones. Esto será un mensaje de esperanza para todos, no simplemente una esperanza para los judíos. Todas las naciones son cubiertas por las bendiciones de Dios y su evangelio.

Mateo 15:21-28. Jesús trata con una extranjera, exclamando sobre su fe y utilizándola como un ejemplo de que es su voluntad tratar a todos en gracia sin referencia a nacionalidad, estatus o preocupaciones de pureza ritual. Las preocupaciones de pureza ritual tenían que ver con distinciones religiosas que apartaban a unos como teniendo valor o dignidad mayor que otros. Jesús no se preocupaba con tales temas.

Mateo 25:31-46. El juicio final de las naciones reflejará cómo ellos trataron a los que tenían hambre, los que tienen sed, los pobres, los desconocidos, los desnudos, los enfermos y los encarcelados. Este juicio cubre a todas las naciones del mundo y su tratamiento de todos. Es un juicio tanto para condenación como para bendición.

Marcos 5:18-20. El ministerio de Jesús se extiende más allá de las fronteras de Israel, enviando un hombre en una misión hacia una región completa de no-judíos. No hay aquí ningún principio de respetar fronteras, sino que el evangelio se presenta como un beneficio para cualquier y para todos.

Marcos 7:24-28. El ministerio de Jesús lo lleva otra vez afuera de las fronteras de Israel. Él hace hincapié en ministrar a una que era considerada inferior dado a su estatus de no ser judía. La gracia se extiende a todos sin cualquier distinción.

Lucas 2:32. El Mesías se figura aquí como siendo una expresión de luz y esperanza para todas las naciones, no solamente para los judíos. Este es un mensaje de aceptación, ya que los gentiles son determinados estar bajo las bendiciones, promesas y provisiones de Dios.

Lucas 4:16-20. Los oprimidos (incluyendo a los inmigrantes) eran el objetivo esencial de la proclamación de Jesús en lo tocante a la redención, liberación y libertad. Jesús no se preocupaba con temas de nacionalidad o estatus migratorio, pues el amor de Dios es para todos.

Lucas 4:25-27. Elías había sido enviado para cuidar de una viuda en el exterior, no a una israelita. Naamán, otro extranjero, fue el único leproso que se curó en la historia de Israel. Dios no guardó sus bendiciones en base a la nacionalidad del recipiente.

Lucas 10:33-35. Es el extranjero samaritano quien se paró para ayudar al hombre herido en la parábola. Él es la respuesta a la pregunta, "¿Quién es mi vecino a quien debo amar como a mi mismo?" Desde la perspectiva de Jesús, la nacionalidad no tiene consecuencia en las bendiciones de Dios.

Lucas 17:18. El extranjero es aquél que aquí establece el patrón para dar gracias. Los nativos judíos estaban demasiado involucrados en seguir las exigencias del protocolo. Los samaritanos era considerados inalcanzables por la redención a los ojos de los judíos, pero Jesús no ve ningún impedimento en extenderla a ellos.

Hechos 9:15. Los propósitos de Dios para Pablo incluían enviarle como emisario del evangelio hacia las naciones más allá de los judíos. Él sería tanto un inmigrante, como también un portador del mensaje de esperanza para todas las naciones del mundo.

Hechos 10:45. Fue un choque para los judíos descubrir una validación para que no solamente se compartiera el evangelio a los gentiles, sino que ellos recibieran también la unción del Espíritu Santo. Este carácter de la respiración de Dios fluir en sus vidas era para ellos prueba contundente de que Dios bendecía estos esfuerzos para predicar la gracia ante todas las naciones, sin ninguna distinción.

Hechos 11:1. El mensaje del evangelio siendo predicado por Pedro a personas que aun eran gentiles regresa a Jerusalén. Era una gran crisis para estos creyentes judíos, pues no habían esperado que el evangelio cubriera a poblaciones que no se habían convertidos al judaísmo.

Hechos 11:18. Al escuchar los reportes que los convertidos gentiles habían experimentado la llegada del Espíritu de Dios sobre ellos, estos creyentes judíos fueron silenciados. Ellos estaban incómodos con compartir y la fe en Jesús con los gentiles, pero reconocieron que Dios les llamaba a extenderse más allá de los límites de su comodidad.

Hechos 13:43. Gente judía y no judía quienes se habían convertido, seguían a Pablo. Él sí empezaba su predicación y enseñanza entre los judíos en las ciudades donde enseñaba, pero rápidamente se trasladaba a los gentiles cuando los judíos se enojaron con él. Él les aceptó a los gentiles bajo el evangelio sin reserva alguna.

Hechos 13:46-48. A los judíos que escuchaban a Pablo y Bernabé, no les gustaban que estos misioneros llevaran su mensaje más allá de los límites del judaísmo. Ellos deseaban mantener este mensaje adentro del judaísmo, y no les gustaban que fuera compartido y disponible a cualquiera sin que primero se tornara judío. Los gentiles, entretanto, quedaban entusiasmados al oír y recibir las palabras de Pablo y Bernabé.

Hechos 14:27. Pablo reportaba referente a la expansión del evangelio a las naciones más allá del judaísmo. Esta noticia se recibió bien por muchos, aunque fue un paso muy estruendoso para que la iglesia primitiva lo aceptara. Recibir a gentiles exigiría aceptarles en su medio sin distinción, lo que les era muy incómodo.

Hechos 15:3-23. Pablo y Bernabé regresan aquí hacia Jerusalén para reportar sobre su ministerio entre los gentiles, tanto como para pedir dirección en lo tocante a un conflicto que había surgido a luz de su ministerio. La asamblea en Jerusalén no estaba completamente feliz con los detalles del ministerio entre los gentiles, pero se encontraron obligados a reconocer la presencia y acción de Dios entre esos convertidos quienes no habían adoptado el judaísmo. El resultado final del concilio era que los gentiles no estarían obligados a tornarse judíos, sino que vivieran de acuerdo a la fe y la gracia ofrecidas por Jesucristo que ya les habían cubiertos.

Hechos 17:19-21. A los atenienses y a los inmigrantes residentes, les gustaba escuchar las nuevas ideas presentadas. Pablo les predicó tanto a la población residente, como a los inmigrantes que allí estaban, que distinciones nacionales no hacían diferencia bajo el evangelio.

Hechos 18:6. Pablo se sintió obligado a tomar una posición en contra de algunos judíos que bregaban en contra de su enseñanza. En su respuesta, él comparte abiertamente que su ministerio procederá entre los gentiles, ya que los judíos de la sinagoga no se disponían por aceptar su enseñanza. A ellos no les gustó que él se dirigiera hacia la comunidad gentílica.

Hechos 21:19. Otra vez encontramos a Pablo reportando su ministerio entre otras naciones. Las completas bendiciones y participación en el evangelio se hacían disponibles a todos los grupos nacionales diferentes a lo largo del ministerio de Pablo, todo desde un punto de partida en Dios.

Hechos 21:25. Aquí hay afirmación en la decisión del concilio de Jerusalén en lo tocante a los convertidos gentílicos. A ellos no se les presiona a que se tornen judíos, pero se pide que honren ciertas prescripciones judías en contra de la idolatría, comer sangre y la inmoralidad sexual.

Hechos 22:21. Lucas describe aquí una ocasión en que Pablo narra la historia de su llamado para servirle a Jesús. Él cuenta como Dios le llamó con la misión específica de enviarle a las poblaciones gentílicas alrededor del mundo.

Hechos 26:17. Pablo enfrentaría persecución a lo largo de su ministerio. Esto vendría tanto desde gentiles como de judíos. Dios le protegería, entretanto, a lo largo de su camino, ofreciendo guía y protección en el curso de su ministerio fiel.

Hechos 26:20-23. Pablo narra elementos de su ministerio de llevar el evangelio hacia personas desde muchos lugares y fondos. Él predicó en Damasco, luego alrededor del Imperio Romano, siendo llamado por Dios a predicar tanto a judíos como también a gentiles.

Hechos 28:28. Finalmente en Roma, Pablo tiene la oportunidad de presentar su evangelio otra vez a los judíos. Como ellos rechazan su mensaje, él otra vez regresa a predicar el evangelio de Jesucristo entre aquellos que no son judíos.

Romanos 1:13. Hacia mucho tiempo que había sido el deseo de Pablo predicar en Roma, así como había predicado en muchas otras naciones. Él estaba seguro de que Dios pretendía que el evangelio fuera un mensaje abierto para todos, sin importar las definiciones o identificaciones nacionales.

Romanos 3:29. Pablo recuerda a sus lectores romanos que Dios no es simplemente el Dios de Israel, como si fuera eso un título exclusivo. Dios es también Dios para todas las naciones alrededor del mundo. En lugar de ser propiedad de alguna nación, Dios es soberano sobre todos.

Romanos 9:22-30. El propósito del evangelio es en parte tornarnos justos, específicamente para justificarnos ante Dios en base de la gracia mediante la fe. Esto no viene como alguna iniciativa humana, como si los gentiles hubieron procurado a Dios. Al contrario, esto vino desde la iniciativa de Dios, Dios deseando ofrecer libremente la salvación y redención a todas las naciones del mundo.

Romanos 11:11-13. Pablo aquí argumenta en lo tocante a las distinciones entre los judíos y los gentiles. Él no está listo para considerar que los judíos son basura con cualquier definición más que lo sean los gentiles. El evangelio les vino desde la iniciativa de Dios. Tal contrario, tanto los judíos como los gentiles encuentran aceptación de Dios con la misma base.

Romanos 11:25. Pablo no quiere que los gentiles crean que son más importantes que los judíos, como también no quiere que los judíos piensen ser más importante que los gentiles. La salvación de Dios ha sido ofrecida libremente sin relación a la nacionalidad. Como la salvación es un regalo basado en la gracia, no tiene nada que ver con cualquier categoría humana de ser más digno o de más valor que el otro.

Romanos 12:13. El creyente debe compartir con otros creyentes, tanto cuanto debe invitar a extraños hacia su hogar. El término aquí para la hospitalidad realmente indica el amor hacia el extranjero o desconocido, o sea, el ajeno. El amor del evangelio debe extenderse más allá de las preocupaciones por nacionalidad y hasta las preocupaciones de conocer las personas hacia los cuales ministramos.

Romanos 15:9-18. La salvación de Dios se extendía hacia los gentiles en la misma forma que se había extendido hacia los judíos. Pablo menciona a varios pasajes del Antiguo Testamento que hablan hacia el cuidado de Dios por redimir a personas desde todas las naciones.

Romanos 15:27. Pablo consideró propio que los creyentes gentiles reconocieran su responsabilidad por cuidar por los judíos quienes sufrían aflicción económica dado a un hambre regional. Él une esta responsabilidad a un sentido de una obligación hacia aquellos por medio de los cuales había llegado el mensaje de la salvación de Dios.

Romanos 16:4. Había otros creyentes presentes en Roma quienes habían hecho sacrificios para llevar el evangelio hacia los gentiles. Ellos habían colocado sus vidas en riesgo, así como lo había hecho Pablo, reconociendo junto con él que el evangelio extendía las bendiciones y la provisión de Dios hacia toda categoría de persona.

1ª Corintios 14:21. Dios hablaría por medio de inmigrantes y extranjeros en idiomas desconocidos, pero aun así sería ignorado. Dios estaba listo para utilizar a las personas sin consideración de su nacionalidad, pero la cuestión mayor era si aceptara o no el mensaje y la bendición que Dios les extendía.

2ª Corintios 11:26. Pablo había estado en peligro igualmente desde paisanos que desde extranjeros. Él les predicaba a todos, pero recibió la afronta de la persecución de los judíos y de los gentiles. La nacionalidad no era factor determinante en respuesta a Pablo y el evangelio.

Gálatas 1:16. Dios reveló Jesús a Pablo con el propósito bien específico de que llevara el evangelio hacia los gentiles alrededor del mundo. Esto no era ningún propósito secundario de Dios, sino algo importante lo suficiente para comisionarle a Pablo.

Gálatas 2:2. El ministerio de la predicación de Pablo entre los gentiles no era algo que se escondía de otros creyentes. Él tenía el apoyo de los ancianos de la iglesia en Jerusalén, ante los cuales él había explicado en detalle el mensaje que compartía. Ellos le habían respaldado con su bendición.

Gálatas 2:8-9. El ministerio gentílico de Pablo fue apoyado por varios líderes de la iglesia en Jerusalén. Ellos reconocieron el ministerio de Pedro esencialmente entre los judíos y comprendían a lo de Pablo ser semejante entre los gentiles.

Gálatas 3:8. Pablo recuerda a sus lectores en Gálatas que Dios había hablado del mismo mensaje de salvación por gracia desde los primeros tiempos de Abraham. El mismo modo por el cual Abraham encontró gracia con Dios y salvación es el modo por el cual los gentiles habrían de encontrar la salvación.

Gálatas 3:14. Como Dios le había prometido a Abraham que todas las familias de la tierra serían bendecidas por medio de él, así los gentiles del ministerio de Pablo estaban recibiendo la bendición del Espíritu de Dios derramado en sus vidas.

Efesios 2:11-19. Ante Dios, los efesios ya no eran extranjeros, sino que pertenecían al pueblo de Dios, la familia de Dios. Dios se ocupa de cambiar las categorías de nuestra pertenencia, como somos llamados a pertenecer primeramente y mayormente a Dios y solo secundariamente a alguna nación o entidad política.

Efesios 3:1-8. Dios ha llamado a todas las naciones para que participen igualmente en Jesucristo de la misma herencia. Las distinciones nacionales no tienen realidad desde la perspectiva de Dios. Ellas son categorías de la invención humana a las cuales Dios no da importancia.

Colosenses 1:27. Era la voluntad de Dios ofrecer el evangelio a las naciones. La esperanza de estas buenas nuevas era un mensaje de redención, por la cual Jesucristo viviría en el creyente. Esto era una novedad, desde la perspectiva de los judíos, pero cubría a todos los gentiles quienes aceptarían la ofrenda de Dios para su redención.

1ª Tesalonicenses 2:16. El ministerio de Pablo a los gentiles no era sin oposición seria. Él designaba las acciones de sus opositores como pecado. Ellos no tendrían que responder a Pablo, sino a Dios por colocarse en oposición a los propósitos de Dios para redimir a todos.

1ª Timoteo 2:7. Fue Dios quien había designado a Pablo como predicador y apóstol a los gentiles. Esto no era ninguna posición que él había asumido por su propia iniciativa. De veras, el propio Pablo en conjunto con muchos judíos había luchado en contra de tal mensaje. Al contrario, esta era una iniciativa nueva de Dios que les hacía muy incómodos a muchos.

2ª Timoteo 4:17. Pablo recuerda algo de la persecución que había sufrido para que proclamara el evangelio entre los gentiles. Él había sido rescatado de violencia en contra suya en más de una sola ocasión por la intervención de Dios. Dios aun quería que él cumpliera con ese propósito.

Hebreos 13:2. La hospitalidad debería ser extendida a extraños, aun como algunos héroes de la fe habían hecho en el pasado y así recibieron a mensajeros de Dios como sus huéspedes. Somos convocados a compartir las bendiciones de Dios con todos bajo el concepto que al hacerlo recibimos la plenitud de las bendiciones de Dios.

Se Debe de Tratar a los Inmigrantes con Igualdad
(73 Pasajes)

Uno debería de tratar a los inmigrantes como iguales a los demás.

Podríamos separar esta segunda agrupación de textos de acuerdo a dos temas, el primer referente al tratamiento general debido a los inmigrantes y el segundo referente a las prescripciones legales que una sola ley debería aplicarse igualmente tanto al inmigrante como al nacido en Israel. Muchos des estos textos de veras denotan específicamente estos ideales bíblicos y exigen que todos sean tratados con igualdad, sin referencia a las convenciones nacionales, políticas y sociales. Como un todo, entretanto, un mandamiento para tratar a inmigrantes y extranjeros como uno trataría a un nativo es aun un solo mandamiento que sigue el mismo principio de un tratamiento parejo.

El amor y la gracia de Dios quedan a la disposición de todos, por lo cual somos convocados a trabajar por la igualdad de tratamiento de cualquier y toda persona, sin importar las definiciones sociales. "Pues en Cristo no hay ni esclavo ni libre, ni judío ni no-judío, sino que todos son uno en Cristo." Este es el mismo principio al centro de estos variados pasajes.

Estos textos no simplemente se refieren al hecho que la ley debería tratar a inmigrantes y nativos de forma igual. Ellos se preocupan con lo específico de la aplicación práctica de esto principios, como se puede ver en el conflicto entre los judíos y los samaritanos en los evangelios. Aun así, estos textos son bien claros sobre lo que debería haber sido las actitudes del pueblo escogido de Dios.

Esta segunda agrupación de pasajes bíblicos utilizando terminología para inmigrantes, extranjeros, errantes, naciones o refugiados exige un tratamiento de igualdad para inmigrantes, extranjeros y la población residente de Israel. Hay poco espacio aquí para cualquier sentido de privilegio especial en beneficio de la población residente en contraste al inmigrante. Todos deberían ser aceptados como iguales en respeto tanto a beneficios, como ante las exigencias de la ley.

Este principio queda directamente en contra de la ley romana, como también las leyes de las demás naciones alrededor del Israel Antiguo. En la época de Abraham, cada ciudad tenía sus propias leyes, aunque la norma era que solamente sus ciudadanos encontraban protección por estas mismas leyes. Este mismo concepto se extendía a las entidades políticas mayores que se criaban alrededor de la Palestina en los siglos subsecuentes. Mientras que Israel compartía una definición de la justicia en vista de cómo se trataba a los sin voz, parece haber sido la única nación cuyo código legal defendía un concepto de igualdad.

Génesis 17:3-13. El pacto de Dios incluye que Abram sería el padre de muchas naciones (nacionalidades/etnias). La tierra en la cual él era un inmigrante pertenecería un día a sus descendientes. La regla referente a la circuncisión debería ser aplicada a hijos, esclavos y extranjeros (esclavos o siervos de su séquito), pues una sola ley aplicaría igualmente a todos sin distinción.

Éxodo 12:14-20. El festival central de identidad hebrea (la Pascua) debería ser celebrada por todos como un requisito para la presencia en Israel. Ninguna distinción debería ser hecha en lo tocante al estatus residente de un individuo. Había una sola ley que debería ser aplicada a todos igualmente.

Éxodo 12:43-49. El extranjero no debería participar en comer de la oveja sacrificada, si no hubiera participado en la redención de los hebreos de Egipto. En un sentido, ellos aun quedaban esclavizados con un estatus menor, esperando aun su redención. Si ellos hubieran ingresado a la nación por medio de la circuncisión, ellos serían considerados plenamente parte y deberían participar de forma completa. La única distinción que aquí se concede tiene que ver con la participación personal en el proceso de redención. De otra forma, todos son iguales ante Dios, la nacionalidad en si no tiene ninguna importancia. Los inmigrantes residentes y los israelitas deberían todos obedecer a la misma ley.

Éxodo 20:10. El sábado fue dado como una bendición y descanso hacia los hebreos con base en poder confiar en Yahvé por provisión suficiente para que tomaran un día para descanso. Esta bendición se extendía hacia el inmigrante, quien normalmente no habría esperado gozar de las mismas libertades y bendiciones cómo lo demás de la población. Hay aquí una prohibición en contra de tomar ventaja del inmigrante, tratando a trabajadores como perteneciendo a una clase inferior de persona con derechos reducidos.

Éxodo 22:21. Aquí hay un mandamiento para respetar y no maltratar (oprimir) a refugiados dado a su estatus como inmigrantes. La base para protección otra vez se relaciona a la empatía desde la experiencia hebrea de haber sido oprimidos cómo inmigrantes y extranjeros.

Éxodo 23:9-12. Los refugiados no pueden ser esclavizados u oprimidos por consecuencia de su estatus migratorio. Los trabajadores inmigrantes no podrían ser colocados en una categoría inferior a la de los animales de carga. Ellos deberían recibir la misma categoría de protección y bendición como los residentes nacionales. Mientras que hay reconocimiento que los inmigrantes son blancos naturales para la opresión, ni ellos ni los animales deberían sufrir trabajo forzado más que cualquier persona protegida por pertenecer a la tierra.

Levítico 16:29-31. El mismo mandamiento serviría tanto para el refugiado como para el nativo. Hay exigencias aquí para igualdad de tratamiento, específicamente mencionando a las poblaciones de refugiados inmigrantes.

Levítico 17:8-16. Se hace una distinción entre el vivir en la tierra y pertenecer al pueblo de Dios. No hay ningún sentido por el cual un inmigrante no debería ser dejado participar del pueblo de Dios, pero la conversión debería ocurrir antes que pudiera gozar de plena participación de la alianza. Las protecciones de la alianza aun se extendían así como ciertas exigencias éticas y restricciones que se aplicarían a todos. Debería haber respeto igual ofrecido a Dios. Las preocupaciones de pureza ritual se aplicarían igualmente a todos.

Levítico 18:24-26. Un mandamiento aquí se aplica tanto a inmigrantes como a la nación para que sigan el mismo código de conducta. No hay ninguna distinción hecha en sentido de responsabilidad ante la ley o las exigencias de Dios.

Levítico 19:10. La rebusca (el fruto que queda en el campo luego de la cosecha) en las huertas deberían ser dejada para los pobres, incluyendo a los refugiados inmigrantes. La misericordia no se debería limitar por cuestión del estatus migratorio de uno. Hay un reconocimiento aquí que la provisión de Dios tiene intención de proveer para todos sin distinción.

Levítico 19:33-34. Los refugiados e inmigrantes deberían ser tratados tan bien como cualquier otro miembro de la nación, amados así como cualquier otro con base en una experiencia empática. Como uno desearía ser tratado en la condición de inmigrante o refugiado en otro sitio, así debería de tratar a los demás en su medio.

Levítico 20:2-3. El juicio sobre un inmigrante debería obedecer a las mismas reglas como sobre un nativo. No hay ninguna distinción que hacer. La inferencia es que la tendencia sería de ser permisible hacia el nativo y prejuicioso en contra del inmigrante. Esto queda completamente inaceptable.

Levítico 22:18-25. Aquí se dan mandamientos referentes a sacrificios aceptables que debería aplicarse a todos, sin importar su condición migratoria. Dios específicamente cede espacio para la participación de inmigrantes el la vida cúltica de Israel, aun si no hubieran llegado a participar en la alianza con Yahvé.

Levítico 23:22. La rebusca debería ser dejada para los pobres, incluyendo a los refugiados (inmigrantes). No debería haber distinción en referencia a quienes podrían beneficiar de la rebusca dejada atrás en el campo. La preocupación de Dios es proveer por las necesidades de todos, sin distinción.

Levítico 24:22. Hay no más una ley que debería aplicar igualmente a todos, sea nativo o inmigrante. La ley no debería ser utilizada para oprimir o beneficiar a un grupo arriba de otro grupo, sin dar importancia a preocupaciones sobre ciudadanía o estatus inmigratorio.

Levítico 25:4-7. La cosecha del séptimo año debería ser lo suficiente para cuidar de los esclavos, siervos y refugiados. Estas clases menores de la sociedad deberían recibir los beneficios de la provisión de Dios, así como lo demás de la población.

Levítico 25:35. Un israelita llegando a la pobreza debería ser tratado con la misma misericordia debido a cualquier refugiado. No hay ninguna distinción. Parece un tanto extraño que un inmigrante sería tratado mejor que un pobre nativo, pero lo importante aquí es simplemente la igualdad, sin dar importancia al estatus.

Números 9:14. Los inmigrantes deberían celebrar la pascua en conjunto con todos los israelitas. Hay una sola ley que debería aplicar igualmente a todos. Aunque la Pascua es un festival especial de identificación hebrea con la redención de Dios desde Egipto, todos deberían ser aceptados en la misma base.

Números 15:11-16. Debe haber una sola ley que se aplica igualmente a los nativos y los inmigrantes. Todos deberían ser tratados de acuerdo a la misma medida de valor ante Dios.

Números 15:24-29. Hay una sola ley que se aplica tanto a los nativos e inmigrantes. Ellos deberían encontrar tratamiento igual ante la ley en base de su valor igual ante Dios, y su estatus en la sociedad exigía un grado mayor de protección para ellos.

Números 19:10. Las leyes de pureza ritual deberían aplicar tanto a la sección nativa como la sección inmigrante de la población. Ellos compartían igualmente en la responsabilidad para acercarse a Dios en honor, obediencia y respeto.

Deuteronomio 1:16-18. La ley debería operar con igualdad, demostrando que no había preferencia para rico o pobre, nativo o inmigrante. Todas las clases y categorías de personas deberían ser tratadas de acuerdo a las mismas normas como iguales.

Deuteronomio 5:14. Hasta los inmigrantes deberían participar del día de descanso sabático, en conjunto con los nativos y los animales de carga. Estas bendiciones de descanso garantizadas y decretadas por Yahvé deberían ser compartidas en igualdad.

Deuteronomio 14:27-29. Ofrendas dadas para el cuidado de los levitas en el templo se deberían extender para cuidar de los huérfanos, las viudas y los refugiados (o inmigrantes) de toda la sociedad. No se da espacio para un tratamiento preferencial de cualquier clase de persona.

Deuteronomio 16:9-11. La fiesta de la cosecha debería ser compartida con viudas, huérfanos, levitas y refugiados (inmigrantes). Debería haber una comprensión de igualdad en relación a la provisión de Dios para cubrir las necesidades de todos.

Deuteronomio 16:13-15. La fiesta de tabernáculos debería ser celebrada en la compañía de familias, esclavos, huérfanos, viudas, levitas y refugiados (inmigrantes) Todos deberían ser incluidos como participantes de la comunidad de Israel.

Deuteronomio 24:14-15. Hay aquí una repetición de la regla de igualdad entre los nativos y los inmigrantes. Los pobres, sin respeto a su estatus inmigrante, deberían ser pagados diariamente con la alerta que si hubiera injusticia en este sentido sería respondida por la intervención de Dios.

Deuteronomio 24:17. No se debería maltratar a un inmigrante o a un huérfano, ni pedir el abrigo de una viuda como garantía. El sentido es tanto que los sin voz en la sociedad son los más probables a sufrir abuso, como que ellos deberían de ser aceptados con la misma igualdad de valor que se le ofrece a todos los demás en la sociedad.

Deuteronomio 24:19-22. Se debe dejar la rebusca en el campo para los pobres, los refugiados, los huérfanos y las viudas. La gente debería recordar que eran antes esclavos en Egipto. Las clases más bajas son tanto una parte de la sociedad de Israel como cualquier otra y de valor igual como recipientes de la provisión de Dios.

Deuteronomio 26:11-14. A esta fiesta de acción de gracias, deberían invitar a los sacerdotes y refugiados (inmigrantes) en la tierra. El diezmo de cada tercer año se debería de entregar a los sacerdotes, los refugiados, los huérfanos y las viudas. Esta era una distribución de la provisión de Dios para todos en igualdad.

Deuteronomio 27:14-26. En medio a una lista de maldiciones en contra de aquellos que maltratan a los que carecen de protección, una maldición se anuncia sobre aquellos quienes maltratan a refugiados, viudas y huérfanos. Estos son los más probables a sufrir opresión en cualquier sociedad, pero son aquí designados como gozando de la protección especial de Dios.

Deuteronomio 29:11. Todos fueron congregados para la ratificación de la alianza, incluyendo a los trabajadores inmigrantes quienes eran colocados a trabajo forzado en beneficio de la nación. Ellos deberían disfrutar de las mismas bendiciones de la inclusión y aceptación de Yahvé concedidas a cualquier otro miembro de la comunidad.

Deuteronomio 31:12. Todos deberían celebrar la fiesta, incluyendo a los refugiados (inmigrantes), para que aprendieran a respetar y obedecer a Dios. Las bendiciones de Dios reflejadas en la fiesta deberían ser compartidas con igualdad para todos.

Josué 8:33-35. Los inmigrantes fueron incluidos en la congregación de Israel para la bendición sacerdotal ante el arca de la alianza. Ellos fueron cargados con los mismos términos de obligación, como por los mismos términos de bendición para con todos los demás.

Josué 20:9. Las ciudades de refugio como protección desde la persecución y venganza deberían aplicarse para el beneficio de los inmigrantes, bien como para los nativos. Había solamente una ley que se aplicaba igualmente a todos, aplicando protecciones, así como responsabilidades iguales.

2ª Samuel 22:44-46. David reconoció que Dios le estaba fortaleciendo y respetando más allá de las extensiones del nacionalismo. Las bendiciones y el alcance de Dios incluían a los extranjeros que vivían dentro y fuera de las fronteras de Israel.

1ª Reyes 8:41-43. Salomón pidió a Dios que usara el templo para alcanzar a todas las naciones, a partir de su impacto entre los inmigrantes viviendo dentro de Israel. Todos deberían ser recipientes del conocimiento de Yahvé, como también invitados a participar de las bendiciones de su alianza.

2ª Crónicas 6:32-33. A Dios se le pidió atender a las oraciones de los inmigrantes cuando oraran en el templo, contestándoles para llevarles a la fe en Yahvé hacia todas las naciones. Hay aquí un interés mayor en compartir las bendiciones y alianza entre Yahvé y las demás naciones como gozando de valor igual ante Dios.

2ª Crónicas 30:25. La celebración de la Pascua aquí se extendió por una semana completa, ya que la celebración fue aceptada con regocijo por todos, incluyendo a la población inmigrante. Ellos obviamente fueron invitados a participar, mirándose a sí mismos como habiendo sido redimidos desde la opresión en conjunto con los hebreos.

Ester 4:11-14. Hablando y actuando en beneficio de una nación oprimida es una exigencia de la justicia y de mayor importancia que la autoconservación. El término para extranjero aquí se utiliza en referencia al hecho que todas las naciones del imperio bien sabían de la prohibición para entrar a la corte interior del rey en penalidad de muerte.

Job 29:16. La protección y defensa del pobre e inmigrante aquí se definen como una señal de justicia y rectitud. El estatus inmigratorio es de naturaleza opresiva, pero la justicia real exige una igualdad de tratamiento ante la ley.

Salmo 94:6. La injusticia aquí se trata en relación a matar viudas, asesinar huérfanos y masacrar refugiados (inmigrantes). La justicia clamaría por igualdad de tratamiento y valor concedido a todos sin ninguna distinción de valor.

Isaías 11:12. Dios juntaría a las naciones y los refugiados de Israel y Judá. Hay un sentido aquí que es el deseo de Dios tratar a todas las naciones desde la misma definición de valor. Ya no hay privilegio o consideración especial para la gente escogida.

Isaías 14:1. En ocasión de la restauración de Israel por Dios, muchos inmigrantes vendrían como refugiados a juntarse con la nación. Esto recuerda la formación original de Israel desde los demás esclavos que salieron de Egipto en conjunto con los hebreos, como también la voluntad mayor de Dios para ofrecer redención a todas las naciones sin distinción.

Isaías 14:32. A Dios se le anunciaría como proveyendo refugio para los más pobres de la gente en Jerusalén. Entre los más pobres está siempre la comunidad inmigrante, ya que son generalmente blancos más fáciles para la opresión e injusticia económica y social.

Isaías 56:3, 6-7. Hay una promesa de seguridad para el inmigrante quien viene para adorarle a Yahvé. Dios desea ofrecer seguridad a todos, sin preferencia al residente nativo adelante del inmigrante en la tierra.

Isaías 58:7. La justicia significa proveer comida y refugio, ropa y otras ayudas a cualquiera que esté pasando necesidad. El intento aquí es que se incluya a todo y cualquier sin cualquier referencia a las categorías sociales que se usan para definir el valor del individuo. La razón mayor aquí es simplemente que se identifique la necesidad.

Jeremías 7:3-7. Una porción mayor del arrepentimiento incluye el hacer justicia por los oprimidos, incluyendo a los refugiados (inmigrantes), las viudas y los huérfanos. El arrepentimiento en lo tocante a la opresión implícitamente significa aceptar el hecho que todos son del mismo valor y que nuestra opresión es contraria a los principios de igualdad.

Jeremías 22:3. Las exigencias de Dios referente a la justicia se resumen en cuidar de los oprimidos, los inmigrantes, las viudas, los huérfanos y proteger a los inocentes. El estatus inmigrante es naturalmente opresivo, así como las demás condiciones humanas alistadas aquí. La rectitud, o la justicia, requiere un tratamiento basado en igualdad.

Jeremías 25:20. El juicio de Dios hacia las naciones incluiría a los inmigrantes viviendo en aquellas naciones. Ellos participaban de las bendiciones que recaían sobre las naciones, también como de sus responsabilidades.

Jeremías 46:21. Los soldados mercenarios inmigrantes de Egipto también huirían del juicio de Dios. Dios no discriminaría en sentido de las bendiciones, ni en términos de castigo, ya que los principios de igualdad se aplicaban tanto al bueno como al malo.

Jeremías 50:37. La decaída de Babilonia incluiría la fuga y la muerte de sus soldados mercenarios extranjeros. Ellos eran cómplices en las acciones de Babilonia y responderían igualmente ante Dios como cualquier nativo.

Ezequiel 14:7. Anuncio del juicio de Yahvé incluye a los inmigrantes en la tierra como responsables en conjunto con Israel por desobedecerle a Yahvé y por su participación en la idolatría. La igualdad de tratamiento se refiere tanto a la bendición como a la responsabilidad.

Ezequiel 22:7. La justicia del pueblo encontró expresión en cómo cuidaban por aquellos con menos representación. Esto era una falta y motivo de condenación. Ellos estaban dejando que los sin voz permanecieran desprotegidos, incluyendo a la comunidad inmigrante.

Ezequiel 22:29. La justicia otra vez se define en cómo cuidar de los blancos comunes de la opresión: los pobres, los necesitados y los refugiados inmigrantes. Esto era un refrán común en Israel, como también entre las demás naciones del Antiguo Oriente Medio.

Ezequiel 47:21-22. La distribución de la tierra debería incluir a los inmigrantes, quienes disfrutarían de los mismos derechos y responsabilidades que los israelitas. Debería haber una sola ley que se aplicaría en igualdad a todos, sin distinción con base en el estatus migratorio.

Abadías 16. El juicio de Dios caería sobre todas las naciones, no solamente sobre Israel. Todos deberían responderle a Yahvé, sin dar importancia a su nacionalidad, etnicidad, idioma o cultura. Ante Dios, todos quedaban con la misma responsabilidad, bien como la posibilidad de bendición.

Zacarías 7:10. Se le exigía a la población que cuidara por las viudas, los huérfanos, los pobres y los refugiados en contraste a la maldad. Este refrán se usaba como una regla común por la cual se medía el carácter de la justicia de una nación.

Mateo 4:15. Aquellos en tierras de extranjeros también deberían escuchar al pronunciamiento de Dios en conjunto con Israel. El deseo de Dios era anunciar la redención y la inclusión a todos, sin cualquier distinción entre las naciones.

Mateo 8:10-12. Jesús encontró a un inmigrante cuya fe (confianza) era mayor que la de cualquier otro en Israel. Él declaró que otras naciones serían aceptadas adelante de muchos de Israel en el juicio final. Aquí no hay cuestión de igualdad ante Dios, solo de diferencias en cómo nosotros respondemos al llamado y la aceptación de Dios.

Mateo 15:21-28. Jesús trata con una extranjera, exclamando sobre su fe y utilizándola como un ejemplo que es su voluntad tratar en gracia sin referencia a nacionalidad, estatus, o preocupaciones de pureza ritual. Estos principios de igualdad sobrepasan la nacionalidad o estatus migratorio, incluyendo a las preocupaciones de la pureza ritual religiosa.

Mateo 25:31-46. El juicio de las naciones reflejará como ellos trataron a los hambrientos, los sedientos, los pobres, los desconocidos (inmigrantes o extranjeros), los desabrigados, los enfermos y los encarcelados. Jesús utiliza aquí la definición de justicia en referencia a los sin voz y sin poder en la sociedad. Él refuerza su concordancia con la definición básica de la justicia ser esencialmente el tratar a todos cómo siendo de valor igual.

Mateo 27:7. Se compró un terreno para sepultar a extranjeros o inmigrantes. Aquí existe un sentido de provisión para todos, sin dar importancia a su origen nacional. Los inmigrantes llegando hacia Jerusalén desde toda parte del Imperio Romano era una ocurrencia común, ya que muchos judíos deseaban vivir sus últimos años en Jerusalén, aguardando la llegada del Mesías. La comunidad comprendía una necesidad para proveer por aquellos quienes no podrían costear los arreglos para su propio entierro. Hay aquí un recuerdo de Abraham comprando un terreno para sepultar a Sarah como inmigrante.

Marcos 5:18-20. El ministerio de Jesús se extendía afuera de las fronteras de Israel, aquí enviándole a un hombre en misión a una región de no judíos. No hay ningún respeto aquí por fronteras políticas. El evangelio toma prioridad sobre preocupaciones políticas de fronteras y distinciones relacionadas.

Marcos 7:24-28. El ministerio de Jesús le lleva afuera de las fronteras de Israel, haciendo hincapié por ministrar a una mujer considerada inferior por no ser judía. Jesús enseñó aquí que la gracia alcanza a todos, sin espacio para las distinciones que hacemos entre clases de personas.

Lucas 4:16-20. Los oprimidos (incluyendo a los inmigrantes) eran blancos esenciales para la predicación de Jesús en lo tocante a la redención, la libertad y la liberación. Fueron estos con los cuales Jesús estaba más preocupado por alcanzar con el mensaje de la aceptación de Dios.

Lucas 4:25-27. Elías había sido enviado para cuidar de una viuda extranjera, no una israelita. Naamán, un extranjero había sido el único leproso curado en Israel por Eliseo. Jesús no se preocupaba con el hecho que estas intervenciones de Dios habían sido con extranjeros, pues los ve como de valor igual a cualquier otro en Israel. Él mismo había apenas sanado a un inmigrante, bien conociendo el estatus del hombre.

Lucas 10:33-35. Fue el extranjero samaritano quien se detuvo para ayudar en la parábola. Él es la respuesta a la pregunta, "¿Quién es mi vecino, a quien debería amar como a mí mismo?" Jesús estaba enseñando aquí que todas las personas eran igualmente dignas del amor y la atención de Dios por medio nuestro.

Hechos 13:43. Había convertidos entre judíos y no judíos que seguían a Pablo. Él predicaba y ministraba a judíos y gentiles de forma igual, ya que los consideraba de valor igual ante Dios y Dios le había llamado a ese mismo ministerio.

1ª Corintios 14:21. Dios hablaría por medio de inmigrantes y extranjeros en idiomas desconocido, pero aun sería ignorado. Dios no se preocupaba con consideraciones de nacionalidad, sino con anunciar el evangelio de la redención por medio de la gracia.

2ª Corintios 11:26. Pablo había estado en peligro igual desde paisanos y extranjeros. Como el evangelio era igualmente accesible a todos, sus mensajeros también eran igualmente blancos para la opresión y persecución desde uno y cualquier sitio.

Efesios 2:19. Ante Dios, los efesios ya no eran extranjeros, sino que habían llegado a pertenecer al pueblo de Dios, la familia de Dios. Dios les había incluido en la familia de fe en Cristo, sin atención al hecho de su estatus de extranjeros al judaísmo.

Efesios 3:6. Dios llamó a todas las naciones para que participaran igualmente en Jesucristo de la misma herencia de fe. Dios les ofrecía inclusión en la promesa a y en la alianza con Abraham, aunque ellos no eran de linaje abrahámica.

Los Inmigrantes Son Normalmente Oprimidos
(64 Pasajes)

El estatus de inmigrante hace a uno un blanco natural para la opresión.

Este tercer grupo de pasajes demuestra que el hecho de ser un inmigrante se le hace a uno un blanco natural para la opresión y el abuso. Abraham tenía pocos derechos entre las naciones en medio de los cuales peregrinaba, así cómo los hebreos no tenían muchos derechos en Egipto. La implicación aquí sería que para que se diera tratamiento igual a todos, sería necesario dar atención especial a las poblaciones inmigrantes, ya que la inclinación natural o los procesos de decisión tendrían a trabajar en contra de los intereses de los inmigrantes.

Aunque el libro de Ester casi no contiene términos específicos para inmigrantes y extranjeros, aun así trata con el tema de los judíos encontrándose en exilio y encarando gran oposición y opresión dado a su estatus inmigrante. En su totalidad, el libro llega a ser un ejemplo para la nación en lo que corresponde al tratamiento debido para otros que lleguen a ser inmigrantes en Israel.

En el pasaje de Hechos 6 referente a la elección de diáconos, encontramos que la iglesia primitiva comprendía esta temática del tratamiento desigual entre inmigrantes y nativos. Eran las viudas inmigrantes que estaban siendo pasadas por alto por los creyentes nativos, aunque no fuera intencional. La iglesia optó por seleccionar a creyentes judíos helénicos para supervisar el programa de distribución de comidas, simplemente porque eran ellos quienes estaban más atentos al problema de pasar por alto a ciertas viudas en la distribución diaria de comida. La igualdad es un reto difícil de alcanzar, pues somos predispuestos a maltratar a aquellos quienes son diferentes que nosotros, aunque no tengamos la intención de hacerlo. Más común que no, esto sucede simplemente por una falta de reconocimiento de las necesidades de aquellos de una clase, idioma o cultura diferente que la nuestra.

Génesis 4:12-15. Caín temía que su identidad como errante causaría que cualquiera que le encontrara desearía matarle. Él reconocía que el simple hecho de ser extraño es una condición peligrosa, pero Dios intervino y le ofreció protección, aunque él había recién asesinado a su hermano.

Génesis 15:2-13. Abram empieza el pasaje despreciando el hecho que un extranjero sería heredero de su riqueza. Dios le contesta que tendrá a su propio hijo, pero concluye el pasaje con el alerta que sus descendientes un día serán extranjeros en otra tierra, adonde ellos serían oprimidos.

Génesis 17:3-13. El pacto de Dios con Abram incluía que él sería padre de muchas naciones. La tierra en donde vivía como inmigrante un día le llegaría a pertenecer a sus descendientes. Esta declaración viene como un alerta que no todo le pasaría bien a sus descendientes.

Génesis 23:4. Abraham reconoció a su estatus inmigratorio y en humildad pidió por derechos que se aplicarían normalmente solo a los residentes reconocidos. El statu quo era opresivo, como también era el valor exigido para la venta del terreno, pues sus derechos para negociar eran limitados por su estatus inmigratorio.

Génesis 47:9. Jacob habla de su propia vida como empezando en la categoría de un errante. Hay un sentido en la narrativa de su historia que el vivir como inmigrante le había sido una vida difícil, tal como se esperaría.

Éxodo 20:10. La bendición sabática fue extendida específicamente a los inmigrantes, quienes normalmente no habrían esperado gozar de las mismas libertades y bendiciones que gozaban lo demás de la población. Esta prohibición contra tomar ventaja del inmigrante, tratando a tales trabajadores como perteneciendo a alguna clase inferior con derechos inferiores, viene en reconocimiento que los inmigrantes más naturalmente se encontrarían siendo los blancos para la opresión y gozando de beneficios y protecciones menores.

Éxodo 21:8. Aquí encontramos una protección para las mujeres israelitas en referencia al abuso en manos de un extranjero. Hay pleno reconocimiento que si ella llegara a ser una inmigrante en la tierra natal de su esposo, ella probablemente sufriría por su condición de inmigrante.

Éxodo 22:21. Este es un mandamiento para respetar y no maltratar a los refugiados, de su condición de inmigrante. Como los hebreos habían experimentado opresión inmigrantes en Egipto, así ellos deberían comprender la tendencia natural para oprimir es un abuso que deberían evitar.

Éxodo 23:9. Tenemos aquí una repetición del mandamiento para no oprimir ni esclavizar a los refugiados inmigrantes por causa de la experiencia empática de los hebreos como esclavos. Hay un motivo subyacente aquí de que hay razón para recordarles de forma consistente a no oprimir a los demás.

Levítico 19:33-34. Los refugiados e inmigrantes deberían ser tratados tan bien como los demás miembros de la nación, amados como cualquier otro en base de la experiencia empática. Así como le gustaría a uno ser tratado en la condición de inmigrante o refugiado en otra parte, así mismo se debería tratar a los demás.

Números 32:13. La experiencia israelita de vagar errante por lugares inhabitados aquí se ve como un castigo, ya que la vida de un inmigrante es una vida de dificultad.

Deuteronomio 26:5. "Mi padre fue un arameo errante," es la declaración de identidad y fe más antigua hebrea que se conoce. Esto era una expresión central de los orígenes hebreas como una gente inmigrante. En el contexto aquí, hay una referencia a cómo Dios había cambiado el estatus de la nación, trayendo sobre ellos bendiciones desde sus orígenes humildes y difíciles.

Deuteronomio 28:41-44. Empezando con el versículo 15, encontramos una serie de maldiciones en contra de personas, aunque ellos desobedezcan a Dios. En particular, sus hijos llegarían a ser refugiados e inmigrantes en otras tierras, mientras que los inmigrantes en Israel llegarían a la prosperidad en medio de la pobreza israelita. Este pasaje refleja una comprensión clara de la carga del inmigrante como un blanco fácil para tornarse víctima de la opresión.

Josué 14:10. Caleb habla de los 40 años de errantes en tierras inhabitadas como una experiencia difícil para los hebreos, aunque Dios les había preservado la vida a lo largo de ese período de tiempo difícil.

Jueces 12:4. Los de Galaad aquí son considerados como simples refugiados en Efraím y Manasés. Esto es un retrato despectivo de ellos, lo cual les concede un estatus menor como extraños a la sociedad, aunque son israelitas.

Jueces 17:7. Un levita aquí es clasificado en el texto como un inmigrante en la tierra de Judá. Hay una plena comprensión aquí que su estatus como inmigrante es por naturaleza opresiva, y esto que es un israelita.

Rut 2:10. "Soy sola una inmigrante." Aquí encontramos un reconocimiento de la categoría secundaria que se normalmente atribuye a los inmigrantes. Ella sería blanco fácil para el abuso, como ella no tenía a nadie para hablar de su parte. Ruth es un recuerdo a Israel de las raíces inmigrantes de David, específicamente como un descendiente de Moab.

2ª Samuel 15:20. A Itai se le dice permanecer atrás para que no llegara a ser errante en conjunto de David dentro de Israel, como inmigrante, bien como sin tierra. David comprende que ya le sería difícil vivir como errante en la tierra. Sería mucho peor esa vida para quien también era inmigrante.

2ª Reyes 21:8. Dios promete no colocar a Israel otra vez en la condición de ser una gente errante e inmigrante, si ellos simplemente obedecieran. Hay una comprensión clara aquí que tal condición de inmigrante o errante sería difícil.

2ª Samuel 4:1-4. Se hace aquí una distinción referente a algunos israelitas nativos siendo considerados como inmigrantes en otra parte de la nación. Esta mención subraya la norma de una consideración desigual dada a los inmigrantes.

1ª Crónicas 10:4. Saulo no deseaba morir a manos de extranjeros idólatras por miedo de ser burlado. Era sentido común que la victoria en la batalla venía desde los dioses, no desde la actuación de los soldados. Era también muy esperado que el ejército victorioso no trataría bien a sus opositores, sino como blancos para opresión.

1ª Crónicas 29:15. David menciona su falta de esperanza, semejante a aquella de sus antepasados, quienes vivieron como inmigrantes. Es común o natural para los inmigrantes que vivan en una situación desesperada dado a una norma de opresión.

Job 12:24. El juicio de Dios puede causar que los líderes del mundo se transformen en inmigrantes errantes. La figura aquí es de Dios causando una inversión de fortunas desde una posición de poder hacia una posición de ser impotentes y blancos para la opresión ajena.

Job 15:23. Los inmigrantes, caminando errantes en busca de comida como resultado de sus caminos perversos, pueden transformarse en comida de buitres. La condición de un inmigrante o errante es generalmente una condición difícil, llena de incertidumbre e inseguridad.

Job 38:41. Los niños aquí son descritos como carentes, con la descripción de su caminar sin rumbo en busca de comida. Este es el retrato del cazador-recolector, el errante sin tierra y sin lugar para pertenecer en seguridad.

Salmo 55:7. La experiencia de vagar en lugares desérticos se figura aquí como una vida difícil. Aquí se la utiliza como un ejemplo de gran dificultad contra cual el salmista mide la calamidad que estaba enfrentando en su época.

Salmo 59:15. Los enemigos del pueblo deberían llegar a ser errantes. La condición de un inmigrante es visto aquí como un castigo, ya que es normalmente una existencia difícil y opresiva.

Salmo 107:4, 40. El vagar por lugares desérticos es figurado como opresivo y difícil, pero Dios se muestra listo para rescatar al errante dado a su necesidad. Al final, Dios utiliza la condición de errante como disciplina, ya que es una condición difícil.

Salmo 109:10. Siendo un errante aquí se figura como una condición de castigo para los malvados, ya que les coloca en una situación difícil.

Salmo 119:176. El salmista se retrata aquí como un errante en necesidad de rescate. La condición inmigrante es difícil por hacerle a uno dependiente en las estructuras de poder, las cuales no se diseña para su protección.

Salmo 137:4. Esto es una expresión de dificultad encontrada en adorarle a Dios como inmigrantes bajo opresión. El estatus de inmigrante es naturalmente opresivo, causándole a uno estar inseguro referente a cómo vivir dentro de la sociedad al su entorno.

Isaías 8:21. Los errantes quedarían con hambre, pues la vida de un inmigrante es difícil e incierta. Aquí el tornarse inmigrante es el resultado de una maldición que se hecha sobre los idólatras.

Isaías 17:2. El texto específicamente se refiere al vagar de manadas en las ciudades de Aroer, pero el contexto describe que la población se ha transformado en errantes por otra parte. El ser errante o inmigrantes es secundario a la destrucción de su nación.

Isaías 19:14. El vagar de Egipto aquí se usa como símbolo de la destrucción de Egipto, de haber perdido su camino. Suya es una situación de impotencia, resultado de encontrarse en la condición normal de una comunidad inmigrante.

Isaías 32:20. El ganado aquí son los que están vagando como parte de un retrato mayor de la tranquilidad de la población asentada y viviendo en seguridad. Esto es la antítesis de la realidad normativa para una población inmigrante.

Isaías 63:17. Vagar aquí es un vagar desde los caminos de Yahvé. Es un retrato de cómo vivir contrario a los propósitos de Yahvé es semejante a vivir la vida de un errante vagando en necesidad de seguridad.

Jeremías 2:31. La figura de un errante se utiliza aquí en una ocasión en la cual Dios habla a Israel de estar perdida y descuidada. El inmigrante comúnmente encara gran dificultad para suplir sus necesidades básicas.

Jeremías 5:19. La razón para el exilio era que la población estaba sirviendo a dioses extranjeros, con el resultado de que la nación serviría a naciones extranjeras como una nación inmigrante. Este castigo se basa en la comprensión que vivir como un inmigrante es muy difícil.

Jeremías 22:26-27. Joacím y su madre vivirían el resto de sus días en juicio como inmigrantes deseando regresar a su tierra natal. Ellos serían removidos de su estatus de poder hacia una posición de impotencia y dependencia.

Jeremías 30:7-8. Al final del juicio del exilio, el pueblo de Dios jamás sería oprimido otra vez, esclavizados a extranjeros. Esa es la condición más natural para el inmigrante, el vivir bajo servicio a la población mayoritaria.

Jeremías 31:19-20. El texto habla del vagar errante como distanciarse desde la provisión y protección de Yahvé. Viviendo como inmigrantes, extraños o errantes, le coloca a uno en un estado de mayor necesidad de protección y seguridad.

Jeremías 35:7. Judá debería aprender una lección de fidelidad desde un pueblo errante, inmigrantes quienes eran fieles en no asentarse debido al mandamiento de un ancestral. Este grupo era despreciado, pero Yahvé llamó a Jeremías para que les colocara de ejemplo para la nación de Judá.

Jeremías 50:6. Vagar se contrasta aquí a tener un sitio de descanso, pues se comprende que la vida inmigrante es difícil. Es una vida que por definición es insegura y vulnerable. Descanso costumbra ser un retrato bíblico de recibir y disfrutar las bendiciones de Dios. Aquí el vagar se contrasta a tales bendiciones.

Lamentaciones 4:14-15. El vagar en el exilio fue impuesto a Judá en castigo por su infidelidad. Ellos encontrarían la opresión como compañía natural de la vida del inmigrante.

Lamentaciones 5:2. Se pronuncia un ay, dado al hecho que la tierra y la nación se cayeron en manos extranjeras. Hay una comprensión básica que esto ocasionaría opresión sobre la nación mientras que perdieran su independencia política.

Lamentaciones 5:18. El vagar de los chacales en Sión aquí se contrasta a la población siendo esparcida lejos de Jerusalén en exilio. Al paso que se tornaron inmigrantes en exilio, serían removidos desde la seguridad de su propia tierra.

Ezequiel 7:21-22. Al ser abandonado por Yahvé, la tierra y el templo caerían en manos de ladrones extranjeros. Este retrato habla de una pérdida de seguridad, de opresión pendiente y de la impotencia de la población residente.

Ezequiel 11:9. El juicio caería en manos de extranjeros, dados la libertad de su acción concedida por Dios. Su presencia y poder hablan naturalmente de una expectativa de opresión a ser visitado sobre los israelitas.

Ezequiel 20:32-38. El juicio caería sobre Israel aun en su condición de inmigrantes en exilio. Se esperaba plenamente que su estatus inmigrante diera entrada a una situación de opresión y dolor. El juicio de Yahvé, entretanto, se extendería aun más allá de su experiencia de exilio e inmigración.

Ezequiel 34:6. Israel se figura aquí como un rebaño andando errante sin guía, ni dirección, ni seguridad. Esto habla de la experiencia común de una población inmigrante, pues normalmente se desconoce los patrones de vida de la tierra desconocida.

Oseas 9:17. Vagar entre las naciones en exilio queda retratado aquí como un castigo de Dios sobre la nación. Hay un claro concepto de que vivir como inmigrantes es una experiencia difícil.

Amós 8:12. El pueblo se transformaría en errantes por su necesidad de procurarle a Dios. La categoría de ser desterrados aquí es colocada como una dificultad pendiente, ocasionada por el juicio y en consecuencia de un abandono de Yahvé.

Mateo 17:25-26. Era práctica común obligar a extranjeros a pagar tributo, no a los nativos. El tributo era una categoría de impuesto específico al aceptar la posición de un poder conquistador y la subordinación de la población cuya tierra había sido invadida.

Mateo 18:17. Jesús instruye a los discípulos que ellos deberían hacer todo lo posible para estar reconciliados el uno con el otro. Si la otra parte no aceptara hacer parte de una reconciliación luego de traer otros miembros de la iglesia en medio, entonces deberían tratarle como un ajeno o un gentil. El motivo aquí es que el ajeno es naturalmente tratado como irrelevante. Jesús no estaba tanto condonando tal tratamiento de ajenos, sino notando que aquellos que se recusan a ser reconciliados se aíslan de lo demás de la comunidad creyente, una decisión que debería ser respetada.

Marcos 5:5. El endemoniado de Gadara es descrito como un errante, no teniendo un sitio al cual pertenece. Él ha sido echado fuera de la sociedad, haciéndole falta un sistema de seguridad y apoyo, un blanco fácil para el enojo y la inseguridad de la sociedad a su vuelta.

Juan 8:48. Algunos judíos utilizaron el epíteto de "extranjero indeseado" para Jesús como un insulto. Había amplio reconocimiento que un inmigrante o extranjero tiene un estatus menor que la población residente.

Hechos 7:6. Como inmigrantes, los descendientes de Abraham serían esclavizados y tratados de forma áspera. Esto es una expectativa normal para una población inmigrante, ya que son blancos fáciles sin nadie para pleitear su caso en las estructuras políticas de la sociedad.

Hebreos 11:9. Abraham confiaba lo suficiente en Dios para vivir como inmigrante. Dios le llamaba no simplemente para entrar en un territorio desconocido, sino a una vida de dependencia en Dios en medio de varias estructuras políticas que le tratarían de oprimir.

Hebreos 11:13. La muchedumbre de testigos comprendía que ellos vivían en este mundo en la condición de inmigrantes. Su sentido de pertenecer no podría ser definido de acuerdo a estructuras, sino solamente de acuerdo a la provisión y protección de Dios.

Hebreos 11:38. Se describe la muchedumbre de testigos aquí como errantes sin sitio para nombrar como su hogar. Esta condición se les hacía blancos para la violencia y abuso por las poblaciones residentes.

James 5:19. Vagando de la fe habla de ser distanciado de las modales de Dios, su protección, provisión y de pertenecerle. Esta es una condición vulnerable natural de la condición de las comunidades inmigrantes en todas partes del mundo.

1ª Pedro 1:1-2. Pedro escribía a judíos viviendo como inmigrantes en la dispersión luego de la destrucción de Jerusalén. Él reconoció que vivían como extranjeros en las varias naciones del Imperio Romano en las cuales se encontraban. Ellos no gozaban de las protecciones de vivir dentro los cuidados de sus propias estructuras políticas.

1ª Pedro 2:11-12. Pedro escribía hacia los discípulos como inmigrantes en este mundo. Por implicación, el creyente no es ciudadano de ningún estado político, dado a su lealtad prioritaria al reino de Cristo. Él lleva esto más allá de una condición temporera de los creyentes en la dispersión, considerándolo ser la norma para todos los creyentes, necesitando confiar en Dios a la luz de su condición común de ser recipientes de la opresión y persecución ajena.

1ª Pedro 2:25. El vagar de ovejas se utiliza como símbolo de una población apartándose del camino y la voluntad de Dios, actuando como si ya no pertenecieran a Dios. Hay una conexión aquí entre ser un errante y tener dificultad para suplir sus necesidades.

Recuerdos y Declaraciones que el Pueblo de Dios Ha Comúnmente Sido Inmigrantes
45 Pasajes)

Encontramos muchos textos que sirven de recuerdo que la nación de Israel era una nación inmigrante, y por lo tanto debería tratar a otros con empatía en reconocimiento de su propia historia.

Una sorprendente variedad de textos utilizando términos específicos para referirse a inmigrantes o refugiados (mayormente inmigrantes), trabaja para recordar a la nación que trate a extranjeros como necesitando de justicia de la misma forma que cualquier otro sin voz política en Israel, como a los pobres, las viudas y los huérfanos. El cuidado y la preocupación de Dios para los sin voz y sufriendo opresión es un tema consistente en estos textos. La nación debería cuidar por los inmigrantes sin distinción referente a sus estatus residente. Las bendiciones y la provisión de Dios deberían ser lo suficiente para cuidar las necesidades de todos por igual.

La condición inmigrante en estos pasajes se trata como parte del plan de Dios para los hebreos, la nación de Israel y la iglesia. Como ellos antes eran inmigrantes, los fieles comúnmente serían inmigrantes en otros períodos históricos. Muchos vivirían sus vidas como inmigrantes para cumplir con los propósitos de Dios para sus vidas, como Pablo, Moisés y Abraham. Sus experiencias pasadas y sus expectativas futuras deberían llevarles a tratar a inmigrantes y extraños con cuidado y protección.

Génesis 17:3-13. El pacto de Dios incluye que Abram sería el padre de muchas naciones. La tierra en la cual vivía como inmigrante pertenecería un día a sus descendientes. Ellos a veces vivirían como inmigrantes en otras tierras, conforme a su propia experiencia.

Génesis 20:13-14. Abraham fue enviado por Dios a tornarse un errante en otras tierras. Él debería ser un inmigrante sin un sitio para llamar suyo, dependiendo a lo largo del camino en la dirección, el cuidado, la provisión y la protección de Dios.

Génesis 28:4. La promesa de Dios para pertenecer a la tierra se extiende en esperanza para las generaciones futuras, en conjunto con un recuerdo del estatus inmigrante de los patriarcas. Isaac extiende su preocupación que su hijo Jacob pase más allá de su condición de inmigrante para tornarse reconocido como un residente en la tierra.

Génesis 37:1-2. Este pasaje reconoce y nos recuerda del estatus inmigrante de Jacob (Israel) e Isaac en Canaán. Esto era parte de una serie de recuerdos constantes a Israel que ellos ni siempre habían vivido en la tierra de Israel.

Génesis 37:15. José se encuentra vagando por los campos, aparentemente perdido, aunque de hecho estaba en busca de sus hermanos. El texto aquí parece prefigurar que José sería echado afuera de su propia tierra, transformándose en un inmigrante en tierra ajena.

Génesis 47:9. Jacob habla de su propia vida como la de un errante en una tierra a la cual realmente no pertenecía. Hay un sentido aquí que vivir como un inmigrante es una existencia difícil. Él suspiraba pertenecer a la tierra, reconociendo que el ser un residente es una categoría de experiencia completamente distinta a la suya.

Éxodo 2:22. Moisés reconocía su estatus inmigratorio, habiendo dejado Egipto y viviendo ahora en exilio en la tierra de Madián. Él menciona el ser "solamente un inmigrante," ya que tal estatus le coloca a uno en una categoría de inferioridad, siendo despojado de ciertos derechos pertenecientes a otros.

Éxodo 6:4. Dios recuerda la promesa para hacer de los hebreos dueños de la tierra en donde antes habían sido solamente inmigrantes. Dios estaba cambiando a su condición y estatus, pero al hacerlo ofrecía otro recuerdo de que sus antepasados también habían sido inmigrantes y errantes.

Éxodo 18:1-5. El hijo de Moisés fue nombrado en reconocimiento de que Dios le redimió desde una opresión de inmigrante. Esto hace parte de un pasaje haciendo hincapié para recordarles a los hebreos otra vez de sus orígenes inmigrantes en conjunto con las de sus líderes.

Éxodo 22:21. Aquí hay un mandamiento para respetar y no maltratar (oprimir) a los refugiados dado a su categorización como inmigrantes. La base para la protección es otra vez relacionada a la empatía desde la experiencia hebrea como inmigrantes oprimidos en Egipto.

Éxodo 23:9. Esto es una repetición de un mandamiento para no oprimir o esclavizar a refugiados como inmigrantes. La experiencia hebrea de la esclavitud debería haber provisto razones suficientes para comprender lo que significa ser oprimido como inmigrantes. La empatía debería ser un motivador para no tratar a otros de la misma forma.

Levítico 19:33-34. Los refugiados e inmigrantes deberían ser tratados tan bien como los demás de la nación, amados como a cualquier otro en base de una experiencia empática. Cómo a uno le gustaría de ser tratado en la condición de inmigrante o errante en otro lado, así uno debería tratar a los demás.

Números 32:13. El vagar de los israelitas en lugares desérticos se figura como un castigo desde Dios, ya que la vida de un errante inmigrante es difícil en lo mejor de los tiempos.

Deuteronomio 10:18-19. Dios es misericordioso hacia los huérfanos, las viudas, y los refugiados, quienes son los más vulnerables en la sociedad. Yahvé los coloca como un ejemplo para la gente. También debería de servir como recuerdo de su experiencia de haber vivido como refugiados y después como esclavos en la tierra de Egipto.

Deuteronomio 23:2-4. Se hace aquí una distinción en términos de entrada hacia la parte interior del santuario de Dios. A los inmigrantes, no se les permiten entrar dado a su falta de participar en la alianza. Ciertas naciones son específicamente excluidas por su denegación para ayudar a los hebreos cuando eran inmigrantes errantes.

Deuteronomio 24:19-22. La rebusca debería ser dejada en el campo para el beneficio de los pobres, los refugiados, los huérfanos y las viudas. Recordando que eran esclavos en Egipto debería servir de alerta de la importancia de obedecer al mandamiento referente a la misericordia. Hay un tema subyacente que la tierra pertenece a Yahvé, y la gente podría ser sacado de la tierra por no obedecer a los mandatos de Yahvé referente a cómo deberían tratar a los demás.

Deuteronomio 26:5. "Mi padre fue un arameo errante" es la expresión más antigua conocida de la identidad y fe hebrea. Esto era una expresión central de los orígenes de los hebreos como una nación inmigrante. Debería servir de un recuerdo de las necesidades de inmigrantes como un todo, así como ayuda para que Israel se identificara con el apuro de los inmigrantes en medio suyo.

Deuteronomio 29:16-28. La población fueron inmigrantes en Egipto y luego pasaron a una generación de errantes antes de entrar a la tierra prometida. Dios les había rescatado desde una situación de inmigración y opresión.

Deuteronomio 30:1-5. La nación sería llevada a exilio por abandonar a Yahvé. Solamente después de reconocer y colocar de lado su idolatría serían regresados a la tierra de la promesa a Abraham.

Josué 14:10. Caleb habló de los 40 años de errantes en el desierto como siendo una experiencia difícil para le pueblo hebreo. Dios le había preservado durante ese período de tiempo, tal como Dios continúa deseando tratar en misericordia otros inmigrantes.

Rut 2:10. "Soy solamente una inmigrante." Aquí hay un reconocimiento del estatus secundario normalmente atribuido a los inmigrantes. El estatus inmigrante es por naturaleza opresiva. Rut es un recuerdo a Israel de que el rey David era de origen inmigrante, como los inmigrantes en su medio actual.

2ª Samuel 15:20. A Itai se le dice que se quedara atrás para que no se transformara en un errante en conjunto con David dentro de Israel y a la vez como inmigrante. David comprende que sería difícil lo suficiente su vida de errante como israelita, pero sería aun peor para uno que era también inmigrante.

2ª Reyes 21:8. Dios promete no colocar a Israel otra vez en la condición de ser un pueblo errante e inmigrante, si simplemente a obedecieran. Esto sirve como otro recuerdo de su historia como una nación inmigrante.

1ª Crónicas 29:15. David ora en memoria de sus antepasados siendo extranjeros y extraños, viviendo sin esperanza, aun como él estaba experimentando. Esto sirve para recordar a Israel otra vez de sus orígenes inmigrantes.

Job 1:7. El siervo de Dios aquí ha estado viajando por el mundo como errante, no como alguien que pertenece a un sitio específico. Mientras que la tradición puede figurarle a este siervo como Satanás, el texto le describe como uno de los ministros de Dios, reportando de forma regular conforme su práctica normal.

Job 2:2. El siervo de Dios otra vez se figura como viajando por el mundo como errante, sin pertenecer a ningún sitio. Hay un sentido en que este siervo ve la totalidad del mundo, bien como el hecho de que no pertenece a ningún lugar específico en donde se debería quedar.

Salmo 55:7. La experiencia de vagar en lugares desérticos se ve como una vida difícil. Este vagar de inmigrante aquí se nota como un ejemplo de gran dificultad, contra el cual el salmista mide la calamidad que enfrenta.

Salmo 114:1. Esto es un recuerdo de que Dios trajo el pueblo desde otras tierras donde vivían como inmigrantes. Esto habla de la protección y la provisión de Dios al inmigrante, pero es también un recuerdo de la dificultad que enfrenta el inmigrante en general.

Salmo 119:176. El salmista se clasifica como un errante perdido en necesidad de rescate. Hay amplio reconocimiento aquí que la condición del inmigrante es difícil, pero a la vez que Dios se preocupa por el inmigrante, así como lo debería el israelita.

Salmo 137:4. Esta es una expresión de la dificultad para adorarle a Dios en celebración como inmigrantes bajo opresión. El estatus de inmigrante es por naturaleza opresiva y esto se extiende a cuestiones de servicio y culto a Dios.

Isaías 11:12. Dios reuniría a las naciones y refugiados de Israel y Judá dondequiera que estuvieran. Esto es un reconocimiento que una vez más en exilio la gente viviría como inmigrantes, pero que Dios les prometía otra inversión de sus fortunas cuando estuvieran listos para asumir sus responsabilidades bajo la alianza con Yahvé.

Isaías 17:2. El texto se refiere específicamente al vagar de los rebaños en las ciudades de Aroer. En la situación, entretanto, la población residente se había transformado en errantes en otros sitios. Que ellos habían llegados a ser errantes o inmigrantes fue resultado de la destrucción política de su nación.

Isaías 52:3-12. La gente había pasado una temporada en Egipto, pero más tarde habían sido vendidos libremente a Asiria en exilio. Dios les regresaría, entretanto, a una nueva realidad de libertad. Dios volcaría su condición de inmigrantes, esclavos y oprimidos en una nueva condición de libertad.

Isaías 63:11-14. El vagar de los israelitas en el desierto fue bajo los cuidados y la provisión de Dios. Yahvé proveía por sus necesidades. Mientras que era un tiempo de conflicto y ansiedad, Dios aplacaba las condiciones adversas de la experiencia errante.

Hechos 7:6. Como inmigrantes, los descendientes de Abraham deberían esperar ser esclavizados y tratados de forma cruel. Esto viene siendo un alerta desde Génesis que Esteban retocó como un tema plenamente reconocido en el Israel de su propia época.

Hechos 7:29. Esteban recuerda a sus oyentes que Moisés había vivido como un inmigrante en la tierra de Madián. Él estaba utilizando este tema para llegar a la declaración de que Jesús era la manifestación de Dios más allá de los símbolos nacionales del templo.

2ª Corintios 11:26. Pablo había enfrentado peligro de paisanos como también de extranjeros. Parte de este peligro se debía a que vivía como inmigrante y errante en la extensión del Imperio Romano. Era lo suficiente común para él encarar opresión como un inmigrante en medio de otros inmigrantes.

Hebreos 11:9. Abraham confiaba lo suficiente en Dios para vivir como un inmigrante. Esto era una vida con un grado menos de seguridad, en la cual tendría que depender más completamente en Dios que en las estructuras políticas humanas. El recuerdo aquí sirve para enfatizar el carácter inmigrante de los fieles a lo largo de los siglos.

Hebreos 11:13. La muchedumbre de testigos comprendía que vivían en el mundo con un estatus de inmigrante. Ellos eran inmigrantes políticamente, pero también en el sentido de no pertenecer realmente al orden de este mundo.

Hebreos 11:38. Esa muchedumbre de testigos se describe aquí como errante sin sitio para llamar suyo. Este tema de ser errantes sin tierra sirve como recuerdo para la nueva generación de creyentes sin tierra de sus orígenes de fe.

Santiago 5:19. Vagar de la fe habla de ser distanciados de los caminos de Dios, su protección, provisión y un pertenecerle a Dios. Habla de ser necesitado y a la responsabilidad de los fieles para cuidar de los demás sufriendo la misma situación.

1ª Pedro 1:1-2. Pedro estaba escribiendo a judíos viviendo como inmigrantes en la dispersión. Ellos habían sido obligados a salir de su tierra como en exilio más una vez. En esta ocasión, entretanto, hay un sentido de que su futuro será continuamente en la categoría de errantes sin tierra.

1ª Pedro 2:11-12. Pedro estaba hablando a discípulos como inmigrantes en este mundo, no simplemente en una tierra en particular. Por implicación de sus palabras, el creyente no es ciudadano de ningún estado político, dado a su lealtad prioritaria al reinado de Cristo.

1ª Pedro 2:25. El vagar de ovejas se utiliza aquí como símbolo del pueblo desencaminarse del plan y la voluntad de Dios, actuando como si ya no perteneciera a Dios. Hay aquí una conexión entre el ser errante y encarar dificultades para llenar sus propias necesidades.

Inmigrantes, Refugiados, Pobres, Viudas, Huérfanos y Extraños Son Todos Una Sola Clase
(42 Pasajes)

Estos pasajes hacen iguales a los inmigrantes, las viudas, los pobres, los huérfanos, los extraños, los errantes y los extranjeros, colocándoles en una misma categoría como necesitados, sin voz y desprotegidos.

Estos pasajes aquí mencionados no incluyen otros textos semejantes que utilizan otras listas omitiendo términos para inmigrantes, extranjeros o refugiados. Si todos esos pasajes fueran incluidos, la lista crecería hasta 56 pasajes. Estos otros textos, entretanto, bien podrían ser considerados para ser agregados con estos, pues probablemente deberíamos verlos como formas abreviadas de una misma fórmula básica. Estos pasajes son básicamente referencias a los sin voz o sin poder en cualquier sociedad. La expresión más completa de estas listas de los vulnerables incluiría a refugiados, inmigrantes, pobres, viudas, huérfanos, enfermos, leprosos, ciegos, esclavos, sin hogar, errantes, viajeros, desconocidos, cautivos, prisioneros, hambrientos, sedientos, estériles y hasta los muribundos. En algunos casos, listas cómo estas incluyen a los levitas y sacerdotes, ya que ellos no recibieron una porción de la tierra como el resto de Israel. Eso era razón suficiente para considerarles vulnerables, ya que vivían a la misericordia de la fidelidad de otros.

No hay ningún texto, entretanto que incluye esta lista completa de los sin voz, vulnerables e impotentes. Hay, entretanto, varias versiones más cortas de este tema. La versión más común que parece ser repetida sin los demás componentes es de viudas y huérfanos. Alternado a estas designaciones son los pobres y extraños (desconocidos). Dado a que tan repetidas veces son incluidos en el contexto con inmigrantes y otros grupos oprimidos, parece bien probable que deberíamos aplicar el concepto de vulnerable o sin voz a la mayor parte de los textos que realzan estos términos. Esencialmente todos de estos pasajes extienden preocupaciones acerca de los maltratos que recibían estos grupos variados de gente vulnerable.

Génesis 17:3-13. El pacto de Dios incluye que Abram sería el padre de muchas naciones. La tierra en la cual vivía pertenecería a sus descendientes. En el pacto de la circuncisión, entretanto, se incluiría además de sus descendientes biológicos. Incluiría a sus esclavos y a los extranjeros, no haciendo ninguna distinción entre ellos. Serían incluidos en la misma categoría que los descendientes de Abram y con ellos serían recipientes de las bendiciones prometidas por Dios. Aquí los esclavos y extranjeros (inmigrantes) son vistos como de una sola categoría, pero esa se coloca del lado de los descendientes legítimos de Abram, sin hacer distinción.

Éxodo 12:14-20. El festival central de identidad hebrea (Pascua) debería ser celebrado por todos como una exigencia para su presencia en Israel. Ninguna distinción debería ser hecha referente al estatus residente de un individuo. Había una sola ley que debería ser aplicada igualmente a todos.

Éxodo 12:43-49. El extranjero no debería participar en comer del cordero pascual si no hubiera participado en la redención de los hebreos de Egipto por aceptar el pacto con Dios. En un sentido, ellos quedaban esclavizados con un estatus reducido, aguardando la redención. Si ellos habían sido ingresados a ser parte del pueblo por medio de la circuncisión, ellos también eran considerados parte de la gente y deberían participar completamente. La única distinción que se permite aquí tiene que ver con la participación plena de uno en el proceso de redención. De otra forma, todos eran iguales ante Dios, la nacionalidad siendo ignorable. Los inmigrantes y residentes deberían obedecer a la ley igualmente.

Éxodo 20:10. El sábado fue dado como una bendición y descanso para los hebreos con base en que podían confiar en Yahvé por provisión suficiente para que tomaran un día de descanso. Esta bendición debería extenderse al inmigrante, quien normalmente no gozaría de las mismas libertades y bendiciones que los demás de la población. Hay una prohibición en contra de tomar ventaja de los inmigrantes, por tratar a tales trabajadores como perteneciendo a una clase inferior de personas con menos derechos.

Éxodo 22:21-25. Los extranjeros, las viudas, los huérfanos y los pobres son mencionados en una serie de versículos referente a las protecciones legales para los más susceptibles al abuso. Ellos son todos tratados como siendo de una sola categoría.

Éxodo 23:6-9. En una sección de leyes referentes a la equidad, los extranjeros y los pobres son colocados lado a lado como participando de una misma clase como los más vulnerables. Es esta vulnerabilidad que queda por detrás de la necesidad en que se basan estas mismas leyes.

Éxodo 23:11-12. Las leyes del sábado aquí tienen la intención de beneficiar a los pobres, los esclavos y los extranjeros, bien como lo demás de Israel. Estos grupos específicos son mencionados aquí por causa de la tendencia de arrojarles lejos de la provisión de Dios.

Levítico 19:10. La rebusca debería ser dejada para los pobres, incluyendo a los refugiados inmigrantes. La misericordia no se debería limitar por el estatus inmigrante, sino que se aplica específicamente a todos cuyas situaciones de vida les hace vulnerable y carientes de misericordia.

Levítico 19:33-34. Los refugiados e inmigrantes deberían ser tratados tan bien como a cualquier miembro de la nación, amado como a cualquier otro en base de la experiencia empática. Así como uno desearía ser tratado bajo la condición de ser inmigrante en otra parte, así mismo se debería tratar a otros.

Levítico 23:22. La rebusca debería ser dejada para los más vulnerables de la sociedad, tanto los pobres como los inmigrantes o refugiados. Todos ellos son de una sola categoría y carientes de esta provisión y protección debido a su estado de no tener tierra.

Levítico 25:4-7. Dios haría que la cosecha no plantada del séptimo año fuera lo suficiente hasta para cuidar de los esclavos, siervos, y refugiados inmigrantes. Estas son las personas que normalmente serían los menos capaces de proveer para su futuro.

Levítico 25:35. Los pobres e inmigrantes ambos deberían encontrar ayuda económica desde la comunidad de Israel. En este texto, son los pobres de Israel que son realzados, ya que se presume aquí que la nación sabe cuidar de la población inmigrante.

Deuteronomio 1:16-18. La ley debería operar con igualdad, demostrando ninguna preferencia para rico o pobre, nativo o inmigrante. Estas distinciones sociales no sirven ningún propósito real, a no ser para hacer vulnerables a las poblaciones pobres e inmigrantes, en contraste a las exigencias de la ley.

Deuteronomio 10:18-19. Dios es misericordioso hacia huérfanos, viudas y refugiados, colocando un ejemplo ante la nación al recordarles de su vida como refugiados en Egipto. Cada una de estas categorías simplemente reflejar un grupo con un grado menor de voz y poder.

Deuteronomio 14:27-29. Ofrendas para cuidar de los levitas deberían extenderse para cuidar de los huérfanos, las viudas y los refugiados. En este pasaje, es notable que los levitas fueron también clasificados como vulnerables, dado a que no eran participantes en la distribución de la tierra.

Deuteronomio 16:9-11. El festival de la cosecha debería ser compartido con las viudas, los huérfanos, los levitas y los refugiados. Se comprende que la tierra se le pertenece a Yahvé, así como la producción de la tierra. Su abundancia debería ser compartida, por lo tanto, con todos los miembros de la sociedad, incluyendo a la comunidad inmigrante.

Deuteronomio 16:13-15. La fiesta de tabernáculos debería ser celebrada en la compañía de familias, esclavos, huérfanos, viudas, levitas y refugiados. Hay una expansión aquí en la lista que hemos visto de los vulnerables de la sociedad.

Deuteronomio 24:14-15. Aquí hay otro caso de la ley para cuidar los más vulnerables de la sociedad. Los pobres deberían ser pagados diariamente con la alerta que cualquier injusticia en referente a esto sería respondida por la intervención de Dios.

Deuteronomio 24:17. No maltrate a un refugiado o a un huérfano, ni tome el abrigo de una viuda como garantía de un préstamo. Estos tienen necesidades más obvias que carecen de protección mayor por la sociedad al su alrededor, pues no tiene la misma voz que gozan los demás.

Deuteronomio 24:19-22. La rebusca debería ser dejada en los campos para beneficio de los vulnerables: los pobres, los refugiados inmigrantes, los huérfanos y las viudas. Recordando que los hebreos habían sido esclavos debería servir de razón suficiente para tener empatía con los más vulnerables de la sociedad.

Deuteronomio 26:11-14. A esta fiesta de acción de gracias, la gente debería invitar a los sacerdotes, los refugiados, los huérfanos y las viudas. Es interesante notar que esta palabra fue dirigida a la porción de la sociedad que era dueño de tierras, y por lo tanto daba la fiesta para los sin tierra.

Deuteronomio 27:14-26. En medio de una lista de maldiciones en contra de aquellos que maltrataban a los que carecían de protección, se declara una maldición sobre quienes maltratan a refugiados inmigrantes, viudas y huérfanos. Son estos los que pueden menos contar con alguien para tomar su parte.

Deuteronomio 31:12. Todos deberían celebrar la fiesta por cancelar deudas, incluyendo las deudas de los refugiados inmigrantes. Al participar, deberían todos aprender a respetar y obedecer a Yahvé, reconociendo sus propias deudas por causa de la preocupación de Yahvé para con ellos y para con los demás de los vulnerables.

Job 29:11-16. La protección y defensa del pobre y del inmigrante es una señal de justicia y rectitud. Tanto los pobres como la comunidad inmigrante quedan entre estos más vulnerables a la injusticia.

Job 31:16-32. Job habla de su justicia, incluyendo a sus acciones para beneficiar a los pobres, las viudas, los huérfanos y los desconocidos. Esto era una definición común para medir a la justicia personal, la cual se extendía más allá de Israel entre las demás naciones de su entorno.

Salmo 94:6. La injusticia aquí se retrata como matar a viudas, asesinar a huérfanos y masacrar a refugiados. Ellos son colocados lado a lado como de una sola clase, dado a su vulnerabilidad ante lo demás de la sociedad.

Salmo 109:9-16. Los inicuos aquí son maldecidos con una serie de crisis en la vida que hace semejantes a huérfanos, viudas, inmigrantes y pobres, como de una misma clase. Nadie desea tornarse miembro de ninguna de estas categorías, ya que son condiciones de vida difíciles.

Salmo 146:7-9. Dios es descrito como cuidando por los prisioneros, los ciegos, los perturbados, los extranjeros, los huérfanos y las viudas. Esta lista no se debería considerar como completa, sino como representativa de todos los que se encuentran vulnerables aparte de la protección de Dios.

Isaías 14:32. A Dios se le anunciará como proveyendo refugio para los más pobres de Jerusalén. Esta es una declaración del carácter de la justicia y la rectitud de Dios. El carácter de Dios se define por sus cuidados en beneficio de los vulnerables y los privados de sus derechos.

Isaías 58:7. La justicia se define como proveyendo comida, refugio, ropa y otras ayudas. La preocupación aquí no es con lo que nosotros generalmente definimos como la moralidad, sino que se enfoca más en preocupaciones de justicia material, por medio del cual las necesidades de los más vulnerables se atienden.

Jeremías 7:3-7. La mayor parte del arrepentimiento es hacer justicia en beneficio de los oprimidos, incluyendo a los refugiados, las viudas y los huérfanos. Deberíamos leer esto como aplicando a otros quienes comparten su mismo estatus de vulnerabilidad. Este enfoque material de la definición de justicia es normal para los textos proféticos en Israel y en su entorno.

Jeremías 22:3. Las exigencias de Dios para juicio se resumen en cuidar de los oprimidos, los inmigrantes, los huérfanos, las viudas y proteger a los inocentes. El estatus inmigrante de uno le coloca en la misma categoría de carecer protección así como las viudas, los huérfanos y los pobres.

Lamentaciones 5:2-3. Siendo inmigrantes, viudas, huérfanos o sin casa hace a todos iguales como aspectos relacionados de una condición de vulnerabilidad. Entregando la tierra hacia extranjeros es equivalente a vivir como inmigrantes en una tierra ajena, dado a la tendencia humana hacia la opresión.

Ezequiel 22:7. La justicia del pueblo encontraba expresión en su cuidado por aquellos con la menor representación. En Israel, esto estaba faltando y era digno de condenación. Ellos bien conocían sus responsabilidades para con estas clases serviles, pero las ignoraban.

Ezequiel 22:25. El tratamiento de extranjeros, viudas y pobres se trata como siendo del mismo carácter. El asunto importante es la vulnerabilidad de estos grupos quienes no eran representados por las estructuras políticas.

Ezequiel 22:29. La justicia se define otra vez como cuidando de los blancos comunes de la opresión: los pobres, necesitados y refugiados inmigrantes. Esto es un motivo mucho mayor de definir la justicia que los énfasis actuales que se colocan en la moralidad sexual.

Zacarías 7:10. El pueblo fue clamado a cuidar de las viudas, los huérfanos, los pobres y los refugiados como un contrapunto a la maldad. La situación histórica de la gente bregando por sobrevivencia debería hacer esto un motivo comprensible. Su propia existencia dependía en la ayuda ajena.

Malaquías 3:5. Hacer trampa contra trabajadores, viudas, huérfanos e inmigrantes se relaciona a la brujería, el adulterio y el mentir bajo juramento. Desde la perspectiva de Malaquías, el cuidado de los menos servidos es el asunto más importante en definir la justicia.

Mateo 25:31-46. El juicio de las naciones reflejará como ellos trataron a los pobres, los extraños (inmigrantes/extranjeros), los prisioneros y los enfermos. Lo que hacemos en referencia a cuidar de los vulnerables importa y Jesús pone esta categoría de juicio en un plano más elevado que la moralidad sexual. Su definición tiene que ver con la forma que tratamos a los demás, no en referencia a la cualidad de nuestras acciones que tienen que ver con nuestro cuidado propio.

Lucas 4:16-20. Los oprimidos (incluyendo a inmigrantes) eran los blancos esenciales de la predicación de Jesús sobre la redención, libertad y liberación. Vemos esto en el ministerio diario de Jesús, pero también en textos como este en el cual él utiliza sus esfuerzos para cuidar por otros como características definidoras de su ministerio e identidad.

Lucas 4:25-27. Elías fue enviado para cuidar y estar bajo los cuidados de una viuda extranjera, no a una israelita. Naamán, un extranjero, fue el único leproso curado en Israel. Jesús coloca que Dios no hace las distinciones de valor entre personas de acuerdo con su nacionalidad. Más bien, él se dirige a todos de acuerdo a sus necesidades. Es esto que les une en recibir la atención de Dios.

Lucas 10:33-35. Es el extranjero samaritano quien se detiene con motivo de ayudar al desconocido en la parábola. Él es la respuesta a la pregunta, "¿Quién es mi vecino a quien debería amar como a mi mismo?" Vecino aquí se iguala con cualquiera que pudiera estar en necesidad, sin espacio para las distinciones que naturalmente haríamos.

Los Extranjeros y la Condición Inmigrante Son Relacionados al Juicio o Castigo de Dios
(40 Pasajes)

Estos textos conectan una condición inmigrante o errante al juicio de Dios sobre una cierta población.

Semejante a las palabras de Jesús referente a Tiro, Sidón, Corazín y Betsaida, estos pasajes mencionan a inmigrantes o naciones extranjeras como tomando la posición de acusadores de Israel, dado a la infidelidad de Israel para con Yahvé. De hecho, ellos retratan que el pueblo escogido comúnmente se apoyaba en su genealogía, mientras que no seguían las exigencias de la alianza con Yahvé.

Estos textos son un llamado a la fidelidad como la única medida real de estar bien con Dios. No hay ninguna superioridad inherente a pertenecer a alguna nación en particular. Lo que aparentemente es la única señal de valor para consideración ante Dios es cómo nos tratamos uno al otro. Eso no quiere decir que no hay nada más que decir referente a la salvación, pero que lo que importa en estos textos es que se responda fielmente a Dios en contraste a reclamar pertenecer al pueblo escogido llamado por el nombre de Dios.

Números 32:13. El vagar en el desierto por los israelitas se ve como un castigo, dado a que no se disponían a confiar en Dios. En este caso, es también un caso de ser la voluntad de Dios llevarles hacia la tierra prometida a Abraham, mientras que ellos no estaban dispuestos a cruzar hacia la tierra por miedo de la población residente.

Deuteronomio 28:41-68. Empezando con el versículo 15, encontramos una serie de maldiciones en contra de la nación, caso desobedeciera a Dios. En particular, sus hijos llegarían a ser refugiados e inmigrantes en otras tierras, mientras que los inmigrantes en Israel llegarían a ser ricos en contraste a la pobreza israelita. Este pasaje refleja la comprensión clara de su apuro como víctimas fáciles para la opresión de sociedades de otras culturas, idiomas y etnias. La masa de este pasaje habla de castigo, sea por exilio o por la ocupación de fuerzas extranjeras.

Deuteronomio 29:22-28. Los inmigrantes y otras naciones serían testigos del juicio de Dios en caso de que Israel se desviara de seguirle a Yahvé en fidelidad. La gente sufriría aflicción económica que sería claramente visible a todos, llevándoles también al exilio.

Deuteronomio 30:1-5. Dios regresaría a Israel desde el exilio, restaurándole a la tierra después que cayeran en sí por su opresión como inmigrantes. La experiencia de exilio sería el resultado de vivir en contra de sus responsabilidades en la alianza con Dios.

Josué 14:10. Caleb habla de sus 40 años de vagar errante como una experiencia difícil para los hebreos, aunque Dios le preservó a lo largo de ese período de tiempo. Él estaba listo para dejar atrás ese período de disciplina hacia la abundancia de Dios.

2ª Reyes 21:8. Dios promete no colocar Israel otra vez en la condición de una nación inmigrante y errante, si simplemente obedecieran. El rey de Israel estaba, entretanto, indispuesto a seguirle a Yahvé en fidelidad.

Job 12:24. En medio a una serie de comentarios referentes a varias formas que puede tomar el juicio de Dios, Job menciona que Dios puede causar que líderes del mundo se tornen en inmigrantes errantes por su infidelidad.

Job 15:23. Uno de los amigos de Job argumenta que los inmigrantes errantes en búsca de comida lo hacen como resultado de juicio por sus caminos perversos. Pueda que ellos también se transformen en comida para buitres. El sentido aquí es que es una vida difícil que se puede utilizar como castigo. Aunque Elifaz, amigo de Job, se revelará al final estar argumentando en contra de las posiciones de Dios, hay que reconocer que en ciertos casos esto sí ocurre.

Salmo 59:15. Los enemigos del pueblo se transformarían en errantes. La condición de ser inmigrante se ve como castigo de Dios. El contexto declara que en su estatus inmigrante ellos podrían aprender dependencia en Yahvé

Salmo 107:4, 40. Vagando errante es categorizado como opresivo y difícil, pero se coloca a Dios como listo a rescatar al errante por su necesidad. Al final de cuentas, Dios utiliza la condición de errante como castigo para los impíos.

Salmo 109:10. Siendo un errante es otra vez visto como una condición de castigo sobre los impíos. La condición aquí figura como parte de una lista de maldiciones en contra de los malvados, cada una colocándoles en una posición al mínimo vulnerable.

Isaías 8:21. Los errantes pasarán hambre, pues la vida de un inmigrante es difícil e incierta. Este pasaje hace parte de una advertencia de una calamidad inminente que vendría sobre Israel en castigo por su infidelidad al andar atrás de ídolos y hasta la brujería.

Isaías 17:2. El texto específicamente se refiere al vagar de manadas por las ciudades de Aroer, pero en el contexto su población se ha transformado en errantes en otra parte. Tornándose errantes o inmigrantes fue subsecuente a la destrucción de su nación como respuesta de Dios a su infidelidad.

Isaías 19:14. El vagar errante de Egipto es un símbolo de destrucción, de haber perdido su camino. Es una situación de impotencia, como es también la norma de una comunidad inmigrante, aquí como resultado de la intervención de Yahvé.

Isaías 63:17. El vagar aquí es desde los caminos de Yahvé, un retrato de cómo vivir contrario a Yahvé es semejante a vivir la vida de un errante careciendo de seguridad. El vagar era su propio castigo por desencaminarse desde los patrones de Yahvé para la vida.

Jeremías 5:9-19. La razón para el exilio era que la nación estaba sirviendo a dioses extranjeros, por el cual deberían servir a naciones extranjeras como una nación inmigrante. Ellos tendrían una vida difícil en respuesta a su abandono de Yahvé.

Jeremías 22:26-27. Joachim y su madre vivirían sus días en juicio como inmigrantes deseando regresar a su tierra natal. Ellos no habían seguido las exigencias de Dios, las cuales les habrían capacitado a permanecer en su tierra.

Jeremías 30:1-9. Al final del juicio del exilio, el pueblo de Dios jamás sería oprimido otra vez en esclavitud a extranjeros. Suya sería una experiencia difícil de opresión, pero Dios escucharía su llanto y actuaría en redención.

Jeremías 35:7. Judá debería aprender una lección de fidelidad desde una gente errante, inmigrantes quienes era fieles en no asentarse en la tierra de acuerdo al mandamiento de un ancestral. Este era un grupo despreciado a quien Yahvé llamó a Jeremías para aprovechar como ejemplo de fidelidad para Judá.

Lamentaciones 4:12-22. El vagar en el exilio fue impuesto sobre Judá en castigo por su infidelidad. Yahvé les esparcía en su juicio a que caminaran en conformidad a su ceguera. Esto serviría de una señal más que simplemente para Israel; sería un mensaje de juicio que todas las naciones alrededor del mundo comprenderían.

Lamentaciones 5:2-22. El profeta aquí lamenta que la tierra y la nación habían caído en manos extranjeras. La situación de la nación era severa, pero la esperanza aun se depositaba en la vindicación de Yahvé luego de este período de disciplina desesperadra.

Ezequiel 7:21-27. Al abandono de Yahvé, la tierra y el templo deberían caer en manos de ladrones extranjeros. Esta reversión de fortunas para Israel sería en reembolso por la forma que ellos se habían negado de cuidar por los demás.

Ezequiel 11:7-12. El juicio caería en manos de extranjeros concedidos por una libertad de acción de Dios. Este juicio incluiría enviar a Israel hacia sus fronteras como castigo. Extraños y extranjeros serían las herramientas por las cuales Yahvé ejecutaría este juicio.

Ezequiel 20:32-38. El juicio le caería sobre Israel mientras que eran aun inmigrantes en exilio. Su condición de inmigrante se relacionaba con el juicio de Dios, aun cuando se esperaba que ese juicio se extendiera más allá de su exilio inmigrante.

Amós 8:2-14. En medio a esta serie de descripciones del juicio de Dios sobre la nación, encontramos una referencia específica hacia su transformación en una gente errante. Su situación inmigrante se ve conectado al juicio por abandonar a las instrucciones de Dios.

Oseas 9:17. El pronunciamiento de juicio sobre Israel culmina aquí en hacerles errantes entre las naciones. Esto es solamente algo extra entre las demás descripciones del juicio en contra de la nación.

Mateo 5:47. La relación aquí entre extranjeros y el juicio gira en su exhibición de un patrón semejante a las acciones justas de los judíos. La rectitud de aquellos quienes pertenecen a Dios debería ser mayor que aquellos a quienes no le pertenecen.

Mateo 6:7. Jesús utiliza la figura de los gentiles quienes no conocen a Dios en contraste al modo por el cual aquellos que conocen a Dios deberían orar. El tema de juicio aquí es uno de comparación entre aquellos a quienes conocen y los que no conocen a Dios.

Mateo 6:32. Otra vez, Jesús utiliza a los gentiles en comparación con las prácticas normales de los judíos. Él ve que no hay nada de especial en la práctica judía, ya que su práctica se ve demasiado coherente con las normas religiosas de los gentiles, y no llega a sobrepasarlos.

Mateo 8:10-12. Jesús encuentra a un inmigrante cuya fe (confianza) es mayor que lo que encuentra en Israel. Otras naciones serán aceptadas en el día final antes que el propio Israel. Otros serán aceptados en la base de su fe en Dios, mientras que muchos en Israel quedarán infieles.

Mateo 15:21-28. Jesús trata con una extranjera, exaltando sobre su fe y utilizándola como un ejemplo de que es la voluntad de Dios tratar en gracia sin referencia a nacionalidad, estatus social o preocupaciones de pureza ritual que eran tan importantes para los judíos.

Mateo 20:19. Aquí Jesús anticipa ser entregado a los gentiles en liga con líderes judíos para efectuar su venganza sobre él. Esto no es un aspecto del castigo de Dios, pero sí es el juicio de Dios tanto sobre judíos como gentiles en sus acciones y propósitos impíos.

Marcos 10:33. Jesús otra vez anticipa ser entregado a los gentiles por las autoridades religiosas en Israel. Sus acciones en contra de él señalan en el juicio de Dios que ellos realmente son impíos en sus actitudes y acciones.

Lucas 17:18. El extranjero aquí establece los parámetros para dar gracias, ya que los nativos estaban demasiado preocupados con las exigencias del protocolo de sus tradiciones legales. Jesús le alaba como demostrando el tipo de fidelidad y gratitud que los judíos deberían haber estado demostrando en conjunto con sus tradiciones rituales.

Lucas 18:32. Los líderes judíos entregarían a Jesús en manos de los gentiles para castigo, aunque ellos se encontrarían culpables ante los ojos de Dios por actuar en injusticia e iniquidad. Esto llega a ser una reclamación de juicio sobre sí mismos, aunque ellos consideran que Jesús sería el condenado.

Lucas 21:24. Jesús habla de la destrucción inminente de Jerusalén como el juicio de Dios por medio de fuerzas gentiles. Esto queda de acuerdo a lo que los judíos comprendían ser la práctica normal de Yahvé. Dios había utilizado a naciones extranjeras en varias ocasiones como vehículos de su juicio, castigo y disciplina para Israel.

Romanos 2:14. Por comparación entre judíos y gentiles, Pablo hace mención del hecho que las acciones justas de parte de los gentiles claman por juicio sobre los judíos quienes no son tan justos. Muchos de ellos comprenden los principios básicos de la ley, aunque no viven bajo su estandarte.

1ª Corintios 14:21. Dios hablaría por medio de inmigrantes y extranjeros en idiomas desconocidos, pero aun así sería ignorado por muchos del linaje directo de Abraham. La aceptación de estos extranjeros sería en si una declaración de juicio en contra de la infidelidad de Israel.

Gálatas 2:12-15. La ocasión de comer con gentiles en una libertad completa también era razón para que Pedro fuera juzgado por no actuar en conformidad con el evangelio de gracia. Él bien sabía que había sido liberado del legalismo por medio del evangelio, pero aun estaba dejando que su miedo de los legalistas le detuviera de defender la verdad del evangelio. El juicio aquí no viene directamente de, ni se basa en los propios gentiles, sino en un sentido de que los creyentes gentiles estaban viviendo de una forma más justa que la de algunos creyentes judíos.

1ª Pedro 4:3. Aquí se presenta un contraste con los gentiles más allá de la comunidad creyente. Sus vidas son reflejadas como estando afuera de los parámetros y propósitos del evangelio, mientras que los creyentes son llamados a demostrar evidencia de una ética y un propósito superiores en su vivir.

Preocupaciones sobre la Influencia Religiosa de los Inmigrantes
(19 Pasajes)

Preocupaciones son mencionadas en referencia a la influencia religiosa de los inmigrantes sobre la población de Israel.

Esta agrupación de pasajes tiende a igualar a los inmigrantes o extranjeros con la idolatría y su influencia negativa en la vida de Israel. Donde la Biblia hace comentarios negativos en referencia a inmigrantes o extranjeros, estos comentarios casi siempre tienen que ver con cuestiones de idolatría y la falla nacional en adorar a Yahvé o solamente a Yahvé dado a estas influencias exteriores. De veras, este es el único asunto que determina quien es o no un israelita o participante en el pueblo de Dios.

Deuteronomio 17:15. El rey de Israel no puede ser un inmigrante. Es importante notar que el rey representaba a la nación ante Dios y a Dios ante la nación en la capacidad de su suplente, semejante al papel del sacerdote y profeta.

1ª Samuel 17:25-27. Goliat aquí es categorizado como un inmigrante o extranjero. Lo importante de la declaración, entretanto, es que él no adora a Yahvé. Él se pone en oposición directa a Yahvé, insultando al Dios de Israel. Su desafío y su presencia hacen a los israelitas que teman a sus dioses más de lo que confían en Yahvé.

1ª Samuel 31:4. Saulo se refiere a soldados enemigos como inmigrantes y extranjeros, con énfasis en su idolatría, o su falta de adorarle a Yahvé. Esto era tanto una preocupación para Israel, como también era razón para que Saulo les ignorara como no teniendo importancia.

1ª Reyes 11:1-8. La advertencia de Dios que el matrimonio con esposas extranjeras disminuiría la adoración a Yahvé en Israel dio fruto en los matrimonios múltiples de Salomón con sus esposas ajenas. Dado a eses matrimonios, Salomón erigió templos a sus dioses extranjeros.

1ª Crónicas 10:4. Saulo desea no morir en manos de extranjeros idólatras por miedo de ser burlado. Hay un sentido en que esta burla se extendería a de Dios, ya que se interpretaba la victoria en el campo de batalla proviniendo desde los dioses, no desde la actuación de los soldados.

2ª Crónicas 33:15. Los ídolos de los inmigrantes fueron removidos del templo. Estos jamás deberían haber sido dejados entrar al templo de Yahvé, pero dado a la influencia religiosa de inmigrantes y extranjeros que no se integraron al Yahvismo israelita, los ídolos fueron introducidos al templo.

Esdras 10:11-18, 44. Aquí encontramos un desafío para la población de Jerusalén a que se separaran de la influencia idólatra de inmigrantes y de sus esposas extranjeras. La preocupación era el impacto de las esposas extranjeras sobre la adoración de los hombres hacia Yahvé.

Nehemías 9:2. La gente se separó de los inmigrantes en medio suyo como parte de sus acciones para ratificar su estatus en la alianza con Yahvé. Al centro estaba el tema de la pureza religiosa en servicio a Yahvé.

Nehemías 10:28-39. La gente se separó de la comunidad inmigrante en reconocimiento de su alianza con Yahvé y su responsabilidad para seguirla. El pueblo renovó su ratificación de la alianza con Yahvé, incluyendo aspectos pertinentes a los inmigrantes. Ellos determinaron que no dejarían que los inmigrantes les llevaran a extraviarse de servir a Yahvé en su comercio o por medio del matrimonio.

Nehemías 13:3. La gente echó fuera desde en su medio aquellos quienes se habían mezclado en matrimonio con inmigrantes en desobediencia a Yahvé. La preocupación aquí es establecer pureza en adoración a Yahvé para recibir el favor de Dios.

Nehemías 13:25-30. El pueblo reconoció que el pecado mayor de Salomón fue en apartarse de Yahvé, dado a sus matrimonios con esposas extranjeras. El matrimonio con inmigrantes queda prohibido con la intención de protegerle a Israel de caer en la misma trampa que les habían encaminado al exilio.

Salmo 81:9. Los dioses de los inmigrantes no deberían ser adorados. Los inmigrantes deberían ser enseñados a adorar a Yahvé. Los israelitas deberían mantenerse de sucumbir a la influencia de estas formas y objetos competidores de adoración.

Isaías 2:6. El error de Israel se resume en una contaminación de práctica religiosa por influencias inmigrantes. Ellos debería haberse mantenidos puros en su lealtad a Yahvé, pero fallaron.

Jeremías 4:1. Dios utiliza la imagen de un errante en referencia a Israel a desvirtuarse hacia la idolatría. El concepto hace referencia a que habían perdido su camino, distanciándose de la provisión de Dios, no solamente de las exigencias de su alianza con Dios.

Jeremías 5:19. La razón para el exilio era que la gente empezó a adorar a dioses extranjeros. Por causa de esa falla idólatra, ellos servirían a una población extranjera como una nación inmigrante. Ellos necesitarían aprender por medio del exilio a permanecer fieles a Yahvé.

Jeremías 51:51. Los extranjeros no respetaron el templo, echando vergüenza sobre la gente al ser burlada. Dios cambiaría la realidad en Babilonia, llamando la nación a que regresara en devoción sincera a Yahvé.

Ezequiel 14:7. El anuncio del juicio de Yahvé incluyó a los inmigrantes en la tierra como tan responsables como los de Israel por su desobediencia a Yahvé y a su idolatría. La gente debería enfrentarse a las influencias extranjeras y serle fiel a Yahvé.

Ezequiel 44:7-9. La nación estaba dejando la adoración de Yahvé en el templo en manos de inmigrantes quienes no habían asumido las responsabilidades de la alianza con Yahvé. El énfasis aquí queda en la identificación con Yahvé, no con el estatus inmigratorio.

Efesios 4:17. Pablo escribe a los creyentes en medio de la comunidad gentil de Éfeso para asegurar que ellos crearan distancia entre el carácter de sus vidas y las actitudes y el carácter de la sociedad a su alrededor. Ellos necesitaban cuidarse para ser una influencia en la sociedad, en lugar de ser influenciados indebidamente por los demás.

Siendo una Gente Inmigrante o Errante Es Conectado a Perderse el Camino
(13 Pasajes)

Estos pasajes hablan de vagar como perder el camino en la vida o de desviarse de los propósitos de Dios.

En esta agrupación encontramos pasajes que se refieren a Israel o a creyentes, como pasajes haciendo referencia a personas quienes aun necesitan entrar en relación con Dios. Esta distancia desde los propósitos de Dios comúnmente es un factor en la promoción de la injusticia o la idolatría, entre los cuales hay una conexión moral en el pensamiento hebreo. Mientras que podemos enfocar en la moralidad en relación al sexo y la violencia, el concepto bíblico tendría a colocar énfasis en preocupaciones de la justicia económica hacia los pobres y necesitados, preocupaciones cuales (la avaricia y el egoísmo) también comprendían estar detrás de las prácticas idólatras de fertilidad.

Alejándose de la alianza de Yahvé era visto desde la perspectiva de perderse sin dirección, apoyo o dependencia en la provisión de Dios. Lo importante tras esto es que la alianza con Yahvé comprendía que Dios proveería en abundancia para todos, mientras que los cultos de fertilidad eran vistos como haciendo énfasis en proveer por el individuo a costos de los demás de la sociedad. Esta era una distinción entre la fe y el miedo como la motivación básica detrás del culto y los aspectos prácticos de las relaciones sociales y el cuidado de los demás.

Job 38:41. Niños aquí son figurados como necesitados con la frase "vagando a procura de comida." Esto es el retrato del cazador-recolector, el nómada o el de otra forma sin tierra ni lugar para pertenecer y con poca seguridad.

Isaías 63:17. Esta descripción de errante es un desvío desde los caminos de Yahvé. Es un retrato de cómo el vivir contrario a Yahvé y es semejante al vivir conforme a un errante careciendo seguridad, incierto sobre donde y cómo encontrar su próxima comida.

Jeremías 4:1. Dios utiliza la imagen de un errante en referencia a Israel desviándose hacia la idolatría. El concepto recuerda que ellos habían perdido su camino de la provisión de Dios, al andar tras ídolos, pero Yahvé les llama a que regresen a Él en fidelidad.

Jeremías 14:8-10. Se trata a Dios aquí como un desconocido quien no está atado a la tierra. El término para el errante se utiliza aquí en el contexto de que Israel está actuando como si estuviera simplemente de pasada por la tierra como un extranjero de vacaciones. Sus acciones son como si no pertenecieran a Yahvé, mientras que Yahvé se había apartado de ellos dado a su infidelidad.

Jeremías 31:19-22. El texto habla del andar errante como distanciarse de la provisión y la protección de Yahvé. Se le llama a la gente para que se regresen a Yahvé y a sus caminos para que sean restaurados y encuentren la bendición que habían perdido.

Jeremías 50:6-17. El vagar aquí se contrasta con un sitio de descanso bajo la protección y provisión de Yahvé. En el versículo 17, la imagen cambia hacia la dispersión de un rebaño, por medio del cual se pierde su provisión y seguridad por causa de su distancia desde los cuidados y el abrigo de Yahvé.

Lamentaciones 4:14-16. El vagar en exilio fue sobrepuesto a Judá en castigo por su infidelidad. El texto habla de su vagar ciegamente, como de que Yahvé les dispersó de la tierra de su provisión en Israel.

Lamentaciones 5:2-18. El vagar de los chacales en Sión se contrasta a que la población se dispersó desde Jerusalén en el exilio. Su exilio fue resultado de su desvío desde los caminos de Yahvé. El escritor aquí lamenta el error de sus caminos.

Ezequiel 34:6-16. Israel se figura como un rebaño vagando sin cuidado, guía, dirección o seguridad. Este vagar es un retrato de la distancia religiosa de la gente desde Yahvé, semejante al caso de un pueblo inmigrante pasando necesidad de redención y rescate.

Oseas 9:17. Vagando entre las naciones en exilio se trata aquí como un castigo de Dios sobre la nación, dado a su infidelidad. La nación se había desviado desde los mandamientos de Yahvé, y su vagar errante es consecuencia de sus acciones.

Marcos 5:5. Al demoníaco de Gadara se le describe como un errante, no teniendo un sitio al cual pertenecer. Él había perdido su camino dado a la opresión espiritual bajo la cual vivía y lo que se retrata aquí en el lenguaje del errante.

Santiago 5:19. Vagando desde la fe habla del ser distanciado desde los caminos de Dios, desde la protección de Dios, su provisión y cuidado. La distancia desde la comunidad de fe es algo representativo de la distancia en la relación con Dios.

1ª Pedro 2:25. El vagar de las ovejas aquí se utiliza como un símbolo de la gente desviándose desde el camino y la voluntad de Dios, acciones coherentes con el y ya no pertenecerle a Dios. Hay alguna conexión aquí con el contexto en el cual Pedro se refiere a los que actúan como enemigos de Cristo y el vagar de estas ovejas en su necesidad del cuidado del Pastor.

Fracaso en Tratar a los Inmigrantes de Forma Apropiada
(8 Pasajes)

La realidad israelita no alcanzaba al ideal propuesto por Dios.

Estos pasajes demuestran que la realidad de la vida israelita quedaba lejos de estos patrones de igualdad establecidos por Dios. Reyes como David y Salomón oprimían a poblaciones inmigrantes, obligándoles a trabajo forzado como esclavos. Hay también algunas leyes en el propio código mosaico que no llegan a alcanzar a los ideales mayores para ceder hacia los inmigrantes el mismo valor que al israelita. Tales leyes son contrarias a la ética retratada en la multitud de pasajes que ya hemos visto clamando por una igualdad de tratamiento como una medida de justicia.

No deberíamos quedar sorprendidos que la fe israelita fracasó en alcanzar a sus propios patrones, ya que es norma para cualquier sociedad alrededor del mundo y a lo largo de la historia. Nuestra propaganda política y religiosa es una cosa, pero nuestra aplicación práctica de los mismos principios que sostenemos como importantes es comúnmente un tema muy distinto. La diferencia mayor en las Escrituras hebreas es que los profetas eran muy abiertos en llamar la atención de Israel por sus fracasos, así como hizo el profeta Natán con el Rey David cuando del asesinato de Urías y la violación de Betsabé.

Levítico 25:45-46. Esta es la primera instancia de abrir una excepción para un tratamiento distintivo al inmigrante en contraste al nativo. Con esta disminución de los cuidados por los inmigrantes, viene una ley para proteger el nativo de abuso en manos de un inmigrante.

Deuteronomio 14:21. Aquí existe una segunda excepción a la regla que una sola ley se aplica igualmente al nativo y al inmigrante, pertinente al comer la carne de un animal que haya muerto naturalmente. Parece que la distinción aquí se basa en una relación con la alianza con Yahvé que no existe en el caso del inmigrante.

Deuteronomio 15:1-5. Aquí encontramos la tercera excepción a la regla de una sola ley aplicada en igualdad. Esta vez la excepción viene en términos del perdonar las deudas cada séptimo año. Esta es una distinción práctica en términos de justicia, diferente de la hecha en sentido de pureza ritual que abriría la posibilidad para participación en el culto público.

Deuteronomio 23:2-4. Una distinción se hace aquí en sentido de la entrada a la parte interior del santuario de Dios. Los inmigrantes no podrían entrar por no participar en la alianza. Específicamente, ciertas naciones son excluídas por haber negado ayudar a los hebreos cuando eran inmigrantes errantes.

Deuteronomio 23:20. Como una quinta excepción a la regla de una sola ley, se le permite cobrar intereses a un inmigrante, pero no al nativo. Este es más un caso de una definición diferenciada de justicia entre el nativo y el inmigrante, la cual se choca con las preocupaciones de igualdad en tantos otros textos.

1ª Crónicas 22:2-5. David obliga a la fuerza de mano de obra inmigrante a que reúna material de construcción para el templo a ser hecho por Salomón. Este ejemplo es contrario a los principios de tratar al inmigrante en un mismo nivel que el nativo.

2ª Crónicas 2:2-18. Salomón coloca a los inmigrantes a servicio forzado para construir el templo. Ellos fueron también obligados a construir los templos a dioses extranjeros para las esposas de Salomón, aunque no lo menciona específicamente en el texto.

Ezequiel 22:7. La justicia de la nación encontraría expresión visible en el cuidado que tomara por aquellos con un grado menor de representación, específicamente incluyendo la población inmigrante. Esta rectitud estaba en falta y era motivo de condenación a Israel.

Fuerzas Extranjeras Son Percibidas Como una Amenaza
(4 Pasajes)

Se interpreta a las naciones extranjeras como siendo amenazas militares.

Estos textos ven a las demás naciones como fuerzas invasoras ocupando a Israel. Hay alguna mezcla de comentario entre los textos, algunos colocando a estas naciones en la categoría de siervos de Yahvé, y otros como interferencias de amenaza a la nación. La preocupación aquí es mayormente la amenaza en potencial que son estas naciones para la seguridad de Israel. Estos pasajes mencionan la protección de Dios por Israel en respuesta a la percepción de esas amenazas.

Isaías 52:1. Los incircuncidados jamás regresarían a atacar a Jerusalén. Al contrario, la ciudad viviría en paz y libertad. Los poderes extranjeros que les habían amenazado, Egipto y Asiria, serían derrotados por Yahvé.

Isaías 60:10-22. La inversión de Dios para Israel será demostrado aun más poderoso en que los mismos extranjeros quienes habían oprimido a la gente reconstruirían a los muros de Jerusalén. Reyes extranjeros estarían al servicio de Israel, pagándole tributo donde antes habían actuado en guerra y dominio.

Isaías 62:8-12. La promesa de Dios para la seguridad de Israel aquí especifica que enemigos extranjeros ya no la despojarían, tomando para si la abundancia agrícola de la tierra. En lugar de calamidad llegando desde el exterior, Yahvé les garantizaría seguridad.

Joel 3:12-17. La esperanza futura de Israel incluiría la ausencia de cualquier presencia militar. Dios instituiría justicia y concedería protección a la nación en seguridad extranjera. La amenaza de poderes extranjeros ya no existiría más.

Otros
(4 Pasajes)

Estas utilizaciones de terminología inmigrante no encajan en categorías mayores.

Estos textos temáticamente quedan ajenos a nuestro estudio de las actitudes y la enseñanza bíblica referentes a inmigrantes y la inmigración. Ellos se incluyen aquí simplemente por utilizar terminología específica a inmigrantes, desconocidos, extranjeros, refugiados o errantes.

Juan 2:14. Se hace mención aquí de hacer cambio para la moneda de uso en el templo. Esta práctica era técnicamente aceptada por el código mosaico, pero Jesús lo descarta como opresivo a los israelitas pobres a quienes se les cobraba por el servicio.

Hechos 4:24-28. Ambos gentiles y judíos conspiran en contra del ungido de Dios, aunque sus acciones acaban por adelantar la redención planeada por Dios. Hay un sentido limitado que une el juicio de Dios a inmigrantes y extranjeros, pero más que nada es un reconocimiento que ambos judíos y gentiles conspiraron juntos en contra de la voluntad de Dios, aunque sus propósitos no invalidaron a los propósitos de Dios.

Hechos 21:21. Se le acusa a Pablo de enseñar a judíos en tierras extranjeras a abandonar la ley de Moisés. La acusación viene desde judíos, pero se basa en una mala comprensión y representación falsa de la enseñanza de Pablo.

1ª Corintios 14:11. Donde hay una falta de comunicación, se puede presumir un estatus inmigratorio. Pablo parece pensar que hablar en lenguas públicamente puede ser semejante a la confusión de idioma entre personas que no han aprendido bien un idioma que están utilizando.

Resumen de Inferencias desde estas Agrupaciones Textuales:

Cuatro de las categorías de pasajes promueven actitudes de igualdad entre las personas sin referencia a su estatus migratorio. Este tema comprende esencialmente tres cuartos de los pasajes bíblicos que utilizan terminología específica para inmigrantes y extranjeros. Esta es la enseñanza esencial de la Biblia referente a inmigrantes. Nosotros somos todos iguales ante Dios. Debemos, por lo tanto, tratar uno al otro como iguales, sin referencia a etnicidad, inmigración, idioma, experiencia o cultura.

Esto no es simplemente la enseñanza del Nuevo Testamento. Es la enseñanza esencial del Antiguo Testamento. La mayoría de los textos mencionados son del Antiguo Testamento. Si aceptamos la suposición común que la ética de los escritores del Nuevo Testamento es de una calidad y carácter más elevada que la del Antiguo Testamento, hay entonces aun más importancia para dar a esta enseñanza del valor igual de la vida humana entre todas las naciones y categorías de personas. Era la voluntad de Yahvé que Israel de la antigüedad aprendiera a tratar a todas las gentes como iguales en valor ante Dios. Israel simplemente fracasó en realizar este reto. Desafortunadamente, nuestra propia experiencia no es muy diferente.

PARTE TRES

Otros Textos y Temas Pertinentes

Hemos visto unos de los temas más sobresalientes en la Biblia que se refiere a los inmigrantes y a las responsabilidades de la nación o de los creyentes en su tratamiento con inmigrantes o extranjeros. Hemos mirado brevemente a los pasajes bíblicos que utilizan la terminología específica para inmigrantes, extranjeros o refugiados. En este punto, debemos tomar una breve mirada a una serie de pasajes y temas secundarios que pueden o no utilizar terminología específica en referencia a inmigrantes, pero que tiene algo que ver con los imperativos bíblicos referente al tratamiento apropiado y la relación con inmigrantes, extranjeros y extraños.

El libro de Hechos será un texto central para estas líneas, ya que uno de sus temas mayores es el conflicto de los creyentes judíos en aceptar a los creyentes gentiles como iguales ante Dios. Esto era un concepto ya definido en varios pasajes del Antiguo Testamento, pero en la práctica no se le encontraba mucha aplicación. Así como los judíos acostumbraban menospreciar a los gentiles, también los creyentes judíos tendían a hacer lo mismo y las sociedades gentílicas se menospreciaron una a la otra, incluyendo a los judíos. El evangelio de Jesús volcó esta actitud de cabeza, pero llevó mucha reflexión personal para que los creyentes aceptaran y adoptaran los principios del evangelio. De la misma forma, nosotros también tenemos dificultad en dejar que el carácter y las actitudes de Jesucristo encuentren expresión apropiada en nuestras propias vidas.

Hechos 10 — Día de Pentecostés de los Gentiles

En Hechos 10, encontramos a Pedro pasando por la experiencia de tener una visión de animales que jamás había comido. En conjunto, él recibe la orden para que matara y comiera de ellos. Él quedó asombrado por la experiencia de esta visión, ya que estos animales eran vistos como ritualmente impuros para los judíos. Mientras que estas definiciones estaban conectadas a una doctrina de pureza ritual, el tema mayor dando base a este tema era el de mantener a los israelitas lejos de una conexión entre estas comidas con las prácticas de fertilidad.

Desde los días de Moisés hasta los días de los reyes de Israel, la nación luchó con el predominio de los cultos a la fertilidad que los rodeaban. Esas prácticas incluían el uso de la sangre, cocinar novillos en la leche de su madre y el uso de cerdos como símbolos de fertilidad, vida y poder sobre las fuerzas de vida, muerte y procreación. Las prohibiciones alimenticias judías eran generalmente conectadas a abusos de la vida desde estos cultos de fertilidad. Los judíos deberían honrar a la vida como perteneciente a y prestado por Yahvé. Ellos no deberían procurar agarrarse a alguna fuerza vital de una forma que deshonrara la dádiva de Dios.

Al pasar los siglos, especialmente con regreso del exilio, los judíos tuvieron menos problemas con los cultos de fertilidad a su alrededor. Ellos aprendieron y se adaptaron a considerar que éstos estaban en contra de la voluntad de Dios. Ya no se encontraban tentados a participar en estas prácticas como un camino hacia la idolatría. Llegando hasta el día de Pedro, ya era más una cuestión de tradición, de cultura y de una norma como la diferencia que se hace entre comer una ardilla y un ratón. De forma anatómica, hay poca diferencia, aunque el uno se recomienda comer y el otro se define nocivo.

Es en esta situación, entonces, que Pedro escucha las órdenes a comer lo que hasta el momento él había siempre considerado nocivo o demasiado feo, aunque había escuchando a Jesús declarar que todas las comidas eran puras. Jesús acabó con las leyes de purificación, así para extender la mano a todas las personas y llamarles ante la presencia de Dios. Él abolió las definiciones que trataban a ciertas personas como dignas o indignas de Dios. Él simplemente estableció que Dios desea amar y aceptar a todos, sin excepción.

La analogía a la comida en la visión fue diseñada para ayudar a Pedro comprender que los mismos principios que Jesús enseño en referencia a la pureza ritual deberían ser aplicadas a las personas. En contra de la enorme tradición judía de aislarse de los gentiles, Dios indicaba a Pedro que esto no era simplemente abusivo, era también en oposición a la voluntad de Dios. Dios no deseaba que nadie fuera considerado indigno, impuro o no merecedor de la atención y la gracia de Dios.

Para realizar el hecho, Lucas hace hincapié no solamente para describir la sábana que se baja del cielo tres veces en la visión, sino que relata a Pedro contando el mensaje de la visión más tres veces en el pasaje. Lo recontó a los mensajeros que le llegan, en la casa de Cornelio y luego a los creyentes judíos en su regreso. Para los creyentes judíos, esto era una ocasión sin igual. Ellos fueron sorprendidos con la extensión de la gracia de Dios. No era para nada un mensaje a ser ignorado.

Como resultado de la visión, creyentes judíos viajaron como inmigrantes para hablar con extranjeros. Entraron en una casa extranjera, comieron con extranjeros y reconocieron que Dios había decretado no hacer diferencia entre ellos. Todos estaban cubiertos igualmente por la gracia de Dios. Si todas las personas son consideradas de valor igual ante Dios, los discípulos empezaron a reconocer que ellos eran responsables también para tratar a todas las personas con definiciones de valor igual. Significaba reconocer que Dios aceptaba a cualquier y a todos y que, como discípulos, somos obligados a descartar las distinciones que hacemos para hacer lo mismo que Dios.

Hechos 15 — El Concilio de Jerusalén

La misma polémica de la posición de los gentiles ante el evangelio que se vio en Hechos 10 estaba otra vez frente a la iglesia en Jerusalén en Hechos 15. Pablo había empezado su ministerio entre los gentiles sin colocar condiciones sobre ellos que los obligarían a convertirse al judaísmo. A esta altura, los creyentes se consideraban judíos quienes habían aceptado a Jesús como su Mesías. Ellos aun no se consideraban cristianos en el sentido de una ruptura con el judaísmo. Cornelio y los demás en su casa eran vistos como gentiles que se habían convertido al judaísmo de Jesús. La predicación de Pablo, entretanto, había tomado un nuevo rumbo, evitando el tema de una conversión al judaísmo. Él simplemente se enfocaba en que aceptaran a Jesús.

Para los creyentes judíos, esto era mucho más que una simple cuestión de testificar a alguien que entonces se unió a una iglesia de otra denominación cristiana. Ellos estaban batallando con la mera posibilidad de aceptarle a Jesús más allá de los límites del judaísmo, más allá de su concepto de cualquier relación con Yahvé. El tema y la posibilidad no se les hacían ningún sentido, pues no podían imaginar un relacionamiento con Yahvé aparte de sus raíces y tradiciones judías, con su cultura de honrar a Dios y los mandamientos que vinieron por Moisés.

Para estos creyentes judíos, sus tradiciones religiosas no eran simplemente un fundamento sobre el cual Jesús construyó. Quedaban para ellos como la estructura básica de la relación con Dios, una base al cual Jesús simplemente explicó con más claridad. Ellos ya no miraban al sábado como una carga, pero miraban a la enseñanza judía referente al sábado como una expectación básica de servirle a Dios. Ya no lo dejaban interferir con su atención a las necesidades de los demás, pero la seguían en su íntegra. La circuncisión aun era un elemento esencial de su alianza con Yahvé, aunque desarrollaban una nueva dependencia en la fe puesta en Jesús junto a la gracia y el amor generoso de Dios.

Para aceptar plenamente a los gentiles en una relación de fe con Yahvé, sin exigirles que adoptaran al judaísmo como un todo, era más que simplemente difícil para ellos. Exigía que colocaran de lado una completa serie de reglas y valores que ellos percibían como centrales a una vida que le agradaba a Dios. La ropa que vestían hablaba de su lealtad a Dios. Las filacterias que colgaban en su ropa, sus rizos laterales usados por los varones, los "mezuzot" que adornaban las entradas de sus casas y negocios eran más que ornamentales para ellos. Las comidas que evitaban, la manera en que comían y celebraban las bendiciones de Dios hablaban fuertemente a su sentido de bienestar e identidad como una gente apartada a servicio de Yahvé. Al mínimo se les era difícil para que aceptaran que los gentiles entraran en una relación con Yahvé por medio de Jesús, sin que adoptaran estos marcadores de una vida devota a Dios.

Las prácticas alimenticias de los gentiles les eran nocivas. Miraban a la ropa como inmoral. Sus modos de comer, viajar, vocabulario e ignorancia de las Escrituras les marcaban como inmorales, sucios, indignos e inadecuados para los propósitos de Dios. Pedro y Pablo clamaron por su aceptación simple y puramente en base de las demostraciones de gracia y amor de Dios. Para la mayoría, esto les era muy difícil aceptar. Se exigía que los creyentes judíos tomaran una nueva mirada muy cercana y difícil a sus propias tradiciones que habían dado estructura y significado para sus vidas ante Dios.

El evangelio, entretanto, simplemente exigía de ambos judíos y gentiles que aceptaran el amor y la gracia de Dios, no que se tornaran uno en cultura, idioma y tradición. Su unidad no dependería de su identidad cultural, étnica o nacional. No tendría nada que ver con fronteras políticas o definiciones de ciudadanía, estatus o clase. Dependería simplemente del amor y de la aceptación de Dios. Sea que los demás fueran judíos, romanos, griegos, egipcios, etíopes o galeses no hacía ninguna diferencia, ya que Dios no demostraba tales distinciones al ofrecer gracia. Como Dios aceptaba y no categorizaba a la gente, así es el ejemplo establecido para nuestra propia aceptación y categorización de los demás. Somos todos una sola clase, amados por Dios y ofrecidos su plena aceptación.

Génesis 20 & 26 — Abraham e Isaac (esposas hermanas)

"Un arameo errante era mi padre" es uno de las declaraciones más antiguas de la identidad hebrea. Esta confesión construía participación e identidad desde un vínculo con Abraham, el antepasado de la gente que sería llamado para pertenecer a Yahvé. Este errante hizo su camino desde Ur de los Caldeos hacia la tierra de Palestina y hacia Egipto. Al paso, él era un inmigrante sin derechos legales entre los países por los cuales pasó y vivió.

Abraham era un ganadero nómada, un inmigrante quien movía su campamento en conjunto con los animales bajo sus cuidados. Él era líder de una tribu, en cierto punto liderando a unos 300 hombres armados. Su seguridad en las tierras que cruzaba venía de la banda de hombres quienes le seguían, leales a su servicio.

Se esperaría que al pasar los años el número de aquellos que le servían pudiera haber disminuido por una que otra razón. Uno de estas instancias pueda haber sido su entrada en la tierra de Egipto en tiempos de hambre. Es probable que algunos decidieran partir camino con él en un período de hambre en conjunto con el proyecto de entrar en un territorio establecido como era Egipto.

Génesis registra que en su entrada a Egipto, Abraham entrega a su esposa y media-hermana, Sarai, hacia el harén del faraón. Esto no significa lo que muchos presumirían, que ella se tornó en esposa del faraón. Era más bien un acuerdo según los moldes de un tratado de paz establecido entre un hombre de importancia que entrara la tierra dominada por otro hombre de importancia. Entregando a Sarai hacia el harén era un medio de mantener la paz entre Abraham con su tribu y los poderes políticos en Egipto.

Mientras que Abraham participó voluntariamente en esta entrega de Sarai hacia el harén egipcio, el buen sentido ve que él no se sintió completamente libre en lo tocante a esta acción. Hubo mucha presión o amenaza de violencia en contra de él y de su banda acaso se rehusara ofrecer a su esposa-hermana al harén de Egipto.

En la narrativa de Génesis, Yahvé interviene y Sarai es liberada y entregada otra vez a la custodia de Abraham. Esto solo sucede, entretanto, dado a la intervención de Dios al traer una infertilidad sobre la casa del faraón. Abraham entregó a Sarai, pero sin la misma voz o posición que se le hubiera concedido si fuera él uno de los residentes naturales de Egipto. Él era un inmigrante, un extranjero de una tribu desconocida, quien entró a un territorio extranjero y tuvo que someterse a las presiones de la estructura política local.

Unos pocos capítulos más adelante en Génesis, leemos un relato muy semejante referente a Isaac, hijo de Abraham. Este se encuentra viviendo semejantemente en medio de otra sociedad como un inmigrante. Como en el relato de su padre, poco se menciona del séquito que le acompaña, aunque era más que probable que tenía un séquito consigo de los que habían seguido a su padre Abraham.

Isaac entregó a su esposa, Rebeca, hacia el harén de Abimélec. Esperaba así proteger su propia vida y establecer la paz entre sí y las estructuras políticas a su alrededor. Otra vez, la táctica es descubierta por la intervención de Dios, e Isaac es dado en libertad para llevarle a su esposa de forma igual que Sarai le fue regresado a su padre Abraham en Egipto.

Este es otro caso de inmigrantes perdiendo ciertos derechos y voz de igualdad dado a su estatus inferior de inmigrante, extranjero, "otro" o desconocido ante el sistema político establecido. Esto era el aprieto común para un inmigrante en esos días, aun como lo es también en el mundo de hoy. Aquellos afuera de la cúpula del poder no son tratados con la igualdad o solicitud concedida a aquellos de adentro. El segmento más bajo de la sociedad tiende a ser en el inmigrante o extranjero. Ellos son los que no tienen conexiones con los que tienen poder. No tienen quienes tomen su parte o que hasta comprenden la situación en el cual se encuentran.

Abraham e Isaac experimentaban opresión dado a su estatus inmigratorio. Esto sin mencionar a Sarai y Rebeca, quienes, como mujeres, no les era esperado que tuvieran voz, sin contar con su etnicidad o clase social. Como mujeres de hombres quienes eran inmigrantes, sus derechos eran aun menos que los derechos de las mujeres de la sociedad reinante. Entre la gente considerada propiedad, estar atado a un inmigrante o a un nómada se les hacía su posición aun más sujeta a la opresión y al abuso. La buena noticia es que Yahvé intervino para proveerles de su protección y reunirse con sus familiares que les deseaban proteger.

Ester, una Reina Inmigrante en Peligro

El libro completo de Ester es un estudio de lo que puede suceder a una gente inmigrante en exilio desde su propia tierra. Más allá de la intervención de Yahvé para rescatar a la gente escogida de los opresores que enfrentaban, el libro es un estudio de caso de cuan fácil es para que la gente manipule a las fuerzas políticas con la intención de degradar o maltratar a una gente quienes no estaban en su propio patio.

La historia subraya que la gente judía en el exilio era incomprendida, dado al hecho de las diferencias en sus prácticas, costumbres y valores religiosos. Ellos eran vistos por el lente interpretativo de la cultura del país, que les describía de una forma despectiva y distorsionaba elementos de su identidad. Sus tradiciones religiosas también impedían el proceso establecido que pudiera darles una forma de expresar sus preocupaciones y procurar la resolución de su aprieto.

De hecho, algo de la opresión que sentían era intencional, pero otra parte, si no la mayor, era resultado de una falta de comprensión y mal interpretación de señales culturales, étnicas y religiosas. Amán es muy intencional en sus maltratos a los judíos, aunque el rey es quien le da cuerda para sus acciones opresoras y no se da cuenta de gran parte de las consecuencias de las acciones y los propósitos de Amán.

Amán tomó una relación que se había agraviado con Mardoqueo. Utilizó esto como pretexto para exterminar a todos los judíos en el imperio. Él falló en reconocer que las acciones de Mardoqueo no se dirigían específicamente a sí, sino que reflejaban una postura religiosa contra arrodillarse ante cualquier que no fuera Dios. Amán se ofendió con esa acción y la proyectó sobre toda la nación de Mardoqueo. Es un ciclo que hemos visto repetidas veces a lo largo de la historia humana.

El inmigrante, el desconocido, el ajeno tiende a ser visto de forma escéptica por la población mayoritaria. Es común que un grupo mayoritario menosprecie al otro por causa de sus diferencias en pensamiento, acción, hábitos y valores. Las fallas de comprensión cultural se amontonan con una mala experiencia y es meramente natural que se pinte el todo de la población con un solo pincel y mayormente de forma negativa.

Ester dibuja una escena difícil en la cual una animosidad en contra de una población inmigrante se transforma en la base para un genocidio. Amán coloca la base para el genocidio, aunque una intervención llega por medio de Ester y su súplica con el rey. Su gente es rescatada de su muerte inminente, pero aun hay conflicto entre los inmigrantes judíos y otros del imperio.

Amán construye sus planes para genocidio en la base de actitudes existentes en contra de los judíos. Él no empezó su estrategia de la nada, sino que trabajó con las perspectivas negativas que otros compartían en contra de esta gente inmigrante que no se conformaba con las normas culturales de la sociedad mayoritario.

La conformidad habría significado una pérdida de identidad para ellos. La conformidad habría obligado a que se distanciaran de su identidad y los valores que daban sentido y estructura para sus vidas. También habría significado el abandono de Yahvé como el único Dios para que los judíos adoraran.

Podríamos hablar despectivamente de una población siendo asimilada por otra cultura como una cosa natural. La realidad, entretanto, es que hay mucho más por de bajo de la asimilación cultural que las acciones exteriores que se clasifica e identifica como la cultura. Por detrás de cada acción, actitud y dicho cultural existe una serie de valores y conceptos que se distinguirán de cultura en cultura.

Para Amán, el arrodillarse a él en honor le hablaba de aceptar que la posición social del otro era inferior. A Mardoqueo, entretanto, el arrodillarse era señal de adoración y lealtad debidas solamente a Yahvé. Para Mardoqueo, era por la falla de Israel y Judá en arrodillarse solamente ante Yahvé que ellos se encontraban en el exilio en una tierra ajena. Ellos no eran inmigrantes por su propia elección, sino en consecuencia de haber sido infieles en su relación con Yahvé.

Lo que para Amán era una simple acción para demostrarle respeto, era algo completamente diferente para Mardoqueo. Para éste, las consecuencias de fidelidad a Dios eran una preocupación mucho mayor que cualquier consecuencia en relación al fracaso en respetar las expectativas de Amán. Amán pudiera reaccionar en contra de Mardoqueo, pero Mardoqueo se preocupaba con la reacción de Dios, quien había enviado a la nación en su totalidad hacia el exilio.

La reacción de Amán se extendió más allá de lo que Mardoqueo hubiera esperado, pero Mardoqueo aun se enfocaba en una interpretación completamente diferente, no sólo en lo que correspondía a las palabras y acciones de cada cual, sino también en relación a las consecuencias mayores ante Yahvé. En el balance, Amán se preocupaba consigo, mientras que Mardoqueo se preocupaba con su nación. Esto tiende a la vez a ser la diferencia esencial de actitud entre un opresor y su víctima.

Cuando una comunidad inmigrante se ve en la mira de alguna posición opresiva, es más común que los opresores estén más preocupados en mantener su posición de poder, control, superioridad o sentido de valor. El grupo a ser víctima se transforma en el foco del sentido de inseguridad de la población mayor. Ellos procuran incrementar la seguridad de su poder, posición o valor a costos de un grupo caracterizado como "el otro," y luego no merecedor de los beneficios gozados por la mayoría en poder.

El grupo ajeno al poder tiende a preocuparse mucho menos con cuestiones de poder, sino con cuestiones de sobrevivencia y de una seguridad básica. Es solamente después de que se resuelven estas preocupaciones más básicas que se puede tener el lujo de preocuparse con cualquier otro sentido de dominio o poder. Es esa dominación, entretanto, con el cual el poder mayoritario tiende a preocuparse. Las lecciones de Ester parecen ser que es nuestra preocupación por mantener el dominio que abre el camino para la caída de esa posición de poder. Amán pudiera haber evitado una multitud de problemas si hubiera simplemente estado dispuesto a pasar por alto sus propias inseguridades y no los proyectara hacia una gente ya oprimida por su estatus inmigrante dentro de las fronteras de su nación.

Juan 4 — La Mujer Samaritana

Juan 4 es una historia muy conocida y recontada del encuentro de Jesús con una mujer samaritana en el pozo de Sicar. Lo que quizás pasemos por alto, entretanto, es como Jesús ignora tantos tabús nacionales y sociales en este encuentro con esta mujer tan indigna. A la vez, acostumbramos a no tomar en cuenta que Jesús es un inmigrante en esta narrativa. Él había dejado su tierra natal y se cruzó por territorio ajeno, entrando a una tierra poblada por gente que los judíos consideraban responsable por difamar su identidad y el nombre de Dios por casarse con gente de otras naciones.

Hasta donde los judíos lo consideraban, el matrimonio con naciones idólatras era una gran afronta a Yahvé como también el sincretismo religioso que exhibían entre una fe basada en el Pentateuco y los cultos de fertilidad provenientes de otras culturas. Los samaritanos no eran vistos simplemente como enemigos, sino como una gente quien, como una nación, había negado a Yahvé y desistido de su responsabilidad para servirle a Yahvé en pureza y sinceridad de corazón.

Jesús parece demasiado despreocupado con estos temas que eran de tan gran importancia a los judíos en general. Juan, al escribir su evangelio, reconoce una necesidad para explicar en resumen que los judíos y los samaritanos no se hablaban. Lo que él no detalla es que un judío sentía que cualquier contacto con un samaritano profanaría al judío, dado el abandono samaritano de las tradiciones de Moisés en lo tocante a Yahvé.

Cuando Jesús, obviamente un judío, habla con la mujer samaritana, ella es desconcertada que él se bajara para hablar con ella. Ella sinceramente esperaba ser menospreciada, ignorada, o de otra forma degradada por un judío en su proximidad. En lugar de tratarle a ella de acuerdo a definiciones de clase, estatus, importancia o pureza ritual, entretanto, Jesús le habla como igual. Él la trata simplemente como una persona, un ser humano digno bajo la mirada de Dios.

Esto le era completamente inesperado. Primeramente, ella era samaritana y además era mujer. Los judíos no hablaban con mujeres desconocidas. Los judíos no hablaban con samaritanos. Juntando las dos cosas, un hombre judío jamás se bajaría a hablar con una mujer samaritana sin demostrar una actitud de gran superioridad.

Como lectores del evangelio de Juan, reconocemos muy bien la superioridad de Jesús, pero tal no era tema para Jesús. Él queda completamente despreocupado con establecer su estatus en relación a los demás, como si su estatus pudiera ser afectado o contaminado por el contacto con alguien de otra clase. Él prontamente defiende que él es de veras diferente de lo que ella podría esperar, pero no utiliza esa distinción para aplastarla de cualquier forma.

Aunque Jesús aquí es un inmigrante, él no acepta que tal estado le hace inferior de cualquier forma. Tampoco acepta las definiciones judías de inferioridad y superioridad como forma digna de clasificar y tratar a la gente. Al contrario, Jesús va más adelante, enviando a la extranjera, esta mujer, una mujer de baja reputación, hacia la ciudad de la cual sus discípulos recién llegaban. La envía como su emisario especial en lo tocante al mensaje de la gracia y la aceptación de Dios para estos samaritanos odiados.

Los discípulos habían entrado a la ciudad para encontrar comida, pero habían ignorado el hecho de que cargaban un mensaje de mayor importancia que la comida. Ellos estaban ciegos por la identidad de la población de la ciudad. Miraban a esas gentes como samaritanos detestados, y como consecuencia, indignos de Dios y de su gracia. Ellos proyectaron su propio repudio como el repudio de Dios por esa gente. Haciendo así, fracasaron en su misión mayor como discípulos de Jesús, a llevar testigo a su maestro y llamar a otros a seguir sus enseñanzas. Mientras que ellos fracasaron en su responsabilidad, esta mujer samaritana de mala reputación aceptó la tarea ante si, corriendo para cumplir con el propósito de compartir a Dios con su gente.

No solamente estaban ciegos estos discípulos judíos a la extensión de la gracia y aceptación de Dios, sino que también sus tradiciones les impedían mirar hacia los demás con la misma percepción de su maestro. Ellos miraban a la gente de acuerdo a categorías ya establecidas. Jesús trataba a uno y todos sin distinciones de su etnicidad, nacionalidad, idioma, género y cultura. Haciendolo así, estableció una norma para nuestro propio tratamiento de las gentes de las demás naciones, sin importar el sitio en donde nos encontremos.

Marcos 5 — El Demoniaco de Gadara

Marcos 5 nos lleva con Jesús a encontrarnos con otro desconocido, un extranjero de afuera de Israel, con Jesús en el papel de inmigrante. Este era ajeno a su propia comunidad, plagado por unas dos mil deidades extranjeras (el término bíblico se refiere más específicamente a los dioses de religiones paganas). Si alguien podría ser considerado ajeno para un judío, este hombre lo era sin duda. Era poseído por demonios; no era judío; no tenía posición en la sociedad; vivía entre las tumbas, un sitio específicamente impuro para los judíos en sus conceptos de pureza ritual.

Jesús entró al área donde este hombre habitaba y aceptó el encuentro con él. El hombre se hincó a los pies de Jesús y ellos empezaron a conversar, aunque hay alguna confusión si era el hombre o si eran las deidades paganas hablando por medio de él.

Jesús no se parece atribulado por este encuentro. Con plena certeza esperaríamos que los discípulos estuvieron en guardia, inseguros referente a cómo proseguir y muy incómodos con el contacto entre Jesús y este hombre aparentemente trastornado.

A lo largo de este encuentro, haríamos bien recordar que estos discípulos estaban en medio de una experiencia agobiante. Nada referente a este encuentro les era cómodo. Ellos estaban en una tierra extranjera, caminando entre las tumbas de una nación pagana y conversando con un hombre quien estaba abiertamente bajo la opresión de fuerzas espirituales.

Este escenario no comunicaba consuelo, ni pureza ritual, ni una atmosfera en la cual uno esperaría encontrar gente activamente adorando a Yahvé. Eso es, entretanto, exactamente lo que encontramos, al contrario de todas las expectativas. Este hombre gentil, poseído por demonios, ajeno a su propia sociedad pagana, se arrojó a los pies de Jesús en adoración.

Si este hombre pudiera ser aceptado y amado por Jesús, cualquiera debería calificarse para lo mismo. Él había intentado suicidarse; él vivía no solamente una vida de impureza, sino que en un escenario de muerte y corrupción a que un judío tenía la obligación de evitar. El contacto con los muertos descalificaba a un judío de participar en la vida religiosa de Israel. Este hombre vivía entre los muertos, entre las tumbas de una gente pagana. Aun así, parece que Jesús vino específicamente para encontrarse con este hombre y ofrecerle redención, rescate y una nueva oportunidad de vida. No fue solamente eso, pues Jesús también le comisionó para que representara lo que Yahvé había hecho por él entre su propia gente.

El hombre salió de la presencia de Jesús y sus discípulos en contra de sus propios deseos, pero embarcó en una misión para testificar de Jesús en una región de diez ciudades de su gente. Jesús le aceptó, aunque era extranjero. Luego, como inmigrante en el territorio del hombre, le envió a ministrar entre la gente que le había echado fuera, tratándole como ajeno. Son las personas como este hombre quienes la sociedad, todas las sociedades, han categorizados como indignos para servirle a Dios, pero quienes Jesús parecía tener el mayor interés en traer al redil de la nueva Israel que estaba creando. Él los tomó y los comisionó como sus discípulos y emisarios del reino que Dios inauguraba por medio de él.

Jesús aquí tomó a los discípulos en un viaje por medio de una tierra extranjera. Ellos ministraron como inmigrantes a alguien ajeno de entre su propia gente. Jesús luego le comisionó este hombre a ministrar a la misma sociedad que le había rechazado como indigno de su contacto y consideración. En esta aplicación práctica de la aceptación y gracia de Dios, él se extendió más allá de las barreras múltiples que las sociedades en torno del mundo instituyen para mantener a sus miembros en categorías distintas de valor e inclusión. Por su ejemplo, enseñó a sus discípulos que miraran más allá de sus prejuicios y trataran a los demás de acuerdo a un concepto radicalmente distinto de la igualdad bajo la gracia de Dios.

2ª Samuel 11 — Urías el Hitita

El sitio de Urías en la historia de Israel es un caso especial. Él era un inmigrante, un miembro de una nación considerada enemiga de Israel. Aun así, él entra en la numeración de los soldados sirviendo en la defensa militar y la estructura política de Israel.

David ve a la esposa de Urías, quien con gran probabilidad es también una inmigrante, hija de una inmigrante o por lo menos una israelita quien en su matrimonio ha salido de los límites establecidos en la ley de Israel, con sus prohibiciones de matrimonio con extranjeros. Por su nombre, uno esperaría que ella fuera inmigrante de origen del país de Seba, lo que hoy día sería la Etiopía, ya que su nombre significa "hija de Seba." (Probablemente, esto no era su nombre, sino un título que se le identificaba como inmigrante africana.)

En parte, parecería que es por causa de su estatus inmigrante que ella se encuentra como blanco para la atención y abuso de David. Como la esposa de un inmigrante, ella no tendría las mismas protecciones bajo la ley práctica que gozaría un israelita nativo.

Ella debería haber gozado las mismas protecciones que cualquier otro. Su esposo por derecho debería haber tenido la misma voz que se le concedía a cualquier hombre israelita. El problema, entretanto, es que en práctica las cuestiones de igualdad ante la ley jamás fueron implementadas en la vida de Israel, así como la aplicación de igualdad ante la ley no es una realidad para la mayoría de comunidades inmigrantes en el mundo hoy.

Es muy probable que al regresar del frente de la batalla, a Urías se le hizo saber que algo estaba mal entre su esposa y el rey. De cualquier forma, Urías se adhirió a las normas establecidas en Israel que un soldado debería lealtad completa a la guerra, evitando contactos íntimos con su esposa o cualquier otra mujer mientras continuaba la batalla. Urías siguió el patrón, mientras que David, con la responsabilidad para liderar la defensa militar de Israel, no lo siguió.

Era el inmigrante dentro de Israel quien vivió de acuerdo a los patrones establecidos por Yahvé, mientras que el nativo y rey actuaba en contra de estos patrones de conducta.

El ajeno en cualquier territorio o entre cualquier nación se encuentra en una situación vulnerable ante el poder mayoritario. A veces esta vulnerabilidad no tiene importancia y muchas veces no llega a ser realizado de acuerdo a su potencial. En otras ocasiones, esa vulnerabilidad es interpretada por otros como licencia para oprimir, especialmente dado que el inmigrante no es comprendido a participar de la misma categoría que la mayoría reinante.

No es difícil ver como este principio se aplica al mundo. Podemos mirar hacia el tratamiento de los judíos como chivos expiatorios en territorios europeos desde la edad media hasta la Alemania nazista. Podemos mirar a muchas otras naciones alrededor del mundo quienes han oprimido a una nación inmigrante, como los roma en Europa, los nativos en las américas, o las tribus africanas vendidas en esclavitud por tribus guerreras en sus propias tierras. Podemos tan fácilmente considerar como una nación puede deshumanizar a sus propios habitantes, degradándolos como un simple partido enemigo a ser eliminado por algún llamado propósito mayor. Todo lo que se hace necesario es clasificar a alguien como menos que humano o de menor valor.

En el caso de Urías, el profeta Natán entra a la escena después de su asesinato para llamar a David a prestar cuentas por su error en degradar a Urías, el cual había vivido por una ética más elevada que el propio David. David reaccionó en respuesta a la moralidad mayor de Urías por mandar que muriera para apaciguar su propia culpabilidad. El resultado fue que David simplemente complicó sus propios errores para su vergüenza mayor. Él dejó que sus prejuicios en contra de un inmigrante le designaran a sí mismo como de mayor valor que este hombre categorizado como ajeno.

Al final de la historia, David vino a reconocer que el valor de Urías y Betsabé ante Dios eran iguales a su propio valor. La viuda de Urías luego fue elevada al estatus de Reina Madre, y era su hijo quien sería heredero del trono de Israel, como si fuera en pago y pena por los maltratos de David hacia Urías el inmigrante y a su esposa inmigrante que había violado por fuerza social. Que Betsabé fue elevada a esta posición era una declaración alta y fuerte ante todo Israel que David había fracasado en relación a ella y a su esposo en base de su estatus inmigratorio. Ante Dios, los inmigrantes no deberían ser abusados, aunque era fácil hacerlo. Ellos deberían ser protegidos simplemente por ser lo correcto y justo.

Joel 2 y Hechos 2 — "Sobre Toda Carne"

Capítulo 2 de Joel era un pasaje incómodo para los judíos de la época de Jesús, para generaciones anteriores y hasta en la actualidad. Como un todo, a los judíos les gustaban de las palabras de Joel, hablando de un día venidero en el cual Dios derramaría de su soplo sobre todo Israel. Ellos anhelaban ese "Día de Yahvé" como la suprema bendición para Israel. El problema venía de dos frases en el pasaje mayor. La primera frase hablaba de una sociedad sin clases ante la llegada de la bendición de Dios. La segunda frase aplicaba la bendición no solamente a un Israel sin clases, sino también a inmigrantes, extranjeros y a las naciones más allá de las fronteras de Israel.

Pedro toma este pasaje en su sermón explicativo en Hechos capítulo 2. Este es el día de pentecostés, la celebración de la fiesta de primeros frutos, en la cual la cosecha de la primavera se celebraba cincuenta días después de la pascua. En este pentecostés, el Soplo de Dios (Espíritu) fue derramado sobre los discípulos reunidos en Jerusalén, como lenguas de fuego bajando sobre ellos y causando que hablaran en idiomas que jamás habían aprendido. Pedro consideró y declaró este evento ser el cumplimiento de la profecía de Joel referente al Día de Yahvé en la cual Dios visitaba a Israel con su presencia sin respecto a las estructuras sociales establecidas.

Judíos de todas partes del mundo conocido del Imperio Romano estaban presentes en Jerusalén. La mayoría de ellos había llegado en peregrinaje para la pascua y se quedaron para la celebración del pentecostés. La población de Jerusalén generalmente crecía en ese período de 200,000 hasta 1,000,000 para los dos festivales por motivo del peregrinaje religioso.

Es en la presencia de esa multitud de peregrinos judíos llegados de todo el mundo que el soplo de Dios es derramado. Es de entre ellos que unos 3,000 escuchan la predicación de Pedro y aceptan las buenas nuevas de Jesús. En los meses a venir, muchos de ellos regresarían a sus tierras natales, aunque unos cuantos quedarían en la región de Jerusalén para vivir allí sus últimos días en anticipación de la llegada del Mesías o la aparición de Jesús en gloria.

En el sermón de Pedro, entretanto, lo que escuchamos es que las buenas nuevas de Jesús deberían ser predicadas hacia todas las naciones. De acuerdo a la perspectiva de Lucas y los discípulos, ese acontecimiento se había cumplido en ese mismo día con la llegada del Soplo de Dios. Llenó todos los requisitos dados por Jesús como necesarios a ser cumplidos antes de su regreso. El evangelio era para todas las naciones, aun como el Soplo o Espíritu de Dios fuera concedido sobre todas las gentes desde todas las naciones del mundo conocido.

Más adelante, estos mismos discípulos empezarían a reconocer que el evangelio se aplicaba igualmente a aquellos quienes no eran y no se convertirían en judíos. Aun pasaría tiempo antes que compriendieran el concepto que las palabras realmente se aplicaban más allá que todas las definiciones de nacionalidad, etnicidad e idioma. A esta altura, entretanto, el centro de la amplitud del evangelio fue clarificado, aun si la profecía de Joel no se cumplió completamente en este momento. Sería en los capítulos 10 y 15 que otras cosas sucedieran para responder al hecho de que tanto las palabras de Joel como la gracia de Jesús se extendían más allá de la identificación con el judaísmo.

Apocalipsis 7 — "Una Multitud desde Cada Nación"

Juan, escribiendo en Apocalipsis, habla en varias partes de la gente desde las naciones congregándose alrededor del trono celestial en adoración. Esto era un concepto desconsolador, aunque inspiraba esperanza para los judíos y el cristianismo judío. Para la iglesia gentílica, esto era una cuestión de esperanza y confianza en la aceptación de Yahvé sin dependencia en las tradiciones judías y mosaicas.

Hay otras visiones representadas en Apocalipsis que hablan de la salvación hacia los judíos, como de los 144,000 reunidos de las 12 tribus de Israel. La dificultad en este texto, entretanto, es que este número se limita a hombres, vírgenes masculinos de una lista dudosa de 12 tribus. Tal número excluiría las vasta mayoría de creyentes en los primeros dos siglos. Los judíos en esa época eran mayormente descendentes de las tribus de Benjamín y Judá, ya que las demás tribus se habían formado de la nación de Israel luego de la época de Salomón. Estas tribus del norte habían sido mezcladas racialmente en el período de exilio asirio y a su regreso. Ellos habían sido grandemente asimilados entre las demás naciones, el remanente mayor transformándose en los samaritanos odiados.

En la visión de Juan, entretanto, los 144,000 eran mucho más que una representación de la nación pura de Yahvé, quienes no se habían ensuciado por la idolatría. La terminología y el simbolismo de Juan funcionan aquí para enfocar en su pureza religiosa y su devoción a Yahvé como el único Dios. La sexualidad aquí referida tiene más que ver con las asociaciones de la idolatría con sus prácticas de prostitución en los templos de los cultos de fertilidad. La enumeración de las tribus de Israel toma cuidado para aislar una tribu reconocida más que los demás por su idolatría e infidelidad a Yahvé. A la tribu de José se le da extra representación, ya se menciona a José como también el nombre de uno de sus hijos para traer el número de tribus otra vez a 12.

Esto no debería representar una limitación de la gracia de Dios y la extensión del alcance del evangelio. Estos números son nada más que un retrato simbólico que de veras la gracia de Dios alcanza a todos quienes someten sus vidas al servicio de Dios. El número queda de acuerdo con la mención de la multitud incontable de toda lengua y nación de la tierra, de cada tribu. Es la representación del cumplimiento de la promesa de Dios a Abraham en Génesis, que todas las familias de la tierra encontrarían bendición por medio de él. Esta es la visión mayor de Juan, una de las mayores extensiones de participación que podemos encontrar en la Biblia. Como así, todas las gentes, los idiomas, las etnicidades y las tribus son vistos como iguales en importancia ante Dios. Por implicación, ellos deberían ser de importancia igual a todos quienes arrojan sus vidas a servicio y en sumisión a la voluntad de Dios.

Mateo 28 — La Gran Comisión

El pasaje final en Mateo 28 acostumbra ser interpretado como la gran comisión de Jesús. Ha sido utilizado en sermones y textos de misiones alrededor del mundo por lo menos desde los días de William Cary y el comienzo del movimiento moderno de misiones evangélicas. No hay nada necesariamente errado con esa aplicación, a no ser por el hecho que mientras Jesús ofrece aquí una comisión para sus discípulos de todas las generaciones, no es necesariamente una comisión para irnos.

El verbo imperativo aquí no es la tradicional, "Vaya, pues, y hagan discípulos" de tantos sermones. Este es un ejemplo en el cual las versiones tradicionales de la Biblia no hicieron la mejor traducción del texto griego de Mateo. El griego expresa el verbo ir de forma diferente. La frase sería mejor traducida, "Mientras que se vayan, pues, hagan discípulos." En lugar del ir siendo el imperativo, la orden de Jesús aquí es "haced discípulos." Queda subentendido que los discípulos irían, ya que no se quedarían en aquel monte inhabitado. La cuestión es, "al irse," "dondequiera se vayan," "al paso de sus rutinas o viajes," o "dondequiera que se encuentren," deberían llevar a cabo su comisión de discipular a las naciones.

Esta comisión para hacer discípulos, entonces, no se limita a viajar en alguna misión o propósito específico. No es de ninguna forma condicionada a dejar la tierra natal para llevar las buenas nuevas de Cristo a otros. Claro, Jesús hace referencia específica de este mandamiento siendo dirigido a hacer discípulos de todas las naciones, todas las nacionalidades, todas las gentes del mundo. No hay, entretanto, ningún sentido de que esto debe ocurrir por el envío de misioneros a lugares remotos del mundo. Es cierto que se debe llevar a cabo esta comisión mientras haya creyentes quienes jamás han cruzado una frontera nacional y hacen discípulos de los inmigrantes, extranjeros y desconocidos con los cuales tienen algún contacto. No importa el modo de este contacto, esta comisión depende solamente de que haya contacto.

Vemos la aplicación de este principio en Hechos 2 en el día de pentecostés con la presencia de judíos en peregrinaje en Jerusalén provenientes de todo el mundo. A ellos se les presenta el evangelio, el cual llevan en su regreso a sus propias tierras. Vemos a la vez en Hechos 8 con el encuentro de Felipe con el eunuco Etíope, quien lleva el evangelio de regreso a su reina, Candace, en Etiopía. Ella influencia su nación para aceptar el evangelio de Jesucristo. Vemos el principio aplicado en el ministerio de Pablo. No importaba adonde estaba o adonde pretendía irse, cuáles eran sus planes de viaje o cómo estos fueran interrumpidos. Él estaba en una misión para Cristo en la totalidad de sus viajes, dejando iglesias atrás en sitios donde jamás había planeado viajar o quedarse. Mientras viajaba, mientras trabajaba, mientras hacía sus trámites, él estaba en misión para hacer discípulos, sin referencia a su nacionalidad.

El ministerio del propio Jesús demostraba esta misma actitud y misión para traer el mensaje del amor, de la gracia y de la aceptación de Dios hacia todos quienes se cruzaban su camino. De vez en cuando, salía de su camino para que sucediera cierto contacto. Más seguido, entretanto, su propio camino se cruzó por alguien con un propósito, plan o necesidad diferente. Él aprovechaba todos esos encuentros bajo el estandarte de la misión mayor a su frente. Él extendía la mano a samaritanos, judíos y a los demás gentiles, haciendo discípulos a lo largo de su camino.

En cierto nivel, nuestro abuso de este texto como un texto de envío misionero se le hace injusticia a su mensaje y nos distrae del propósito real de Jesús tras esta comisión. Este no es un texto que simplemente se aplica a misioneros en el extranjero. Esta comisión se aplica a uno y a todos los seguidores de Jesús. No es un mandamiento del cual podemos distanciarnos como excepciones a la regla.

Cada uno de nosotros debe estar en la misma misión de hacer discípulos de todas las naciones o gentes. No deberíamos mirar a esto desde la perspectiva de "si por acaso sean de otra nacionalidad, eso es aceptable." En lugar de esto, el mandamiento nos envía en una dirección muy específica, asegurando que nuestros esfuerzos de hacer discípulos entre otros no excluyen a ningún grupo de personas. Somos comisionados a cruzar barreras culturales, étnicas e lingüísticas para hacer discípulos de todas las naciones, no simplemente de aquellos que se nos asemejan.

La comisión incluye a todos desde dos perspectivas. Primero, cada seguidor o discípulo es comisionado. Segundo, estamos todos bajo la comisión de hacer discípulos de cada nación, sin cualquier excepción. La forma más inmediata por la cual esta comisión se aplica a nuestras vidas como individuos tiene que ver con las comunidades de inmigrantes en nuestro medio. Estas son las naciones que encontramos al seguir nuestra rutina diaria en nuestros negocios normales. Esto es donde empieza la gran comisión de Jesús—aquí en casa. Claro, también comprende esfuerzos de misiones en el extranjero, pero el concepto es mucho más extenso que eso. Engloba la responsabilidad de todo creyente de cada nación para alcanzar a extenderse con propósito en llevar el evangelio ante todo grupo de personas, sin cualquier distinción.

Génesis 4 — "Cualquier Que me Encuentre me Matará"

Estamos acostumbrados a leer la narrativa de Génesis 4 desde una cierta perspectiva, la que trata a Caín como el hombre malo, uno a quien Dios le castiga y sobre el cual se le echa una maldición. La tradición nos dice que no hay nada bueno o digno en Caín. Nos dice que debemos aborrecerlo, ya que como asesino no sirve para nada más.

Si leemos la narrativa con atención, entretanto, no es así que Dios se le trata a Caín. Seguro, Dios le avisa a Caín sobre las consecuencias de su pecado. Más que maldecirle, entretanto, lo que Dios hace es colocar una dosis de protección sobre Caín. Dios le cubre con una señal a decir a los demás que nadie debería de matarle a él.

Suena muy raro a nuestros oídos. El deseo humano natural sería más coherente con que le mataran a Caín, ya que éste había asesinado a su hermano. Dios no quiere actuar, ni quiere que los demás actúen de tal forma. Dios interviene en la situación para ofrecerle a Caín cierta protección que seguramente se le hará necesario. Se le hace necesario, porque él ahora será un errante sobre la faz de la tierra, un inmigrante por donde quiera que vaya.

El hecho de que Caín se preocupa por cómo será tratado tiene mucho que ver con la condición de ser errante, y tiene poco que ver con su condición de asesino. A veces perdemos esto de vista, pues estamos leyendo la narrativa y sus acciones para matarle a su hermano Abel están en nuestra frente. En la condición de errante e inmigrante, nadie sabría de sus acciones en matarle a su hermano. Su miedo por ser muerto no tiene nada que ver con venganza por sus acciones. Tiene todo que ver con adoptar la condición de inmigrante, extranjero, desconocido, ajeno.

La tendencia humana es de tratar a cualquier persona ajena con cierta dosis de desprecio e inseguridad. No conocemos al ajeno y cuando se trata de alguien de otra clase, nación, idioma, etnia o color quedamos ansiosos en referencia a ellos. No actúan de acuerdo a nuestras normas. No se visten de acuerdo a nuestros modelos. No habla con el mismo sentido, aunque puedan utilizar las mismas palabras. Su pronunciación es distinta. Su forma de mirarle a otro es diferente. Sus valores, prioridades y acciones nos dicen que debemos estar en guardia en contra de alguna amenaza que desconocemos.

Esta era la situación en la cual Caín estaba entrando. Este era su miedo. Sentía que cualquier que le encontrara le miraría como una amenaza. Se sentía inseguro al entrar en la categoría de errante e inmigrante. Eso, porque la condición de inmigrante es en verdas una condición muy vulnerable.

El inmigrante es vulnerable, porque no conoce las reglas de la sociedad en donde se encuentra. No conoce las normas de interacción de la población. Aunque pueda que hable el idioma, lo habla no simplemente con un acento, no lo utiliza de acuerdo a todas las normas culturales. No comprende las nociones escondidas del lenguaje. No sabe discernir entre un chiste, un elogio y un ataque sarcástico. No comprende cuando se utilizan dobles sentidos para las palabras y los motivos escondidos de los demás.

Puede que aprenda algo de estas cuestiones lingüísticas, pero jamás lo puede comprender de la misma forma que el residente. Es que él no comparte la misma base cultural, social y filosófica de aquellos en cuya presencia se encuentra. Más bien, él utiliza otro sistema de lentes por medio de los cuales interpreta las palabras, acciones e intenciones de los demás.

Lo más interesante aquí, entretanto, es la acción y actitud de Dios referente a Caín. A Dios se le interesa trabajar para protegerle a Caín. Dios reconoce la veracidad de su preocupación por encontrarse como errante e inmigrante. Dios interviene para que él se protegido, aunque Caín es asesino. Aunque él tiene sus fallas éticas y morales, Dios se preocupa por él, específicamente por cuestión de que se encontrará en una condición que tiende a hacerle vulnerable ante las poblaciones residentes y establecidas. Dios ofrece protección a Caín porque él lo necesita.

Esto parece ser la preocupación mayor de Dios en lo tocante a los cuidados por las poblaciones errantes o migrantes. Son las mismas preocupaciones por las viudas, los pobres, y los huérfanos. Las personas que tienden a ser ignoradas por la sociedad y tratadas con algún tipo de desprecio son las personas por los cuales Dios tiende a ofrecer protecciones especiales. Son los más vulnerables, y por eso es que Dios exige que se les extienda un nivel diferenciado de protección. Ellos son vulnerables, y Dios exige que sean protegidos en reconocimiento de esa vulnerabilidad.

Mateo 2 — "Los Extranjeros Sabios"

El evangelio de Mateo se inicia con una lista genealógica de los ancestrales de Jesús. La lista queda esparcida con los nombres de cuatro mujeres quienes reflejan la presencia de gentiles entre los antepasados de David y Jesús. Establecida así una base para reconocer que el evangelio de Jesús no será solamente para el beneficio de los judíos, Mateo agrega otra mención de gentiles en el capítulo 2.

Aquí encontramos un grupo de magos desde el Oriente, más probablemente de la región de Babilonia y reflejando las tradiciones de los caldeos, quienes eran los astrólogos de la corte de Babilonia en la época del exilio judío. Ur era una ciudad en la región de los caldeos, la ciudad desde donde Abraham y su familia empezaron su migración hacia la tierra que se llamaría Israel.

Probablemente Mateo quería que su público judío hiciera la conexión aquí con el peregrinaje de Abraham. Es también probable que él quería que comprendieran una conexión con Babilonia y su historia del exilio y que quería recordarles del aprovechamiento por Dios de Ciro, un rey conocido por su oposición a los judíos, pero quien Dios utilizó como un instrumento para regresar a los judíos desde el exilio hasta Judá.

Haciendo estas conexiones, Mateo también nos lleva en lo que sería un viaje incómodo para cualquier judío. Debemos comprender que Yahvé habló a estos astrólogos mientras que estudiaban las estrellas por informaciones acerca de la voluntad y las acciones de sus dioses. Mientras proseguían con sus ritos y cultos paganos, Yahvé les habló acerca del nacimiento de Jesús, nacido para ser rey de la nación judía.

¿Qué razón tendría Dios para hincarse a hablar con astrólogos paganos? ¿Por qué razón Yahvé les daría información en lo tocante a la llegada de Jesús y no decir nada a los propios judíos? ¿Por qué serían estos extranjeros privilegiados con esa información acerca del nacimiento del Mesías, cuando la propia nación fue dejada en la oscuridad referente a lo que Dios realizaba?

Tradicionalmente, hemos enfocado en estos magos, los hemos tratado como reyes, los hemos contado de acuerdo al número de los regalos que le presentaron a Jesús, pero hemos ignorado las preocupaciones religiosas del hecho que Dios se estaba comunicando con extranjeros mientras guardaba silencio ante Israel en lo tocante a la llegada de su tan esperado Mesías.

Deberíamos quedar perturbados por este pasaje. Aparentemente, eso era por lo menos la intención de Mateo. ¿Por qué razón Dios se comunicaría con una gente que ellos consideraban ser enemigos? ¿Por qué Dios aparecería de cualquier modo a un bando de astrólogos idólatras, quienes pensaban de las estrellas en la noche como dioses a ser adorados? Hasta donde Mateo parece estar preocupado, entretanto, Dios no se preocupa con nuestras categorías humanas de quienes son o no son dignos de ser influenciados por Yahvé. A final, hay muchos pasajes del Antiguo Testamento en que pasó exactamente lo mismo en la historia de Israel.

Rahab era una prostituta, probablemente trabajando con un culto pagano a la fertilidad. Era ella, entretanto, quien comunicó a los espías de Josué el mensaje que ellos necesitaban oír. Ella era la que les dijo que Yahvé tendría la victoria en la batalla anticipada en Jericó. Ella, la idólatra, la extranjera inmoral, conocía la verdad de Yahvé que la propia gente de Yahvé no deseaba o no estaba preparada para aceptar.

Se ve la misma historia en las narrativas de Elías. Allá en 1ª Reyes, encontramos a una viuda en el territorio de Baal que tiene un nivel de fe en Yahvé que parece ser inexistente en Israel. Ella se dispone a confiar en Yahvé, mientras que el rey de Israel y sus siervos están más preocupados con adorar a Baal. En el balance, ella es la que recibe los beneficios de la atención de Yahvé, mientras que el rey de Israel no puede aceptar ni confiar en las bendiciones de Yahvé.

De igual forma, estos magos son sabios, no tanto por causa de su estudio de las estrellas como deidades comunicándose con la humanidad.

Su sabiduría se revela por sus acciones en seguir lo que Dios se revela a ellos y procurar a aquél nacido para ser rey de los judíos.

Ellos muy bien pueden continuar a ser extranjeros idólatras, inmigrantes en la tierra de Israel. Ellos pueden ser ajenos a la alianza de Dios con Abraham y su descendencia, pero Dios no les ha olvidado, ni les ha ignorado, ni les ha echado de lado. En medio de sus fracasos y formas inapropiadas de adorar, Dios intervino para comunicarles gracia y bendición.

Antes del final de la historia, ellos se ven más santos, dignos y rectos que Herodes, quien actuaba como rey de Israel. Aunque Herodes era solamente un rey títere para Roma, él se queda más preocupado con proteger su poder, prestigio y posición que con honrarle a Yahvé. Estos extranjeros, entretanto, entran a la tierra de Israel para pagarle tributo y honra a Yahvé, no desde un sentido de obligación, sino en alegría por la comunicación de Yahvé para con ellos. Ellos adoran y celebran el regalo de Dios, preocupándose con lo que Yahvé está haciendo, no por cualquier cuestión de orgullo, posición o privilegio.

Como en el caso de Rahab y la viuda de Sarépta, son los extranjeros, los desconocidos, los ajenos a la comunidad de Israel, quienes demuestran para aquellos de adentro como debería ser una relación con Yahvé. Estos sabios desconocidos establecen el patrón para la fe real, lo que consiste en pertenecerle a Yahvé. Ellos demuestran que Dios no se preocupa con nuestros conceptos de estatus y preeminencia, sino con un corazón de dedicación, adoración y regocijo con las iniciativas y acciones de Dios.

Herodes liquida a inocentes en Israel para proteger a lo que no puede mantener. Los magos conceden posesiones dignas para honrar a uno nacido para ser rey de una nación extranjera. Ellos demuestran adoración digna, mientras que Herodes solo puede pensar en su autopreservación. Mientras que ellos regresan a casa regocijados, Herodes se mantiene preocupado, ansioso, y muere incompleto y desconectado de Dios.

Hechos 6 — Elección de Diáconos Inmigrantes

Ya mencionamos que la población de Jerusalén crecía a cada año en el período entre la pascua y la fiesta de pentecostés. Judíos de toda parte de Imperio Romano viajaban cuando podían a Jerusalén para las celebración de la pascua, la fiesta más importante del año. Muchos planeaban todas sus vidas para hacer tal peregrinación. Entre ellos, algunos planeaban quedar sus últimos años de vida en Jerusalén, esperando estar presente para la llegada del Mesías. Si murieran en Jerusalén, esperaban ser resucitados a su llegada para participar del banquete mesiánico en la restauración de Israel.

Aun hoy, la mayor parte de los judíos esperan participar en tal celebración. El término tradicional para la fiesta de la Pascua continúa a ser, "¡El próximo año en Jerusalén!" Los judíos hacían peregrinaje a Jerusalén y se migraban a Israel en referencia a tales esperanzas. Cuando murieron y fueron sepultados en Jerusalén, entretanto, mucho dejaban viudas en la región, algunos quienes no tenían de que sobrevivir en sus últimos días. Para la iglesia primitiva, esto resultaba un gran problema.

Sabemos desde los escritos del Nuevo Testamento y de otros documentos históricos, que hubo una serie de hambres en Palestina en los años siguiendo la muerte y resurrección de Jesús. Pablo escribía acerca de iglesias gentiles recaudando fondos para ayudar a alimentar a los hambrientos en Jerusalén. Hechos relata que los creyentes en la iglesia de Jerusalén también se dieron trabajo para proveer por los hambrientos de su comunidad por la venta de tierras y bienes para comprarles comida. Aun así, había otras dificultades. Algunas de las viudas en la comunidad estaban siendo olvidadas. Ellas no eran conocidas por muchos de la población residente.

Estas siendo pasados por alto eran las viudas de inmigrantes judíos que se quedaron en Jerusalén en. Ellas no habían crecido y criado sus familias en Jerusalén. La mayoría no tenían familiares para cuidarles en su mayor edad. Ellas eran ajenas, aun si judías. Muchas, si no la mayor parte, hablaban idiomas diferentes que hablaban los judíos palestinos. Hablaban griego, que era la lengua común del Imperio Romano, y esto causó otro nivel de separación y distancia de la comunidad asentada en Jerusalén.

La iglesia de Jerusalén no estaba procurando pasar por alto a esas viudas. No había ninguna intención para oprimir u ofender, pero el hecho de que eran inmigrantes significaba que no tenían la misma facilidad de enlaces para conseguir la ayuda que necesitaban. Era una simple inadvertencia.

Cuando se trajo el tema ante los apóstoles, hubo cierta incomodidad y preocupación en lo tocante al problema ante ellos. La resolución al cual llegaron los apóstoles, entretanto, era muy inusual por su forma. Lo que determinaron hacer era elegir siervos (diáconos) para la iglesia que cuidarían de administrar la distribución de alimentos de tal forma para asegurar que nadie fuera pasado por alto. Eso parecía una sugestión razonable, como los apóstoles tenían otras prioridades para su responsabilidad. Había mucha otra gente que pudiera cumplir con los requisitos para asegurar una distribución justa.

Trajeron nombres, por lo tanto, para colocar sobre la distribución. Cada uno de ellos era un judío inmigrante. Esto no era nada comparado con las definiciones políticas utilizados en los Estados Unidos para responder a las dificultades con los derechos civiles y la discriminación. Este procedimiento fue mucho más allá de las tácticas políticas en los EUA. Los apóstoles encargaron a la comunidad inmigrante que escogieran entre si siete hombres de buena reputación para supervisar el proceso. Ellos eran los que estaban atentos a la injusticia que se hacía, aunque el problema no era intencional. Como los que conocían la situación, a ellos se les daría la responsabilidad de resolver la inadvertencia. Deberían tomar cuidado para que no solamente las judías helénicas no fueran pasados por alto, sino que tampoco se pasara por alto a las judías palestinas.

Esto era una estrategia alarmante por los apóstoles. "Les escuchamos. Reconocemos que hay un problema. Les agradecemos por traerlo a nuestra atención. Queremos que ustedes, los más atentos al problema, sean los responsables por resolverlo. Elijan entre ustedes gente en quienes tienen confianza para supervisar la distribución de comida. Nosotros les consagraremos o comisionaremos para tener seguridad que el proceso se torne más justo e igual, y que a nadie se le pase por alto."

Parece que la iglesia no tenía problema con la propuesta de los apóstoles. Ellos comprendían la sabiduría de la respuesta. Son aquellos que sufren la injusticia quienes son más hábiles para comprender como se ve y se siente la injusticia. Son ellos quienes deberían ser parte de la solución. Ellos son los que tienen algo en juego en el proceso. Son ellos quienes están atentos a las preocupaciones. Son ellos que comprenden las preocupaciones desde adentro. Así, son ellos quienes pueden de forma más apropiada recibir la tarea e identificar soluciones reales.

La iglesia no parece que estaba muy preocupada con cualquier concepto de discriminación inversa. Ellos no se preocuparon que un grupo de inmigrantes les volviera la toma. Ellos no estaban preocupados en ceder poder a un grupo que estaba pasando por problemas como gente ajena a la comunidad. En lugar de eso, estaban preocupados con atender a las necesidades de aquellos a quienes no se les estaban sirviendo de forma adecuada. Ellos cedieron poder a ellos como ajenos para que se transformaran en la solución a las dificultades que ellos mismos reconocieron y que trajeron a la atención de otros.

Por darles a estos ajenos la responsabilidad y poder para corregir las dificultades reconocidas, ellos les trajeron hacia el centro de la comunidad mayor. Los apóstoles y lo demás de la iglesia hicieron de la comunidad de creyentes inmigrantes igual al resto de la comunidad de creyentes. Ellos les elevaron en estatus de inmigrantes, extranjeros y desconocidos hacia miembros responsables de la comunidad, tan centrales al funcionamiento de la iglesia como a cualquier otro individuo o grupo.

Esto es un retrato de lo que significa incluir a otros en la formación de una comunidad. Es un retrato de lo que quiere decir incluir a extraños, extranjeros e inmigrantes en el corazón de una comunidad, amándolos y tratándolos como a nosotros mismos. Es esto lo que significa amar como Jesús nos enseñó, ofreciendo aceptación y gracia tras el modelo establecido por Jesucristo.

Hechos 8 — El Eunuco Etíope

Hechos capítulo 8 cuenta la historia de un inmigrante de Etiopía quien leía un texto de Isaías en su viaje de regreso desde Jerusalén. Este hombre era un prosélito al judaísmo, habiéndose convertido, pero procurando una mejor comprensión de su fe judía.

Mientras que Felipe se aproximaba del carruaje y reconoció que leía las Escrituras hebreas, le preguntó si comprendía la lectura. Esa pregunta abrió las puertas para un diálogo en lo tocante a Jesús y el evangelio que Jesús había proclamado. Felipe tomó esa oportunidad para compartir su fe y comprensión con este hombre.

El resultado de la conversación no se relata en el libro de Hechos. De acuerdo a lo que Lucas conoce, el hombre pidió ser bautizado por su fe en Jesús (un rito de conversión como aquel que le hizo un prosélito al judaísmo) y continuó su viaje de regreso a Etiopía, donde servía a la reina Candace como mayordomo.

Hay mucho más de la historia que Lucas no relata en Hechos. Lucas quizás no se interesaba por compartir todos los detalles, o posiblemente no conocía las demás consecuencias de aquel encuentro en un lugar desértico. Él puede simplemente haber presumido que sus lectores ya conocían las demás implicaciones de su historia, sin tener que mencionarlas. Él solo se preocupó en mencionar lo que le ayudaría adelantar su caso por llevar el evangelio por etapas hacia las comunidades gentílicas en todo el mundo.

Los creyentes en Etiopía conocen consecuencias mayores para esta historia en Hechos 8, así como los lectores originales de Lucas que pueden también haberlas conocido. Este encuentro "por acaso" entre Felipe y el eunuco tuvo consecuencias a muy largo plazo.

De inicio pareciera que el envío de Felipe hacia el medio de una zona incivilizada y despoblada sería un desperdicio severo de recursos. ¿Por qué gastar el tiempo para salir y hablar con un solo individuo, cuando había ciudades llenas de personas que también necesitaban escuchar las buenas nuevas de Jesucristo?

Dios tenía un plan con un propósito mucho más largo tras su envío de Felipe a ese sitio desértico de lo que Lucas nos relata. El eunuco en cuestión era un alto funcionario de la reina Candace. Como resultado de su conversión al judaísmo de Jesús, las buenas nuevas entraron a la corte de Etiopía, donde este eunuco tuvo acceso a la reina y a una posición desde cual tenía gran influencia entre toda la nación a la cual servía.

Candace vino a ser creyente como resultado del testigo de Felipe por medio del eunuco. Ella no simplemente aceptó a Jesus, sino que llevo su nación completa a que adoptara el cristianismo como el primer país oficialmente cristiano en el mundo.

Resulta obvio que todos los individuos de Etiopía no cedieron sus vidas en sumisión a Cristo, entrando en una relación de compromiso con Dios por medio de Jesús. El impacto de esa conversión, entretanto, influenció a toda una nación hacia la aceptación del evangelio.

Los judíos como una nación no volvieron a Jesús en aceptación de su posición e identidad como Mesías. Etiopía, entretanto, lo hizo.

Más que esto, entretanto, la historia tradicional de Etiopía reclama que la nación ya era un centro del judaísmo desde los días de la visita de la reina de Seba hacia Salomón en Jerusalén. Por esa historia, el eunuco en Hechos 8 no simplemente regresaba a Etiopía como un individuo convertido al judaísmo y a Jesús. Él era parte de una nación que había aceptado al judaísmo y regresó con el complemento del mensaje que Jesús era el Mesías prometido y anhelado.

Eusebio, uno de los padres de la iglesia primitiva, escribió de este eunuco como el primer gentil a convertirse al cristianismo y el fundador de la iglesia en Etiopía. Hay evidencia que algunos de los ritos y las tradiciones del cristianismo etíope y de su judaísmo se extienden hacia fechas anteriores al exilio, como hay una historia de celebrar festivales con fechas de esa época. Por lo menos parece haber un intercambio e influencia con el judaísmo de épocas remotas.

El judaísmo tenía dificultades con la conversión de un eunuco, pero Lucas no parece tener preocupaciones con tales temas. Él parece mucho más preocupado con la adoración del eunuco en relación a la fe hebrea y su aceptación de Yahvé como el único digno de adoración. Es desde esa perspectiva que Lucas habla de su conversión al cristianismo.

Felipe no trata con este eunuco de acuerdo a las normas de la tradición judía. Él lo trata como un igual ante Dios. Le habla en base de las Escrituras que se leían. No encuentra ningún impedimento para su bautismo en la presencia de agua. Aunque técnicamente no era digno para una conversión al judaísmo por ser eunuco, Felipe no ve ningún impedimento para bautizarle como creyente y seguidor de Jesús.

El resultado de esta conversión parece no haber sido solamente una prefiguración literaria de Lucas en lo tocante a la llegada del evangelio a Cornelio. También prefigura el ministerio de Pablo ante reyes y autoridades en todo el Imperio Romano. Antes que Pablo pudiera empezar su ministerio entre los gentiles, Felipe, uno de los diáconos helénicos de Jerusalén ya era responsable por la presentación del evangelio encaminarse hacia Etiopía, considerada una de las tierras más remotas por los judíos y los romanos.

Encontramos aquí un judío helénico inmigrante comunicando el evangelio a un inmigrante desde otra tierra. Este hombre con una conversión dudosa al judaísmo encuentra plena aceptación en el evangelio de Cristo. Es por medio de su aceptación de este inmigrante pasando por

Israel que la comisión establecida por Jesús en Hechos 1:8 se ve realizada en la tierra de Etiopía, "los confines de la tierra" en la mente de los lectores de Lucas. Este inmigrante no solamente recibe el evangelio para si mismo, sino que aparentemente lo lleva de regreso a otros, asumiendo la plena responsabilidad del discipulado. Son los inmigrantes aquí que son transformados en los emisarios del evangelio hacia inmigrantes, comunicando el mismo evangelio a otras naciones.

Pablo, El Apóstol Inmigrante Judío

El mismo Pablo es un personaje muy interesante en relación a su estatus de inmigrante. Él era ciudadano romano y judío, pero su nacimiento fue en Tarsos, afuera de la Palestina. Como romano, él era ciudadano del poder mundial. Como el hijo de judíos, él era judío desde la perspectiva de su etnicidad, religión y educación. Habiendo nacido afuera de Palestina, entretanto, le hacía un inmigrante en Jerusalén, un ajeno que hablaba griego tanto como el arameo, según los moldes del diácono Felipe.

Aun con esas consideraciones, Pablo se hizo parte de las estructuras de poder en Jerusalén en sus esfuerzos tempranos para aplacar la creciente popularidad de los seguidores de Jesús. A la vez, su ministerio como judío y luego como creyente le llevó mayormente a otras tierras donde era clasificado como ajeno, sea por su nacimiento e identidad como judío o por haber nacido afuera de Palestina.

Esta identificación con el judaísmo le clasificó como ajeno por todo el territorio del Imperio Romano. Su ciudadanía romana le definía como ajeno entre los judíos. Su trabajo y vida entre las naciones gentiles creó un sentir a que abandonara sus raíces judías, creando enemistad desde judíos y creyentes judíos. Ambos su nacimiento y el carácter de su ministerio le hacían ajeno entre romanos, griegos, judíos y hasta los creyentes convertidos con los cuales ministraba.

Él Era ajeno en Jerusalén y notablemente no tenía una posición entre el concilio de la iglesia en Jerusalén. Allí es Pedro quien habla con autoridad en conjunto con Santiago. Aunque Pablo puede ser acreditado con escribir la mayor parte del Nuevo Testamento, él lo hizo como un ajeno, un inmigrante trabajando entre muchas poblaciones, pero siempre como uno que no pertenecía en sentido religioso, cultural, político, étnico y nacional. A veces su estatus inmigratorio le era benéfico a su ministerio, pero en la mayor parte le costó personalmente y físicamente, como le colocó en la posición de ser un blanco fácil para servir de chivo expiatorio por cualquier percepción de amenaza por el crecimiento de la comunidad creyente.

Pablo era visto como una amenaza al judaísmo por las poblaciones judías alrededor del mundo, pero más notablemente en su regreso a Jerusalén después de un emprendimiento misionero de impotancia. Allí, la acusación es que había llevado gentiles hacia las cortes del templo donde no deberían ser dejados entrar. En tierras gentiles, Pablo era visto como ajeno y culpado por poner el mundo al revés. Era visto como anarquista y antisocial, pues que no participaba en las normas de la idolatría.

Como ajeno, él era un blanco fácil para abuso, desde aprisionamiento, flagelos, látigos y ser arrastrado afuera de la ciudades para ser apedrejado. Era comúnmente echado de una ciudad por las autoridades locales, aun cuando eran ellos quienes quebraban la ley romana e ignoraban los derechos de Pablo como ciudadano del Imperio Romano.

Es este ajeno, un inmigrante en muchas tierras, a quien se le da crédito como siendo la mayor influencia singular en el crecimiento del cristianismo en el primer siglo. De la misma forma que tratamos a inmigrantes, extraños, y ajenos, somos capaces de estar tratando a otros como a Pablo, pues él habría estado entre aquellos quienes consideramos más allá de las definiciones de quienes pertenecen a la población residente y establecida.

Fue su ministerio a Cristo que le llevó a tantos lugares y le clasificó como ajeno. Él era ajeno a los judíos, atenienses, corintios, romanos, efesios y filipenses. Fueron estas gentes, entretanto, quienes tanto le maltrataron dado a su miedo e incertidumbre de su estatus de ajeno, que por otro lado dieron crédito a sus palabras, aceptando el llamado de Dios para descansar en la gracia y el amor de Dios retratados en Jesucristo. Era su estatus de ajeno que le ayudó a ver como el evangelio podría cambiar la gente a los cuales predicaba. Era también su estatus ajeno que tanto le dio audiencia por algunos y causó que otros procuraran formas de silenciarle para siempre.

Al final, entretanto, eran aquellos quienes corrieron a Pablo de sus ciudades quienes eran más responsables por el crecimiento del evangelio. Eso no quiere decir que Pablo no ministró y compartió el mensaje del evangelio de forma efectiva. Es simplemente que cuando le obligaron a dejar primero una ciudad y luego otra, otros se vieron obligados a tomar posiciones de liderazgo dentro de la comunidades de creyentes nuevos. Si Pablo hubiera quedado mucho más tiempo, es probable que su liderazgo y crecimiento en el ministerio jamás hubiera ganado el mismo impulso. Al ser obligado por asumir responsabilidad para dar continuidad a lo que Pablo empezó en su medio, esas comunidades crecieron de una forma que probablemente no lo habrían hecho de otro modo.

Gálatas 3 — "Ni Judío Ni Griego"

Pablo famosamente escribió que en Cristo no hay distinciones entre judíos y griegos, hombre y mujeres, esclavos y libres. Estas palabras son llamativas, pero a la vez suenan muy conocidas al oído moderno y occidental. Mientras que aceptamos las palabras con su valor aparente, nuestra aplicación de las mismas palabras a lo largo de los siglos ha sido mucho menos vislumbrante. Los hemos reclamado para nuestra propia igualdad, pero las hemos rechazado en relación a la igualdad de los demás. Deseamos nuestros derechos y beneficios que tales palabras nos pueden comunicar, pero muy difícilmente dejamos que sirvan de beneficio hacia los demás. Actuamos como si la gracia de Dios no fuera suficiente en sustancia para extenderse a todos, trayendo beneficio a todos hasta el mismo nivel.

Para Pablo, estas no eran simplemente palabras. Había mucha importancia por detras de las frases que escribió hacia las diversas iglesias a quienes dirigía sus cartas. De muchas maneras, estos conceptos de igualdad eran explosivos. No solo eso, sino que él también aplicó estas palabras de modo que chocaron a las comunidades de los fieles. Esto era parte de la polémica que enfrentaba con los judaizantes quienes le perseguían de ciudad en ciudad.

Estos judaizantes eran enfáticos sobre la superioridad distintiva no simplemente del evangelio, sino también por su estatus ante Dios como judíos. Para ellos, la cuestión de su identidad judía era mucho más que una simple identidad étnica o cultural. Se les comunicaba algo referente a su importancia ante Dios. Era fuente de orgullo para ellos que eran judíos. Más allá, entretanto, su judaísmo les distinguía de lo demás de la población del mundo. Les hacía santo. Les hacía aceptable ante Dios. Era casi un sustituto por cualquier dependencia en la gracia. De veras, esa es la crítica mayor de Pablo en toda la temática levantada por la comunidad judaizante. Si uno depende de su judaísmo, ya no queda espacio para la gracia.

Como resultado, Pablo determinó que no hay ningún valor inherente que difiere entre aquellos que son o no son judíos. Ante Dios, no hay absolutamente ninguna diferencia. Su argumento en Romanos es que todos son pecadores y nuestros mejores esfuerzos de rectitud son como trapos inmundos ante Dios. El código mosaico puede haber revelado una mejor manera por la cual vivir, una ética más elevada por la cual conducirnos, pero no nos hace y no puede hacernos más dignos de la atención, del cuidado y del amor de Dios.

Una vez que aceptemos la salvación y la redención por medio de la gracia, debemos reconocer que no estamos llegando hacia Dios en la base de cualquier calificación personal, valor o merecimiento. Simplemente llegamos ante Dios en la base de sus calidades de gracia, amor, misericordia y perdón. Como esto es todo lo necesario para una vida en la presencia de Dios, inmediatamente no hay ninguna distinción entre nosotros según preocupaciones de valor o importancia. No hay distinciones étnicas, culturales, lingüísticas o de designaciones nacionales para hacer de algún grupo superior o inferior a otro.

De hecho, Pablo extiende el concepto más allá de las limitaciones de identificación religiosa, étnica o lingüística. Él aplica los mismos principios a distinciones de género y estatus social. Él dice que no hay ni judío ni griego, ni hombre ni mujer, ni esclavo ni libre. Tales palabras cortan al corazón de las estructuras sociales del mundo en medio del cual vivía. Si uno las tomara en su valor literal, habrían sido suficientes para destrozar no solamente la estructura social de Israel, sino también la de todo el Imperio Romano.

Mujeres, esclavos y extranjeros no eran considerados tener el mismo valor que los hombres en poder. Para que Pablo simplemente eliminara esas distinciones dentro del evangelio de Cristo era un mensaje perturbador. Era más que simplemente revolucionario, como para muchos sería un ataque a las estructuras básicas de la sociedad. En un sentido muy real, esto era exactamente lo que las palabras de Pablo referente a la igualdad significaban. Ellos definían que no había ninguna diferencia de valor de acuerdo a las categorías en uso por las culturas y estructuras sociales de la época.

Religiosamente, quizás la distinción entre judío y griego era la distinción más importante, pero Pablo no deja el tema en ese punto. Él habla a todo aspecto de la división entre categorías o clases de personas. Él elimina completamente la definición de aquellos que pertenecen y que no pertenecen, los con poder y los oprimidos dentro de los límites del evangelio de Jesucristo.

Si esta cuestión es un tema tan importante en el evangelio como Pablo lo afirma ser, no hay ninguna razón razonable para continuar a hacer distinción entre clases y categorías de personas sobre cualquier base. La posición de uno como inmigrante, desconocido o extranjero se torna en cuestiones risorias ante el evangelio. Se tornan frases ridículas siendo aplicados donde por derecho no existen. Se transforman en definiciones que luchan en contra de los propósitos del evangelio de la gracia de Dios en Cristo. Llegan a ser ataques a las iniciativas de Dios para formar una sola nación desde todas las naciones, clases y categorías de personas.

No pueden existir tales distinciones dentro de la iglesia de acuerdo a la reivindicación de Jesucristo como Señor, pues los propósitos de Dios son hacernos uno. Echan fuera toda y cualquier categoría de distinción o valor. Cualquier discusión de nacionalidad, etnicidad, género o estatus social en referencia al valor o la importancia se transforman en más que simples discusiones afuera del reinado del evangelio. Ellos efectivamente se transforman en discusiones que corren contrario al evangelio. Quedan en oposición a las categorías del evangelio, la gracia bajo cual nadie tiene más mérito que otro. Mérito, valor y estatus son conceptos de una calidad completamente ajena a esta igualdad que origina con la gracia de Dios en Jesucristo.

Juan 17 — La Oración de Jesús por Unidad

En este capítulo del evangelio de Juan, encontramos a Jesús orando por sus discípulos. Él ora tanto por los discípulos a su frente, como también por sus discípulos a lo largo de los siglos. Él expresa tanto un deseo que sus discípulos sean unidos en un solo cuerpo, como también que Dios les moldara a sus discípulos en aquel mismo cuerpo.

Conocemos bien este tema de unidad como una categoría central de la enseñanza del Nuevo Testamento, pero quizás pasamos por alto el grado de la unidad hacia el cual Jesucristo llama a sus seguidores por las épocas. Tradicionalmente hemos mirado a la unidad en tantos términos, pero la mayoría de ellos quedan por el camino cuando miramos a cuestiones de la práctica, como también el grado de unidad al que ambicionamos.

Hay muchos clamando por unidad por medio de una conformidad doctrinaria. A ellos les gustaría que creyéramos las mismas cosas, aceptemos un conjunto básico de verdades y que apliquemos el evangelio de una forma coordinada a nuestra comprensión de Dios y preocupaciones doctrinarias y teológicas. Hay un problema con esta categoría de unidad. Empieza y acaba con nuestros patrones de pensamiento. Jamás se extiende más allá de las cosas que se puede memorizar, clasificar o sistematizar. No tiene la flexibilidad inherente necesaria para adaptarse a nuevos contextos de vida, nuevas situaciones que jamás imaginamos y las experiencias de la vida que nos sorprenden.

Otros claman por la unidad de una estructura organizacional. Quieren que todos los creyentes en toda parte del mundo entren en membresía a una sola institución que será la representación única y singular de Dios y del evangelio de Cristo. El problema aquí es que Jesús jamás estableció cualquier estructura institucional para la iglesia. Él estableció a una comunidad de fe dinámica, viva y multifacética. También habló de otras ovejas de otros rediles que aun necesitaban ser juntados. Habló de la fe afuera de los límites de Israel y comisionó a individuos para compartir su testimonio de la misericordia de Dios lejos del centro de la fe en Jerusalén y aparte de comunicación con cualquier estructura jerárquica. El otro problema mayor con este tipo de unidad es que depende de algún tipo de realidad política, por medio del cual individuos o grupos hacen decisiones que deben ser aplicadas a situaciones desconocidas por los que hacen las decisiones. Jesús jamás aceptó esa clase de estructura de poder. Él comisionó a individuos para depender de Dios por su dirección, mientras que aplicaban el principio de relatar a otros lo que Dios había hecho en sus vidas, sin establecer cualquier sistema de supervisión.

Otros claman por unidad en sentido de procedimientos y procesos identificables. Ellos miran a grupos como los Testigos de Jehová, quienes utilizan una estrategia global para evangelismo y educación. Ellos desean tomar un único modelo y que todos se unan en la aplicación y el uso del producto. Cuando miramos al ministerio de Jesús en Juan, entretanto, encontramos que su conversación con las personas cambiaba de forma considerable a cada evento y con cada individuo. Él habla las buenas nuevas con referencia a agua viva, transformando agua en vino, un renacer, el pastoreo de ovejas, pan de vida y a un gran grupo de otras presentaciones que responden a las preocupaciones de sus oyentes. Él no emplea ninguna estrategia singular que se aplica en todo caso, a no ser el encontrarse con personas en el punto de su necesidad y formular su mensaje dentro de su contexto de vida.

Estos tres conceptos de unidad fallan tanto en unir a los creyentes en todo el mundo, como en alcanzar el grado de unidad a lo cual Jesús nos llama. Estas son respuestas superficiales a preguntas mucho más hondas. Ellos son las respuestas de aquellos que quieren una respuesta simple, una definición rápida, con la cual trabajar. No logran accesar los temas más hondos que tienen un impacto en la unidad. Tampoco logran respetar las palabras de Jesús en lo tocante a la calidad de unidad a la que nos llama.

En Juan 17, Jesús ora que seamos uno de la misma forma en que Jesús y el Padre son uno. Esto requiere una apreciación muy distinta de la unidad a la cual debemos aspirar. Nos llama a unirnos en propósito, carácter, deseo, visión y enfoque. Nos llama a dejar de lado cualquier sentido personal de valor, ambición, dignidad y consuelo para agarrarnos a una unidad por el sentido del propósito declarado por Pablo en Filipenses, considerando a todo lo demás como desechos para que alcanzáramos el llamado siempre más elevado de Dios en Jesucristo.

Parecería que la unidad al cual Jesús nos llama tiene mucho más que ver con el carácter y propósito. Es más el unir nuestras vidas al propósito de Dios, dejando que Dios viva por medio nuestro, tanto individualmente y corporalmente. Dado a la variabilidad y diversidad inherente de la creación de Dios, no esperaríamos que esta unidad fuera un elemento exterior visible de una institución, una metodología o un pensamiento grupal. En contraste, sería una unidad de propósito y carácter, una unidad basada en el amor de Dios. Es esta unidad que nos juntaría en una búsqueda para implementar los principios de las buenas nuevas de una relación con Dios y uno con el otro. Es una unidad que nos llevaría más allá de los límites de nación, etnicidad, cultura, idioma, género, estatus, riqueza, influencia y poder. Se nos uniría en cuidar a los de nuestro alrededor.

Este es el carácter de unidad al cual Jesús retrató al hablar y al vivir la voluntad y los propósitos del Padre a lo largo de su ministerio. Él aplicó los principios de esta unidad con Dios y otros de muchas formas, en muchos lugares y en una multitud de situaciones. Le llevó a hablar de aceptación y agua viva a la mujer samaritana. Le llevó a hablar con Nicodemo de un nuevo nacimiento sin dependencia en cualquier sistema de legalismo o descendencia, pero que transformaría su vida de forma radical desde su interior. Jesús no organizó ni publicó un código de análisis doctrinario que pudiéramos memorizar y citar conforme la necesidad. Él no estableció ninguna estructura organizacional del cual podríamos depender. En lugar de eso, nos llamó a la unidad en dependencia de Dios. Esta dependencia rechazaría a todas nuestras categorías por cuales nos aislamos de otros y reclamamos algún tipo de superioridad sobre aquellos que no encajan en nuestras definiciones.

En realidad, es eso que queda en la base de estas definiciones contrarias respecto a la unidad por uno u otro sistema. Es un modo de clasificarnos en el grupo correcto, rotulando a los demás como ajenos. Nada pudiera estar más lejos de los propósitos de Dios en Jesucristo. Él no echa a nadie de lado, a no ser por los hipócritas religiosos quienes reclaman ser algo que no lo son. Aun a estos él ofrece aceptación, si únicamente dejaran de lado su auto importancia. Es lo mismo con nuestras categorías de aislar personas por considerar nuestra incomodidad con ella como un reflejo de que Dios este inconforme con ellos y que Dios no les acepta. El llamado de Jesús hacia la unidad, entretanto, destruiría tales reclamaciones por completo. Nadie es más o menos merecedor que nosotros. El evangelio es, al final de todo, un mensaje de gracia, un mensaje que elimina a todas nuestras categorías de aceptabilidad, dignidad, valor y superioridad.

Esto es un llamado a la unidad bajo la gracia de Dios, una unidad que elimina cualquier sentido de superioridad. Nos coloca en una misma base igual ante Dios, aceptados dado a su amor, no a algún sentido de valor individual. Es en esta aceptación, gracia y amor que nos debemos unir, sin atención a nuestros modos institucionales de categorizar a la gente para que nosotros nos sintamos superiores a los demás. Debemos unirnos a los propósitos de Dios en gracia y amor, reflejando sus propósitos hacia todos, tal cual experimentamos en Jesucristo. Éste es nuestro modelo de unidad, aceptando la mujer samaritana en el pozo, los leprosos, la mujer cananea, el ciego, el demoníaco de Gadara, los pescadores, los cobradores de impuestos, los fariseos y los pobres, también. Bajo esa luz, nuestras definiciones para dividirnos se tornan inválidas y trabajan en contra del evangelio que declaramos preservar y servir.

Mateo 8 — El Siervo del Centurión

En este pasaje, la historia de Jesús es sorprendente en una forma que posiblemente no esperemos. En este caso, es la comunidad judía que viene a Jesús para pedir su intervención en beneficio de un centurión romano y su siervo. Jesús no empieza a enseñar de la importancia de aceptar a uno ajeno a la comunidad, un gentil. De hecho, vemos que la propia comunidad de judíos reconocen en este extranjero quien representa una fuerza de opresión militar ajena, uno quien es justo y digno de la misericordia de Dios.

Estos judíos parecen tener buena razón para ver en el ejemplo de este hombre uno digno de la atención de Jesús. A la vez, sus definiciones de valor están basadas en la ayuda que este centurión ha ofrecido a la comunidad en la construcción de su sinagoga. El hombre había tomado la iniciativa de acercarse hacia la comunidad judía. Los judíos aparentemente no habían hecho nada para justificar su atención positiva y ayuda. Ellos reconocieron en sus acciones y actitudes, entretanto, que él no era como a los demás gentiles, o por lo menos no conforme su concepto de prejuicio de cómo era un gentil, específicamente, como era un soldado romano.

Esto es comúnmente el caso. Somos tentados a clasificar a otros de acuerdo a una perspectiva de prejuicio en contra de una cultura entera. Nuestras ideas referentes a las culturas tienen algo de validez, ya que nos ayudan a comprender lo que podemos esperar de otros miembros de una misma cultura. Al conocer a un individuo dentro de la cultura o sociedad ajena, entretanto, vemos que el individuo no es idéntico a nuestros conceptos predefinidos del todo. Nuestros estereotipos fallan al tomar una mirada más cercana a individuos dentro de la categoría mayor que clasificamos como uno.

Jesús jamás se encontró con el centurión en toda esta narrativa. Él primero tuvo un encuentro con algunos judíos quienes le contaron de la necesidad del hombre y compartieron su comprensión de la razón por la cual era digno de la atención de Jesús. El próximo encuentro, entretanto, es con un grupo de siervos que llegan a encontrarse con Jesús en su ruta para que él regrese a su propio camino. Su mensaje es que no hay necesidad para que Jesús llegue ante el centurión en persona. Todo lo que necesita es enviar su palabra para que su siervo se sane. Él creía que la autoridad de la palabra de Jesús sería lo suficiente, sin cualquier necesidad mayor para preocuparle a Jesús con un viaje para verlo.

En este punto, Jesús queda impresionado con el centurión. Jesús no quedó impresionado con sus obras y donación para la construcción de la sinagoga. Él no quedó impresionado con que los judíos estaban intercediendo por la necesidad de este hombre. Jesús no parece impresionado por la llegada del siervo del centurión para pedir su intervención. Lo que le impresiona es con el carácter de la fe del hombre.

¿Qué tiene su fe de significante? El hecho que el hombre es un gentil no parece figurar en la atención de Jesús. Debería haber provocado alguna molestia, como es evidente por las palabras de los judíos quienes vienen a su encuentro para pedirle que intervenga. Ellos sintieron necesario justificarle a Jesús su pedido en base de las acciones del centurión que estaban en contra de su posición de representar la ocupación militar de Roma. El hombre era gentil. El hombre no se había convertido al judaísmo, conforme lo que sabemos. El hombre era oficialmente un enemigo de la nación de Israel, pues era representante de Roma. Él era parte de las fuerzas de ocupación militar bajo los cuales los judíos estaban sufriendo. Él era más probablemente idólatra, adorando a sus dioses romanos conforme las costumbres de Roma. De cualquier forma, Jesús queda impresionado con él, dado al carácter de su fe, y solamente su fe.

Aquellos otros temas parecen haber sido secundarios a Jesús. Claro que Jesús no promovía la idolatría y la adoración a las deidades paganas. Jesús no animó la opresión a nadie. Jesús no representaba las prioridades de Roma, pero él sí comprendió y concedió valor al carácter de este hombre quien depositó su confianza en Jesús.

Este extranjero, emblema de la opresión y enemistad, vio en Jesús una autoridad que de cierta forma era semejante a su propia. Comprendía que si Jesús podría sanar desde cerca en la base de su autoridad y dependencia en Yahvé, él lo podría hacer también desde lejos. Jesús no estaría limitado por cuestiones geográficas como nos acostumbramos pensar, sino que podría simplemente pedir la intervención de Dios, sin preocuparse por la distancia.

Jesús no parece haberse importado con que el hombre era un gentil, un extranjero, un miembro de una fuerza de opresión en Israel. Todas estas categorías que marcaban al centurión como ajeno no le eran importantes. Él estaba más enfocado en el hecho de la fe del hombre y lo utilizó como ejemplo para los propios judíos. Mientras que ellos se enfocaban en cómo el centurión no pertenecía a la nación de Israel, Jesús se preocupaba en mostrar a los judíos como este extranjero demostraba las calidades que ellos mismos faltaban. Él tenía el carácter de fe que ellos necesitaban alcanzar.

El hecho que este hombre era un extranjero, un oficial que representaba una ocupación militar, no se calificó a Jesús como importante. Estas eran categorías que parecen ser insignificantes a Jesús. Mientras que podrían hablar montones a nosotros como obviamente hacían a los judíos alrededor de Jesus, ellos tuvieron poco impacto en el carácter de su respuesta a este hombre. No deberían haber hecho una diferencia a ellos, ni a nosotros. La única cosa que parece tener importancia a Jesús es el hecho que la fe de este hombre refleja una calidad más alta de lo que había encontrado entre la mayoría de los propios judíos. Si ser un oficial de una presencia militar opresiva es inconsecuente a Jesús, ¿cuánto menos debería un estatus de inmigrante o extranjero tener consecuencia para nosotros?

Juan 1:46 — "¿Puede Algo Bueno Salir de Nazaret?"

Cuando Andrés fue introducido a Jesús, él fue para encontrarse con Felipe y le invitó a encontrarse con Jesús. La respuesta de Felipe es una que demuestra cúan poco Nazaret era considerado en importancia en el área. "¿Puede algo bueno salir de Nazaret?"

Había mucho prejuicio geográfico en Judá, aun entre la gente de sus propias fronteras y nacionalidad. Los judíos tenían prejuicios obvios en contra de los samaritanos, cananeos y romanos, bien como de los extranjeros. Dentro de sus propias fronteras y entre la gente que compartía su mismo fondo étnico, cultural y lingüístico, ellos mantenían otros prejuicios, también.

Habían actitudes que menospreciaban a los pobres, los ciegos, los cojos, los leprosos y los indigentes del día. Habían actitudes en contra de personas de ciertas ciudades o regiones, como la de Nazaret. Felipe no podía creer que Nazaret era lo especial suficiente para dignarse de la honra de ser el sitio de origen de cualquier persona de importancia. Parece haber sido en su mente un sitio sin cualquier estatus especial o preeminencia para ser mencionado.

Jesús vivió con esa clase de estigma. Sus propios discípulos eran galileos, tachados como gente inculta y sin estatus. Era un estigma con la cual él empezó su ministerio y uno que él contrarió por la forma que se dirigió a temas de posición, estatus, poder e importancia. Dibujó la forma que el trataba a las personas, y cómo guió los patrones que utilizó hasta para seleccionar los individuos que llegaron a ser sus discípulos y enviados.

Parecería que Jesús se dio trabajo para llamar como discípulos a personas quienes serían tachados de la misma clase cuestionable como Felipe lo clasificara a él. En el libro de Hechos, los líderes judíos hacen comentarios referentes a que estos discípulos no tenían el fondo y la educación correcta. Había, entretanto un reconocimiento que ellos habían estado con Jesús.

En lo tocante a la sociedad judía, no había absolutamente nada de especial referente a Nazaret. No había nada de especial en el fondo de Jesús y su vida de hogar para que él llegara hacia la preeminencia en la sociedad de Israel. Él no estudió bajo cualquier rabino reconocido de la época. Él no venía de ninguna familia conectada. Él no nació ni creció en las ciudades correctas, los vecindarios correctos o entre los círculos sociales correctos.

Sus orígenes lo designaron como un ajeno, uno que no pertenecía, uno que no estaba preparado para entrar en la escena política, social y religiosa de Judá con cualquier cosa que se asemejaba a importancia o validez. A pesar de sus orígenes sociales, entretanto, algunos como Andrés reconocieron algo de especial en él.

Felipe tuvo que dejar de lado sus conceptos prejuiciosos de Nazaret para tomar una mirada más cercana a Jesús. Él tuvo que colocar sus expectaciones de lado para que mirara a Jesús de acuerdo a su identidad propia, en lugar de juzgarle de acuerdo a las definiciones sociales referentes a la clase al cual pertenecía. Él no estaba preparado para lo que habría de encontrar en Jesús, pero lo habría perdido por completo si no hubiera colocado de lado sus ideas prejuiciosas y tomado pasos para encontrarse con Jesús y escucharle con sus propios oídos.

Esas comúnmente son las mismas barreras que encontramos en nuestros encuentros con personas de tradiciones, culturas y lugares diferentes. Lo menos que les conocemos personalmente, lo más que nuestros estereotipos parecen justos. Al escuchar sus historias y conocerles personalmente, entretanto, encontramos que nuestros prejuicios sociales tienden a caerse de lado. Empezamos a verles como personas, no como a una categoría de personas.

Sin embargo, requiere de alguna iniciativa, apertura e inversión. Debemos abrirnos para realmente escucharles y llegar a conocerles. Es rara la vez que un encuentro rápido como el de Felipe con Jesús sería suficiente para romper estas barreras que hemos construido a lo largo de años de actitudes prejuiciosas. Lo que encontramos en aquellos de fondos diferentes puede ser lo completamente inesperado, igual a lo que Felipe encontró en Jesús.

Aparentemente, Jesús no le culpó a Felipe por su reacción inicial al convite de Andrés para verle a Jesús. Era, después de todo, una pregunta muy esperada. Entretanto, Jesús le llamó a reconocer que habría muchas otras sorpresas esperándole en una vida de seguirle a Jesús. Sería una vida de ser introducido a una serie de conceptos inesperados referentes a Dios, a otras personas y de quienes eran realmente dignos de la redención de Dios.

Felipe empezaría una jornada con Jesús que acabaría con todas sus expectativas sobre personas de acuerdo a categorías de mérito y valor. Reconociendo a Jesús como algo bueno que salió de Nazaret era solo el inicio para Felipe. Jesús le enseñaría a arrojar todas esas categorías a la basura bien como toda la cuestión de mérito.

Jesús no estaba en el negocio de colocar a personas en diferentes categorías de valor. Él se ocupaba de llamar a las personas más allá de esas categorías hacia una vida de dependencia y confianza en Dios. Él les enseñaría a descartar el concepto de merecer la buena voluntad de Dios y arrojar su vida en la gracia de Dios en su lugar. La gracia no considera el mérito y valor. Se enfoca más bien en la calidad de amor que se ofrece.

En lugar de cuestionar si algo bueno puede salir de una de esas categorías de personas que nosotros echaríamos de lado como indignos, debemos considerar que el mismo Jesús vino desde esas mismas categorías y ministraba mayormente a personas de las mismas categorías de valor cuestionable a la sociedad. Si Jesucristo les amó a ellos lo suficiente para redimirles, no tenemos cualquier base para hacer nada menos y reclamar que servimos a Jesús.

Hechos 26 — "Con Excepción de Estas Cadenas"

Luego de los viajes misioneros de Pablo y su regreso eventual a Jerusalén, él fue arrestado y encarcelado hasta que un tumulto al su alrededor pudiera ser investigado. Al escuchar de un complot en contra de su vida, Pablo apeló para que su caso fuera escuchado ante César, así para evitar que fuera liberado hacia una emboscada. En el curso de su espera para ser enviado a Roma, él tuvo la oportunidad en múltiples ocasiones de hablar con oficiales romanos. Fue en una de estas ocasiones que compartió su fe en Jesucristo, ante el cual fue acusado de querer que todos fueran como si mismo. Su respuesta fue, "Sí, con excepción de estas cadenas."

Pablo no se preocupaba con cuestiones de nacionalidad, política, estatus, etnicidad, idioma o fondo social. Él aceptó la acusación de desear que toda la corte fuera transformada de la misma forma en que él había sido transformado. Él trató a todos de acuerdo a la misma perspectiva y propósito. Era su misión compartir el mensaje de Jesucristo con todos, no haciendo ninguna distinción entre sus oyentes.

Lo que quizás pasamos por alto aquí, es que al predicar el evangelio de gracia, amor y aceptación, Pablo descartó cualquier idea de condenación hacia los demás. Esto había sido central en su historia en el judaísmo. Al aceptar el mensaje de Jesus, entretanto, él dio la espalda a esas tradiciones que había seguido, las cuales colocaban a las personas bajo definiciones de condenación.

Pablo podría haber mirado a estos oficiales romanos quienes le mantenían en cadenas como si fueran sus enemigos. De hecho, eran sus carceleros, aunque estuvieron atados por los designios de la ley para enviarle a Roma mientras querían ponerle en libertad. Él vivió encadenado, aunque sus carceleros no le percibían ser cualquier amenaza. Ellos estaban más preocupados con las repercusiones políticas de enviarle a César cuando no tenían ninguna acusación en su contra.

Lucas no dice nada sobre la razón que Pablo no les habló a sus carceleros de la amenaza en contra de su vida. Debería haber sido un tema de importancia para que Roma protegiera la vida de uno de sus ciudadanos contra cualquier complot. En algún punto no mencionado, entretanto, uno de los poderosos romanos quizás estaba en asociación con aquellos que procuraban asesinar a Pablo. Sin tomar en cuenta la posibilidad de tal complicidad contra Pablo y en contra de las leyes romanas, Pablo aun no les miraba como sus enemigos, sino como personas quienes simplemente necesitaban de oír y responder a la gracia de Dios ofrecida libremente en Jesús.

Para Pablo, los enemigos eran simplemente más personas con los cuales se debería compartir el amor de Dios. Él no mantenía una categoría en la cual colocaba personas indignas del mensaje que tenía para proclamar. Claro, él habló bruscamente de los judaizantes quienes querían obligar a los gentiles que primeramente se tornaran judíos y legalistas antes de aceptar la fe en Jesús. Él era claro en su oposición a esa doctrina como contraria al centro del evangelio. Aun así, él no dejó que su desacuerdo con ellos le concediera base para desligarles ante la gracia y misericordia de Dios.

Los oficiales romanos quienes le mantenían cautivo también eran, ante los ojos de Pablo, simplemente discípulos de Jesus en potencial. Ellos no eran diferentes de él, y él quiso que no fueran diferentes, a no ser por las cadenas que le ataban. Era su deseo que ellos llegaran a ser como a él en relación y dependencia en Dios. Él no excluiría a nadie y llamaba a todos hacia la unidad y gracia que había encontrado en el evangelio. Hasta aquellos quienes eran responsables por su prisión, él no estaba preparado para despreciar.

Pablo consideraba que estos oficiales representaban una fuerza imperial opresiva en todo el mundo y eran iguales a si mismo en lo tocante al evangelio. Él no les consideraba amados por Dios en ninguna forma diferente del amor y la gracia que él mismo había recibido de Dios en Cristo. No estaba solamente dispuesto a compartir el evangelio con ellos, sino de no hacer exigencias sobre ellos además de darles la oportunidad de responder libremente a la gracia de Dios en Jesucristo.

A no ser por la condición de su prisión, Pablo miraba a todos como iguales a si mismo. Después de todo, él no se consideraba como nada especial, a no ser en lo tocante a cómo hacía a Jesús visible en sus palabras, actitudes y acciones. Él se negó colocarse arriba o antes de nadie más, sino que también se esforzó a traerles a todos al mismo estatus ante Dios que él mismo gozaba, basado en una simple aceptación de lo que Dios libremente ofrecía en gracia.

Humanamente hablando, Pablo tenía toda razón para mirar a estos su alrededor como enemigos, inmigrantes, extranjeros, extraños y ocupadores, pero él se recusó a verles como nada más que otros individuos a quienes Dios deseaba redimir. Bajo esa luz, ellos eran solamente iguales, y eso le llamaba a tratarles como tal, sin preocuparse hasta con las circunstancias de su prisión.

Romanos 12:13 — "Trae Desconocidos Hacia Sus Casas"

El término utilizado aquí en Romanos 12:13 es filoxenia. Como ya se ha dicho, tiene como sentido básico el amor hacia los desconocidos. La traducción en inglés, New Century Version, traduce la frase como "Trae desconocidos hacia sus casas." Es más normal que lo consideremos un término para hospitalidad, pero el sentido del término aquí va más allá de una simple hospitalidad, tanto aquí como en Hebreos 13. Es una hospitalidad con un nivel diferenciado.

Xenia es el viajante, el ajeno, el otro, la persona desconocida. Esto tiene que ver con el dar la bienvenida a aquellos que no nos son conocidos, trayéndoles hacia nuestras casas como una expresión del amor y el cuidado de Dios por uno y por todos. Este versículo sigue inmediatamente por el comentario de Pablo sobre el hacer el bien a aquellos quienes les gustaría hacernos daño. Esto coloca la frase en un contexto de extendernos más allá de una simple hospitalidad hacia aquellos quienes ya conocemos, en quienes confiamos y a quienes amamos. Esto se refiere a ampliar nuestro círculo de aceptación y amor para incluir a personas que podríamos hasta temer, ofreciéndoles una porción de la abundancia que Dios ha colocado bajo nuestros cuidados.

Bien que Pablo conocía la "filoxenia," como se le habían recibido en muchas casas por el curso de sus esfuerzos misioneros. Sabemos que entró a la casa de Lidia en Filipos como huésped de honra, como también fue introducido a la casa del carcelero de la misma forma en la misma ciudad. No sabemos mucho de los demás sitios en donde viajó, pero se nos comunica alguna comprensión que había recibido de la "filoxenia" en más de una sola ocasión, y en más partes que en Filipo.

Lucas escribe en Hechos 28 de Pablo recibir de la hospitalidad de Publio, aunque utiliza allí otro término para la hospitalidad en esa instancia. Esa es el término más general con el sentido de una actitud amable, gentil hacia los demás. En Romanos 12 y Hebreos 13, entretanto, el término es más distintivo. "Xenia" por si sola es el término griego moderno para la hospitalidad, relacionada en su origen a conceptos antiguos de Zeus como el dios de viajeros y cuidando de aquellos lejos de su hogar.

El mundo romano del día de Pablo era familiarizado con los conceptos de hospitalidad hacia desconocidos como un motivo de justicia asociado a la responsabilidad religiosa. Estos conceptos ya estaban en circulación alrededor del mundo griego hablante desde la época de Homero, hace unos 1,000 años antes del ministerio de Pablo. El motivo aquí expreso en Romanos 12 y Hebreos 13 se cuadra perfectamente con este principio ya en vigor en el panorama religioso gentil. Pablo toma esta misma temática y construye con ella una relación a la responsabilidad de uno hacia Dios en cuidar no solamente por las necesidades de los demás creyentes, sino también por desconocidos, extranjeros, viajantes e inmigrantes.

Amar y cuidar de desconocidos se encaja bien en el contexto de los comentarios de Pablo aquí en Romanos 12. El concepto se relaciona con el mandamiento de Pablo para hacer el bien a aquellos que nos harían daño, siendo amigables con todos, no maltratando a nadie y siendo amigos de gente regular. Esto es un componente social al evangelio que nos impulsa a que seamos transformados en contribuidores positivos de la sociedad en la cual vivimos. No debemos jamás enfocarnos tanto en el cielo que perdamos de vista nuestra responsabilidad de hacer bien en la tierra. Al contrario, como Pablo menciona aquí, nuestra ofrenda de nuestras vidas como sacrificios vivos hacia Jesucristo incluye que seamos siervos de Dios para extendernos el amor, la gracia y la bendición de todos a nuestro alrededor.

1ª Timoteo 2 — "Es la Voluntad de Dios Que Todos Sean Salvos"

Como Pablo le escribe a Timoteo, él es muy específico sobre el alcance del deseo de Dios para ofrecer la salvación. Dios no distingue entre personas de acuerdo a clases de dignos o indignos, aceptables o inaceptables. La misma categoría de la salvación por gracia actúa en contra de cualquier comprensión de la salvación ser limitada por Dios hacia cierta categoría o clase de personas.

Los seres humanos desde hace mucho tiempo establecieron sistemas para colocar personas en categorías referentes a su valor. Hemos determinado quienes pertenecen o no pertenecen a familias, tribus, comunidades, ciudades, sociedades, naciones, grupos étnicos, clases sociales y hasta castas.

El propósito divino para la reconciliación en Jesucristo, entretanto, no utiliza tales categorías. Dios no coloca a personas en cajas, surtiéndolas de acuerdo a su valor y mérito. El mensaje del evangelio es que Dios ama a la creación como un todo, no solamente una parte de la humanidad, sino toda ella también junto a los animales y las plantas.

Mientras que queramos colocarnos en la categoría de los que pertenecen, Dios no tiene tal categoría. Bajo su plan de redención, no hay más que una sola categoría en la cual la humanidad se encuentra. Todos son aceptables a Dios, pues es la voluntad de Dios que todos sean redimidos y entrar a una relación de confianza en Dios.

Fue esto todo el propósito por el cual Jesús llegó hacia Israel de primera instancia. Ellos habían sido escogidos como un bando de gente sin importancia con nada para darles motivo de orgullo de posición o/e importancia. Dios había tomado un bando de harapientos esclavos huidos y de ellos formó una nación. Dios se había bajado al estatus de un ser humano en Jesucristo para retratar ante todos hasta donde Dios estaba dispuesto a ir para rescatar, redimir y restaurar a una nación que había abandonado sus propósitos.

Ahora en el Nuevo Testamento, Dios tuvo que recordarles a los creyentes judíos que los mismos propósitos de transformarles a ellos en una nación estaban en acción en el propósito renovado de Dios para redimir a toda la humanidad. Dios aun consideraba a ellos como no siendo mejores que los demás, ni tampoco peores. Aun así, Dios estaba dispuesto en tomar tanto a judíos como a gentiles y hacer de ellos una sola nación. Desde todos ellos, Dios formaría una nueva gente más allá de las delimitaciones y fronteras de definiciones políticas, territoriales, étnicas, lingüísticas, culturales y de ciudadanía. Desde todas las naciones, Dios criaría una nueva gente, trayéndoles a la existencia sin dar importancia a cualquier de esas distinciones, pues era y es la voluntad de Dios de redimirles a todos.

Si esto es el propósito de Dios, cualquier acción nuestra que actuara en contra de establecer el carácter de esa unidad queda siendo una acción en contra de los propósitos de Dios hacia los cuales hemos sido llamados. Más que esto, es sobre estos mismos propósitos de Dios que se basa nuestra propia salvación y nuestra relación con Dios. Excluir a otra persona es echar de lado a los propósitos de redención por las cuales hemos sido aceptados por Dios.

1ª Pedro — Discípulos en la Dispersión

Pedro escribió sus cartas a los discípulos en la dispersión. Esto era aparentemente después de la destrucción de Jerusalén en el año 70. En la ocasión, los judíos habían parado de ofrecer los sacrificios anuales en beneficio de César en el año 66, lo que era parte de su acuerdo arreglado con Roma para que quedaran exentos de la obligación de hacer sacrificios directamente a los dioses romanos. Cuando el general romano Tito marchó en el templo para sacrificar un cerdo a los dioses romanos sobre el altar a Yahvé, los judíos reaccionaron a esa desolación sacramental del templo de Yahvé por tocarle fuego y empezar a destruirlo. En el caos y confusión subsecuente, Jerusalén fue completamente destruida y los judíos chocaron con las fuerzas militares romanas.

Jerusalén y el territorio vecino fueron evacuados por los romanos y los judíos fueron expulsos de Roma, también. El centro del judaísmo se trasladó hacia Babilonia, donde algunos judíos se habían quedado desde el exilio. Tanto los judíos como los cristianos fueron esparcidos por todo y más allá del Imperio Romano, mientras huían de la violencia en Judea y procuraron tranquilidad. En conjunto con la destrucción de Jerusalén fue roto gran parte de los sueños acerca de la llegada del Mesías para establecer el reinado mesiánico en Jerusalén. Aunque se agarraban al sueño, reconocieron que cualquier llegada del Mesías se tardaría en llegar.

Cuando Pedro escribió a los creyentes en la dispersión, era a esta huída de Judea al cual se refería. Por definición, estos creyentes eran ahora todos inmigrantes o refugiados, habiendo huido de la guerra y la destrucción en Palestina. Ninguno de ellos podría vivir más en su país natal. Los judíos habían sido expulsos de Roma, como también de las demás ciudades mayores del Imperio, y Jerusalén ya no existía.

Los creyentes en esa época aun eran considerados como poco más que una secta dentro del judaísmo, y por lo tanto, judíos de acuerdo al mundo romano. Como judíos o cristianos, ellos no eran solamente inmigrantes en tierras ajenas, eran refugiados en exilio. Ellos huían de la guerra, la opresión, el conflicto y de toda calidad de prejuicio. Los cristianos enfrentaron un segundo nivel de persecución, esta desde judíos quienes no querían que fueran nombrados entre ellos.

Pedro les habló en lenguaje y figuras que recordaban al éxodo, cuando Dios había sacado un bando de esclavos que huyeron de Egipto, formándoles en una nación. De esta vez, entretanto, Pedro declaraba que su estatus como nación no se definía por cualquier ciudadanía terrestre, sino por participación en el reinado de Jesucristo. Era entre esta población esparcida quien vivía como refugiados por todo el Imperio Romano que Dios trabajaría para construir una nueva realidad, moldeándoles en una gente muy aparte de su estatus político o nacional.

Pedro tomó sus palabras un paso más adelante, incluyendo a los gentiles en esta mezcla como porción formativa de esta nueva nación que Dios formaba. Los creyentes eran refugiados, pero sus hileras crecerían desde las gentes entre los cuales vivían. Dios les tomaría a todos, a pesar de sus orígenes raciales, étnicos, nacionales o políticos, creando de ellos una gente completamente nueva con una identidad que se extendía más allá de una identificación nacional.

De muchas formas, puede que eso había sido el propósito del establecimiento de Israel también, aunque el ideal jamás vino a materializarse. Aparentemente, mucha gente esclava salió de Egipto junto con los descendientes de Abraham. Moisés lideró las diez tribus al salir de Israel, pero parece que muchos otros salieron juntos con ellos en este intento por libertad. Gentiles como Rahab, Rut y Urías hicieron su camino para entrar en la nación de Israel en tiempos remotos, siendo asimilados en la vida de Israel. Esto parece haber sido el propósito eterno de Dios, así como Dios le prometió a Abraham que todas las familias del mundo encontrarían bendición por medio de él.

Aun así, Israel jamás alcanzó la calidad de estos ideales, así como también la iglesia con tanta frecuencia ha fracasado por alcanzar la medida. Pedro, entretanto, no tenía remordimiento en elevar estos ideales ante los creyentes esparcidos por todo el Imperio Romano como refugiados en la dispersión. Ellos no eran una nación. Ellos habían perdido cualquier protección que una identidad nacional les había proporcionado. Políticamente, eran gente rechazada, refugiados de una guerra con pocos derechos o esperanzas por un futuro brillante. Aun así, Dios les miraba como dignos de gracia, amor, misericordia y de ser transformados en el centro de esta nueva gente a quien Dios estaba llamando a la existencia.

"Antes ustedes no eran una gente," es parte del tema de Pedro. Ellos habían perdido su identidad, pero Dios ahora estaba trabajando para darles una nueva identidad, una que alcanzaba más allá de los límites de ciudadanía, política y nacionalidad. En su condición de refugiados, fueron comisionados a tornarse un reinado de sacerdotes a Yahvé, una nación colocada aparte para una misión especial de Dios. Por segunda ocasión, vemos a Dios trabajando para llevar una gente rechazada su sociedad, pisoteados por aquellos en poder, y transformarlos en una nueva realidad más allá de las limitaciones y definiciones de las realidades y categorías políticas existentes. De cierta forma, es un paso divino hacia un concepto de globalización de su reinado.

Es este mismo principio que debería guiar nuestras propias actitudes en lo tocante a los inmigrantes, refugiados, extranjeros o extraños. Dios cuida lo suficiente por aquellos quienes nosotros echaríamos de lado para honrarles con participación en el reino de Cristo Jesús. Luego los comisiona como ministros y sacerdotes de este nuevo reinado, para que todos conocieran a Dios. Las categorías que nosotros podríamos utilizar para descartar algunos al basurero de la humanidad, son las mismas categorías con las cuales Dios actuó en por lo menos dos ocasiones para formar para si una gente de todas las naciones del mundo.

Apocalipsis, Distinguiendo Lealtad a César y a Dios

El libro de Apocalipsis ha inspirado una multitud de interpretaciones imaginativas a lo largo de los siglos. Hemos visto predicciones del final del mundo vez tras vez, empezando por lo menos desde hace mil años. Más recientemente, gente como Hal Lindsey lo intentaron utilizar para predecir realidades políticas y predecir el retorno de Jesucristo. Como otros, él reconoció problemas con su interpretación después del hecho y publicó una nueva versión de su interpretación falla.

La carta de Juan, entretanto, es mucho más directa en tantas maneras que estas interpretaciones inventivas que procuran predecir eventos futuros. Juan tenía cosas mucho más importantes a comunicar que ofrecer a los creyentes un relato de cómo Dios acabaría con el mundo a miles de años luego de la muerte de Juan. De hecho, su mensaje fue dirigido a las iglesias de su propia época, los lectores y oyentes de sus visiones narrativas quienes encaraban dificultades reales en su aplicación de la fe hacia la vida real.

Haríamos bien recordar que la mayoría de este tipo de interpretación de Apocalipsis hoy se basa en los modelos frustrados del pasado. Miles han intentado utilizar el libro dentro del patrón de comprender la profecía como revelación del futuro antes que suceda. Bíblicamente, entretanto, la profecía tiene más que ver con comunicar el mensaje de Dios a la gente del día del propio profeta. Este mensaje puede tener un componente futuro, pero en 90 por ciento de los casos se refiere a la época del profeta o a su futuro inmediato. Moisés fue considerado el profeta preeminente de los judíos junto con Elías. Sus ministerios proféticos tenían muy poco que ver con predecir el futuro. Ellos no se preocupaban por predicción, sino con comunicar la voluntad de Dios a la gente de su día.

La preocupación mayor de Juan es como los creyentes en Jesucristo deberían responder y vivir en la situación del las exigencias religiosas del Imperio Romano. Nos gusta hablar de persecución, y de veras hubo cierta medida de eso. La mayor parte de la famosa persecución romana contra los cristianos, entretanto, vino en períodos de tiempo inconsistentes con la época en que Juan escribió. En lugar de una persecución directa y sistemática, los creyentes enfrentaron una cuestión muy distinta: la falta de comprensión.

Si regresamos a la discusión de la destrucción de Jerusalén en el año 70, recordaremos que los judíos se rebelaron contra Roma y la comunidad cristiana se vio capturada en la misma red de acusación arrojada en contra de los judíos. Por el otro lado de la ecuación, los creyentes sufrieron el ataque de aquellos judíos que no les gustaban que los creyentes fueron clasificados como judíos. A final de cuentas, los cristianos habían aceptado a Jesús como el Mesías, y los demás judíos rechazaban tal raseveración.

Tradicionalmente, los romanos habían reconocido que los judíos no hacían ídolos, ni participaban en sacrificios ante los ídolos. Esto había sido tolerado, enquanto que se hacían los sacrificios a Yahvé a favor de César. De acuerdo a los romanos, la seguridad básica del Imperio Romano dependía en mantener felices a los dioses en cuanto a la población. Si un grupo de gente se aislara de cumplir con los sacrificios y ofrendas, temían que los dioses pudieran castigar a todo el Imperio Romano.

De allí la dificultad encarada por los creyentes cristianos. Ellos no deberían participar de los sacrificios rituales, pero los judíos también reclamaban que tampoco eran parte del judaísmo. En algunos casos, ellos eran acusados que el título "cristiano" era lo equivalente al ser antisocial en el sentido de que su existencia y sus prácticas eran estructuradas para acabar con la base de la sociedad, causando que los dioses se enfurecieran con las sociedades de las cuales eran parte. Por otro lado, eran acusados por comer carne humana y tomar sangre humana en sus celebraciones de la Cena del Señor. Luego, eran tachados de caníbales y asesinos de niños. Si un judío trajera una acusación en contra de alguien por ser cristiano, no le era una simple cuestión de participar de un grupo religioso diferente. Era una acusación de trabajar en contra de la orden establecida de la sociedad, de ser una amenaza al Imperio.

Juan establece una agrupación de posibles respuestas que un cristiano pudiera hacer a las acusaciones elevadas en su contra. Primero, él podía morir. Al rechazar participación con los sacrificios romanos, sería condenado culpable y ejecutado. Segundo, uno podría mentir y hacer de cuenta que no era creyente. En tal caso, uno era obligado a renunciar a Jesús y ofrecer los sacrificios ante los oficiales romanos en evidencia de su participación en los sacrificios para asegurar la estabilidad del Imperio.

De acuerdo con Juan, solamente siendo fiel hasta la muerte era la respuesta adecuada para el creyente fiel. Haciendo de cuenta que uno no era creyente era una respuesta infiel. Tomando la posición que Roma simplemente no comprendía y pasar por los modos para aplacar a los oficiales era una infidelidad a Dios. Juan escribió que para ser fiel, uno debería someterse a Jesucristo y posicionarse en oposición a Roma. Uno debería de confiarse solamente a la misericordia y gracia de Dios. Si uno muriera como resultado de la fidelidad a Dios, Juan lo proclamaba como obteniendo la victoria sobre Roma. Después de hacer las cuentas, Roma no tenía autoridad o poder más allá de matarle a uno.

El llamado a la fidelidad, entonces, era para Juan que uno proclamara el evangelio y siguiera sus indicaciones, sin darle importancia a las consecuencias. Si uno fuera obligado a caminar en una manera que estaba en oposición a los edictos del estado, uno tenía una lealtad mayor para seguir las indicaciones de Dios. Uno pudiera morir como resultado de su fidelidad a Dios, pero la promesa del Cristo resucitado era de una vida sobre la cual César no tenía ningún poder. La victoria que le esperaba al fiel jamás podría ser perdida. Podría solamente ser abandonada o rendida al tornarse infiel a Dios.

Los creyentes vivían bajo una amenaza de Roma. Vivían bajo amenaza como extranjeros, extraños, inmigrantes, refugiados y siendo una población mal comprendida. La vida para ellos era incierta. En algunas áreas del Imperio Romano, la vida era un tanto más tranquila. En otras áreas había más conflicto. Ellos no tenían voz ni voto en el proceso político romano, pues eran considerados ajenos. Elevándose en revolución era contrario a la paz al que Jesús les había llamado. Quedaba en contra a los principios de amar a los enemigos y hacer bien a los que persiguen a uno.

Como una gente perseguida, ellos fueron llamados por este profeta para sufrir su persecución de acuerdo a la manera que habían visto en el ejemplo de Jesús. Ellos deberían estar confiados que la victoria real sería suya, dado a la fidelidad de Dios. Ellos deberían vivir sus vidas por fe y dejar los resultados en manos de Dios. Mientras, deberían seguir las direcciones y los propósitos de Dios, aun cuando los llevara a vivir en desafío al estado.

Ellos estaban bajo una ley superior a la de Roma. Claro, tenían que someterse a las leyes por general. Cuando aquellas leyes les indicaban vivir de forma contraria a las exigencias del evangelio de Cristo, entretanto, ellos deberían mantenerse firmes por Cristo y aceptar cualquiera que fuera la consecuencia que les venía. De tal forma, ellos darían testimonio fiel a la suficiencia de Dios en Jesucristo, declarando que el poder supremo y la victoria real no le pertenecían a César, sino a Dios en Jesucristo.

Aquél que es fiel hasta la final recibirá el premio. Él que testifica por medio de su muerte entrará a la vida. Aquél quien muere por su fe en Jesucristo no perderá la victoria que solo Dios puede ofrecer. Este es el mensaje que Juan tiene para nosotros. Somos llamados a esta fidelidad mayor. Somos llamados a vivir de acuerdo con la realidad retratada en las visiones celestiales de Juan, referente a la autoridad suprema de Dios. Somos llamados a vivir las exigencias del evangelio, aun cuando ellos andan en contra de las leyes del estado y abiertamente aceptar las consecuencias de ser fieles a Jesucristo. Después de todo, hay solamente uno a quien deberíamos entregar nuestra completa lealtad y sumisión. Hacer menos es dar la espalda a Dios y el ejemplo de Jesús quien dio su vida por nosotros.

Vivimos una realidad diferente que la de Juan. Vivimos una realidad en la cual las personas comúnmente tienen una voz en el establecimiento de leyes. Tenemos voz, voto y representación. Tenemos poder político que era negado a la iglesia primitiva. Junto con este poder viene la responsabilidad. Mientras que tenemos la habilidad de influenciar nuestros sistemas legales, trabajando por leyes más éticas y justas, también tenemos la responsabilidad ante Dios para ser fieles a los principios del evangelio, aun cuando pueden llamarnos a una acción que se define ser ilegal.

Con la responsabilidad, poder y oportunidad, entretanto, viene también la carga de aceptar las consecuencias de nuestras acciones. Juan nos llamaría a ser fieles a Cristo Jesús por encima de cualquier lealtad a las autoridades humanas. Él nos llamaría para siempre responder de acuerdo a los principios del evangelio, pero siempre estar dispuestos por aceptar la responsabilidad de nuestras acciones caso haya conflicto con las leyes de la tierra. La autoridad suprema es de Dios, no la de cualquier estado.

Lucas 14 — "Oblígales que Entren"

Jesús no siempre predicaba palabras fáciles que eran cómodas para que la escucharan sus oyentes. En lugar de eso, él muchas veces creaba incomodidad. Hablaba una palabra desafiante y establecía parámetros nuevos para el vivir y la interacción que le hacía incómoda a la sociedad a su alrededor. Esto era especialmente el caso en relación al sistema religioso de Israel. Un motivo de entre los aspectos más incómodos de sus palabras era aquellos a quienes él estaba listo por aceptar e incluir en un ofrecimiento de la gracia, la misericordia, el amor y el perdón de Dios.

La parábola en este tema de Lucas 14 no era en nada cómoda para la buena sociedad judía. Jesús refirió la historia de un rey quien invitó a todos los ricos y poderosos de la tierra a una fiesta. Cada invitado se rechasó la invitación con una u otra excusa. Puede que eran excusas políticamente y socialmente aceptables, pero eran igualmente excusas, elaboradas para que no participaran de la fiesta. En respuesta, el rey determinó que ninguno de ellos se les dejaría entrar a la fiesta de ningún modo. Por otro lado, el rey quiso que la fiesta continuara y que estuviera repleta su sala de banquete. Él envió a sus siervos otra vez, en esta ocasión con invitaciones a las bases de la población. Cuando la sala del banquete aun no quedara repleta, les envió otra vez para obligar a los marginados de la sociedad que se juntaran a la celebración.

Hay un tono sorprendente a esta última comisión. Las palabras de Jesús son "oblígales que entren." Esto ya no es una simple invitación. Es una orden del rey que la población mayor participe en las festividades.

Las implicaciones de las palabras de Jesús aquí son múltiples, pero miraremos a tres de ellas. Primero, la sociedad establecida acostumbra a tener lealtades y prioridades en conflicto con las de Dios. Dios quisiera que todos ellos participaran en la vida de la salvación, pero su invitación es más comúnmente rechazada por los poderosos y ricos. Ellos se ven consumidos por si mismos. Sus prioridades no suelen estar de acuerdo a las prioridades de Dios. Consecuentemente, ellos ni siempre gozan o se relacionan a los propósitos de Dios. Aunque la invitación les es extendida, Dios respeta sus excusas y decisiones de no aceptar la invitación, aunque no sea de su agrado.

Segundo, Dios está dispuesto a llenar el salón del banquete con aquellos a quienes la buena sociedad muy fácilmente se sacudiría como indigna o sin importancia. Los principios de Dios son diferentes, pues Dios quiere que se llene el salón de festividades para la celebración programada. Nuestra participación o aceptación ante la invitación de Dios es de una importancia mucho mayor a Dios que tantas otras temáticas que claman por nuestra atención. Aunque pudiéramos ser socialmente indignos, Dios no se preocupa con tales definiciones.

Tercero, Dios envía una invitación forzosa por medio de sus siervos. Es casi una exigencia, si no la es de verdad, para que aquellos designados como indignos vengan a participar, aun en contra de su propia voluntad. La audiencia para esta invitación es específicamente aquellos que desearíamos mantener lejos de las salas de fiesta del rey. Ellos son, entretanto, expresamente invitados a participar, aun cuando sus propios deseos y ocupaciones normales quedarían en oposición a la comunión con Dios.

De acuerdo a los judíos, la gente con quienes Jesús estaba ministrando comúnmente quedaban es esa categoría. Ellos eran la escoria de la sociedad, de acuerdo a los líderes religiosos y políticos. Fue estos a quienes Jesús dirigía su mensaje, específicamente porque la proclamación normal les excluía.

Ellos no eran los educados. No era los conectados. No eran los con una historia de pureza, estatus, importancia y linaje. De acuerdo a la mayoría, ellos eran los judíos quienes vivían bajo la condenación de Dios. Ellos se habían hecho creer que Dios bendecía con poder y riqueza a aquellos que agradaban a Dios, pero castigaba a los indignos con pobreza y enfermedad. Eran considerados inmerecedores, reportados como bajo la condenación y maldición de Dios, a quienes Jesús dio su mayor atención.

En la mayoría de las sociedades, éstos son los extranjeros, los extraños, los pobres, los inmigrantes, los desabrigados o enfermos. Pero son estos a quienes nosotros ignoramos o hasta faltamos en reconocer a quien Jesús dio la mayor parte de su atención. Él los llamaba, específicamente por causa de que la sociedad tendía a ignorarles. Consecuentemente, ellos eran quienes más necesitaban oír la invitación de Dios a la comunión.

De igual forma, excluídos o marginados de la sociedad eran los que más necesitaban ser presionados hacia la inclusión. Ellos sienten su separación de la nobleza con la mayor fuerza. Son ellos quienes más necesitan oír la voz que les llamaba hacia la presencia y celebración de Dios.

Han sido alejados ya tantas veces por la élite social que ellos serían los menos propensos a tomar iniciativa para unirse en la celebración de Dios. Es probable que esta fuera la razón por la cual esta invitación a los marginados se hace con tanta fuerza en la parábola de Jesús. Esta invitación necesitaría sublevar a un grado mayor de prejuicio que cualquier otro, un prejuicio ya internalizado por aquellos en las hileras más bajas de la sociedad. Ellos han "aprendido su lugar," y requiere mucha energía para que acepten un mensaje tan contrario a lo que la sociedad les ha dicho repetidas veces.

Jesús no está menos preocupado con estos marginalizados que con la élite. Él tampoco está menos preocupado por la élite. La diferencia es que sus palabras de aceptación e invitación para "los menores de estos" tienen que superar a las barreras mayores que fueron erigidos por las estructuras sociales, a diferencia de las demás personas. Ellos están acostumbrados a ser ignorados. Ellos están acostumbrados a ser echados de lado. Ellos están acostumbrados a ser pisoteados, olvidados y descuidados. Un sistema tal requiere una dedicación mayor de recursos para ser superado. La élite y los poderosos ya se consideran aceptables, dignos y los recipientes obvios de la invitación del rey. Son las clases inferiores o los marginados quienes deben superar las fuerzas de las barreras sociales que por demasiado tiempo les han mantenido ajenos a lo demás de la sociedad.

Aunque las palabras de Jesús aquí no fueran dirigidas específicamente a la comunidad inmigrante, estas se aplican a ellos igualmente, pues son ellos los quienes más comúnmente se encuentran más allá del alcance del cuidado y la preocupación social. Son ellos los descuidados e invisibles, así como los sin techo, los pobres y los inválidos son tratados como una carga sobre los recursos de los demás, en lugar de plenos participantes en los beneficios que la sociedad tiene para compartir.

1ª Juan 4 — "El Que Ama a Dios no Puede Odiar a un Hermano"

La primera epístola de Juan trata con temas que la iglesia como un todo enfrentaba desde la influencia gnóstica. Estaba en disputa la desunión entre las esferas espirituales y materiales de la vida. Los gnósticos enseñaban que Jesús no podría haber sido realmente humano, dado a su concepto que Dios no pudo tener nada que ver con el aspecto material de la vida. Así, Jesús no se habría preocupado con sanar a las enfermedades físicas de la gente, tocándoles o cuidando de sus necesidades por comida, abrigo, ropa y lo demás. Para ellos, Dios como espíritu no tendría ningún contacto directo con el mundo material. Más bien, la humanidad necesitaba escapar de la esfera física para entrar a la esfera espiritual habitada por Dios. Allí, ellos creían, uno podría gozar de la presencia inmediata de Dios, pero solamente en una disociación con todo lo material.

Juan empieza su epístola dando énfasis en la naturaleza física y terrenal de Jesús. Él habla de Jesús como viviendo de una forma visible, audible e física entre los discípulos. Él habla de temas de vida en la esfera física, de relaciones con personas como entidades de importancia. Él habla de los temas desde los cuales los gnósticos no querían simplemente escapar, sino que querían ignorar la realidad del pecado y su impacto en la vida y las relaciones con Dios y con los demás. Ellos intentaron decir que solo el cuerpo participaba del pecado, y que por lo tanto no tenía importancia. Juan les respondió directamente. Él habló de la aplicación física, material, del evangelio en nuestras interacciones con los demás.

Aparentemente la preocupación mayor para él era nuestra vivencia que impacta las vidas de los demás en demostración del amor de Dios entrando en medio de nuestra existencia y nuestras relaciones. Uno no puede reclamar un amor a Dios mientras que no ama a otro ser humano, era la crítica de Juan. Él simplemente no dejó espacio para crear una distinción entre lo espiritual y las relaciones con los demás. Si uno es de veras espiritual, como reclamaban los gnósticos, su espiritualidad debería alterar la forma por la cual se relaciona con las personas entre las cuales Jesús vivía y demostraba el amor de Dios.

El mensaje de Juan se extendía más allá de una aplicación directa a las tendencias gnósticas dentro de un segmento de la iglesia. Suya era una forma muy práctica de responder a cómo el amor de Dios manifiesto en Jesucristo debería transformar nuestras vidas de acuerdo al patrón establecido y enseñado por Jesús. De la forma que Jesús vivió, predicó e interactuó, así Juan procuraba por su carta extender el mensaje y la presencia de Jesús, aplicando la propia aplicación que hizo Jesús de las buenas nuevas hacia nuestras interacciones, el uno con el otro. Si reclamamos amarle a Dios, eso debe tornarse visible en nuestras actitudes y acciones ante los demás.

No hay lugar en el evangelio de Cristo para que uno ame a Dios e ignore las necesidades de aquellos quienes nos rodean. No hay espacio en el evangelio para amar aquellos quienes más se nos asemejan y no amar a otros quienes podemos colocar en alguna categoría que nos excusa de cualquier responsabilidad de aplicar la misma medida de amor a cualquier otro.

El amor hacia Dios, Juan reclama, se hace visible en nuestras acciones y relaciones con los demás seres humanos bajo el mismo patrón que Jesús estableció ante nosotros. El amarle a Dios requiere que cuidemos por los intereses que le preocupan a Dios. Requiere que juntemos nuestras vidas y propósitos a la vida y al propósito de Dios. No hay, por lo tanto, ningún espacio para definir alguna clase de personas como inmerecedoras de nuestro amor y nuestra atención, cuando Cristo vino igualmente por uno y por todos, sin distinción.

Mateo 5 — "Son la Sal de la Tierra"

La lectura tradicional de las palabras de Jesús en Mateo 5 es que fueron dirigidas hacia los propios discípulos, como para colocar a estos aparte, y por implicación a la iglesia, en distinción a lo demás del mundo. Lo que encontramos, entretanto, es que Jesús estaba enseñando no solamente a los discípulos, sino también a una multitud completa. Sus palabras no eran dirigidas simplemente hacia aquellos en el grupo interior, sino fueron difundidas a toda la gente que le pudiera escuchar. Todos ellos estaban siendo llamados la sal de la tierra y la luz del mundo.

Al inicio del sermón, Jesús detalla los patrones que definirían aquellos quienes eran de veras bendecidos en los ojos de Dios. Cuando él llegó a sus comentarios sobre ser sal y luz del mundo, entretanto, sus comentarios se cambiaron a ser descriptivos de la realidad, aplicándose a todos sus oyentes. Se entiende que había toda clase de personas presentes. Aplicamos estas palabras de Jesús a todas las personas hoy. Luego, el problema. Es allí que este texto empieza a crear cierta incomodidad para la iglesia.

Estamos acostumbrados a leer estas palabras como si ellos se aplicaran a la iglesia, los de adentro, los como a nosotros quienes hemos aceptado a Jesús como Señor y Salvador. Hemos utilizados los términos para trazar distinciones entre nosotros y los demás. Hemos aprovechado el texto para darnos un grado mayor de valor o importancia que los ajenos al evangelio. Estas palabras de labios de Jesús, entretanto, se aplican igualmente a uno y a todos, sin cualquier distinción especial para la iglesia. Jesús estaba llamando a todos que le escuchaban sal de la tierra y luz del mundo. ¡Él no hacía ninguna distinción entre las personas con esta declaración!

Cada uno de los oyentes tenía el mismo potencial para cumplir con los propósitos de Dios. Cada uno de ellos era en su esencia luz y sal para hacer una diferencia en su entorno. Ellos eran todos llenos del potencial para hacer una diferencia marcada, un impacto positivo en lo tocante a los propósitos de Dios. La pregunta que Jesús eleva con estas palabras, entretanto, se aplica a lo que hacemos con este potencial que Dios ha colocado dentro de cada uno de nosotros. Esto es el único sitio en donde podemos encontrar una distinción que importe.

Si cumplimos con nuestro propósito, los demás deben ver la naturaleza distintiva de la presencia y acción de Dios en nuestras vidas. Ellos deberían acordarse a la misma chispa de luz que reside también en ellos. Ellos deberían glorificarle a Dios o revelar a Dios al mirarnos viviendo de una forma por la cual los propósitos de Dios se transforman en realidad en nuestro vivir.

Somos llamados a brillar por otros, así como deberían hacer las luces. Somos llamados a cumplir con nuestra misión y propósito ante otros, no por que seamos mejores, sino por que hemos aceptado a los propósitos y la misión que Dios nos ha dado a cada uno de nosotros.

Inherentemente, todos tenemos el mismo valor ante Dios. La pregunta es, ¿qué haremos con esta posición de valor? ¿Qué haremos con la luz del mundo (no la nuestra propia) que se colocó en nosotros? No es algo para nuestro propio beneficio, sino que es para beneficio de los que nos rodean. Es en conjunto que somos convocados a brillar ante los demás hasta que ellos asuman el mismo propósito de alumbrar el mundo para todos. Es solo por medio de cumplir con esta misión que hay cualquier distinción real entre nosotros y los demás. En sentido de valor y mérito inherentes, somos idénticos.

Lucas 10 — "¿Quién Es mi Vecino?"

Quizás la historia de Jesús y el abogado quien buscaba justificarse es el texto central en referencia a todas nuestras obligaciones hacia inmigrantes, extranjeros y extraños. Jesús había apenas respondido una pregunta referente al mayor mandamiento de Dios. Jesús luego contestó la pregunta a seguir en la cual se radicaba el conflicto real con los mandamientos de Dios. ¿Quién es mi vecino? debería haber sido una cuestión de establecer límites para la definición de quienes debemos amar ante Dios. Debería ofrecer un alivio y una justificación para un tratamiento desigual de la gente, luego que se definieran y defendieran las categorías de quienes eran y no eran dignos. La respuesta de Jesús, entretanto, destruyó toda la base para la pregunta que se hacía.

Jesús se viró al hombre procurando su autojustificación y le obligó a tratar con una nueva definición de vecino que le era muchísimo más expansiva de que cualquier definición que jamás había aceptado, más expansiva que jamás había escuchado.

La parábola del Buen Samaritano trajo nuevos parámetros para la definición de un vecino que el judaísmo había seriamente considerado antes. Un enemigo odiado con el cual los judíos no se bajarían para hablar se figura como el héroe quien cuida por un judío quien fue ignorado por otros judíos por causa de las preocupaciones con la pureza ritual. Este enemigo quien jamás calificaría como ritualmente puro entra en la escena para actuar conforme la gracia y cumplir con los mandamientos que apenas se habían definido ser los mayores mandamientos entre todos.

El samaritano aquí era ajeno. Él era inmigrante. Él era ritualmente impuro. Él era indubitablemente desde más allá de las normas cómodas para la sociedad religiosa judía. Él era, entretanto, la expresión corporal de lo que Jesús procuraba establecer como el modelo para nuestras interacciones con los demás.

Jesús tenía aquí más que un punto. Preocupaciones de la pureza ritual, tan importantes en la vida judía, se echaron de lado no simplemente como irrelevantes, sino como actuando de forma contraria a la importancia mayor de las instrucciones y los mandamientos de Dios en lo tocante al amor hacia los demás. Segundo, Jesús coloca a este inmigrante odiado en la posición de cumplir con los mayores mandamientos de Dios, transformándose en la expresión corporal de la voluntad y el propósito de Dios.

Cualquier razón que encontramos para descartar a clases de personas como más allá de los límites de nuestra responsabilidad personal ante Dios aquí encuentra su fin. Ante Dios, no hay ninguna definición como la que el abogado procuraba de alguien quien se queda más allá de la definición de la pregunta, ¿quién es mi vecino? Jesús no pudiera haber sido más claro a lo que fue en este encuentro. Cada persona es mi vecina. Todos quedan incluidos en los mandamientos de Dios para que yo les ame. Todos son de valor y mérito iguales ante Dios. Cualquier acción que yo pudiera tomar para definir los temas de forma diferente me hace culpable de ignorar los mayores propósitos y mandamientos de Dios.

El inmigrante, el extranjero, el extraño, el ajeno son todos igualmente mis vecinos, bajo las definiciones de Jesús. El mandamiento para amar a mi vecino no respeta, ni conoce limitaciones de fronteras, culturas, etnicidad, idioma u origen. Así como Cristo Jesús llegó para amarles a todos, somos nosotros llamados a amar a todos igualmente y sin distinción.

CONCLUSIONES SUMARIAS

Las visiones de Juan en Apocalipsis hacen referencias a multitudes de cada nación, idioma y tribu ante los pies del Cristo resucitado. Esto es posiblemente el objetivo final de la vida en Jesucristo. Bajo esta visión y perspectiva, no hay fronteras ni límites para cruzar. Bajo el estandarte de Cristo, todos somos uno sin distinción. Es en esta calidad de diversidad que Jesús nos llama hacia una unidad esencial en Juan 17. Dejando de lado nuestras diferencias y distinciones, somos convocados para juntarnos y para que corporalmente nos transformemos en la gente de Dios, el cuerpo de Cristo.

Fronteras nacionales y políticas migratorias son preocupaciones de la política, búsquedas humanas por poder, influencia y control. Las preocupaciones de Dios en lo tocante a los inmigrantes en toda la Biblia son completamente distintas que ellas. Dios se preocupa con temas de justicia, tratar uno al otro con dignidad, respeto, igualdad y amor. Estos son preocupaciones de traer a otros hacia el reinado de Dios, sea de Israel o del Espíritu más allá de las preocupaciones de la nacionalidad, etnicidad, o idioma. Preocupaciones humanas con la inmigración son aquellas de exclusión, mientras que las de Dios son de la inclusión y de igualdad.

Los patrones de justicia establecidas, especialmente por Jesús, van mucho más allá de los límites de los conceptos humanos de justicia "por aquellos que son como a nosotros." Ellos abrazan al ajeno como siendo tan importante como aquellos dentro de nuestro propio grupo, clase, tribu, idioma y nación

Como lo dice Juan, "Pues Dios así amó al mundo...." Dios no ama tanto a mí y los míos, como que Dios ama a todo el mundo, mucho más allá de mis definiciones de nacionalidad, de etnicidad, de idioma, de estatus y de origen. Somos todos amados por Dios y llamados para amarnos los unos a los otros como hijos e hijas del Altísimo, sin cualquier distinción.

—Christopher B. Harbin

PARA MÁS LECTURA

Hay mucho otros textos que tratan con temas en lo tocante a la inmigración. Abajo están algunos de los textos que he encontrado de ayuda en mejorar mi comprensión de lo que significa ser y vivir como un inmigrante. Muchas veces es una vida llena de desafíos que requieren una gran medida de fuerza.

Mis propias experiencias como un inmigrante fracasan en alcanzar lo que significa para la mayoría, pues aunque yo he sido inmigrante, siempre lo he sido como ciudadano de una potencia mundial entre poblaciones de naciones en desarrollo. Tornándose un inmigrante en un poder mundial al venir de un país en desarrollo es una realidad y experiencia muy distinta a la mía.

Sonia Nazario. *Enrique's Journey.* New York: Random House, 2007.
Budos, Marina. *Ask Me No Questions.* New York: Scholastic, 2007.
Linda Sue Park. *A Long Walk to Water: Based on a True Story.* Boston: Clarion Books, 2010.

SOBRE EL AUTOR

Christopher B. Harbin, nacido en Carolina del Sur, ha vivido la mitad de su vida como inmigrante. Fue criado por padres misioneros en Brasil antes de regresar a los EUA para sus estudios de universidad y seminario. Estudió idiomas modernos en Mississippi College, y luego se graduó con maestría en divinidad desde Southern Seminary en Louisville, adonde sirvió como enlace étnico para la Long Run Baptist Association. Chrístopher y su esposa Karina sirvieron de misionaros en México y en Brasil, donde trabajaron en plantación de iglesias, enseñando en seminarios, y donde Chrístopher coordinó un programa de seminario por extensión en Rio Grande do Sul. Desde su regreso a los EUA, Chrístopher pastoreó a dos iglesias en Virginia, donde también trabajó con congregaciones latinas de las asociaciones bautistas locales. Él ahora sirve como pastor asociado para ministerio latino de la Primera Iglesia Bautista de Huntersville, NC. Él vive en Davidson, NC con su esposa y sus dos hijos inmigrantes, nacidos en Brasil. Chrístopher ha escrito de forma extensa para sus alumnos de seminario e iglesias, también publicando sermones en www.sermonsearch.com.

www.theotrek.org — Una jornada electrónica de fe en Dios…

www.ingramcontent.com/pod-product-compliance
Lightning Source LLC
Chambersburg PA
CBHW071654160426
43195CB00012B/1466